LUFTWAFFE
SECRET PROJECTS
STRATEGIC BOMBERS 1935-1945

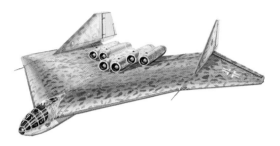

Midland Publishing

**Luftwaffe Secret Projects –
Strategic Bombers 1935-1945**

© Dieter Herwig and Heinz Rode 1998, 2000

First published 1998 in Germany by
Motorbuch Verlag, Stuttgart.

Translation from original German text
by Elke and John Weal

Design concept and editorial layout
© Midland Publishing and
Stephen Thompson Associates.

English language edition published 2000 by
Midland Publishing
(an imprint of Ian Allan Publishing Ltd)
24 The Hollow, Earl Shilton
Leicester, LE9 7NA, England
Tel: 01455 847815   Fax: 01455 841805

ISBN 1 85780 092 3

Worldwide distribution (except North America):
Midland Counties Publications
Unit 3 Maizefield, Hinckley Fields
Hinckley, Leics. LE10 1YF, England
Tel: 01455 233747 Fax: 01455 233737
E-mail: midlandbooks@compuserve.com

North America trade distribution by:
Specialty Press Publishers & Wholesalers Inc.
11605 Kost Dam Road
North Branch, MN 55056, USA
Tel: 651 583 3239 Fax: 651 583 2023
Toll free telephone: 800 895 4585

Printed by Ian Allan Printing Limited
Riverdene Business Park, Molesey Road
Hersham, Surrey, KT12 4RG, England

Illustration on title page, opposite:
The Arado E 555/1 flying wing was designed for
a combat radius of nearly 3,000 miles. Had the
Second World War continued nearer 1950, then
this scene, reproduced from a painting by Keith
Woodcock GAvA GMA ASAA, depicting two exam-
ples being pursued by a P-80 Shooting Star over
Manhattan, might just have become a reality.

LUFTWAFFE
SECRET PROJECTS
STRATEGIC BOMBERS 1935-1945

Dieter Herwig and Heinz Rode

Contents

Foreword

This second volume of the *Luftwaffe Secret Projects* series deals with strategic bomber projects in the period 1935 to 1945.

Compared to the fighter projects (which were described in the first volume of the series), coverage of the bomber projects has proven to be a much more daunting task, there having been very few, if any, strategic bomber developments in Germany prior to 1945. Not until the closing months of the war did the necessity for strategic heavy bombers come to be regarded as vital.

The first part of this second volume describes early bomber developments which were to have been built as so-called prototypes, but which either failed to complete the development stage or which, in a few cases, actually resulted in experimental types commencing flight trials.

The second part of the current work deals with those bomber projects planned, under construction, or completed by the war's end which, in terms of their overall design concept, speed, range and construction, were years ahead of the designs under development by their opponents.

Much of the detail which follows is based upon previously unpublished material.

In an attempt to overcome the delays and protracted processes involved in tendering and the awarding of construction contracts by the RLM (*Reichsluftfahrtministerium*) and the politically-minded committees of the *Ministerium für Rüstung- und Kriegsproduktion* (Ministry of Armaments and War Production) and at the same time provide a decisive weapon for the furtherance of the air war, Germany's aviation industry – aided and abetted by certain members of the Luftwaffe hierarchy – submitted countless design proposals. But the lack of technical understanding displayed by many of those in positions of authority within the RLM, coupled with a supine and unimaginative bureaucratic machine, made it impossible for the industry to develop a suitable bomber – either piston-engined or jet-powered – and get it into production, let alone to the front-line units.

Bombers with speeds approaching the supersonic, new propulsion systems, and with ranges far in excess of 28,000 kilometres (17,500 miles) while carrying a heavy bomb load – aircraft, in fact, which would have been quite capable of reaching the USA in non-stop flight – were fully engineered and ready for metal to be cut. But construction contracts were never awarded.

At the end of hostilities Germany's enormous technical advances in this, as in all other areas of aviation research, fell into the hands of the victorious Allies.

To this day – decades after the end of the war – the results of this research remain the basis of aviation technology in the supersonic age, both on the international civil scene as well as the military.

Luftwaffe Secret Projects is not intended as a latter-day glorification of ground-breaking aviation technology. Its aim, rather, is to rescue from obscurity the truly remarkable achievements of the designers and engineers of Germany's aviation industry.

Dieter Herwig
Heinz Rode

English language edition
March 2000

Acknowledgements

All the original manufacturers' documents, data and photos published in this second volume of the of the *Luftwaffe Secret Projects* series *Strategic Bombers 1935-1945* have come exclusively from the archives and the collection of the *Deutsches Studienbüro für Luftfahrt* (German Aviation Study Bureau) in Frankfurt am Main.

The author has received valuable assistance and support from a staff of friends and colleagues at the *Deutsche Gesellschaft für Luftfahrtdokumentation* (German Association for Aviation Documentation), whose knowledge and files have helped to present an accurate picture of long-range bomber project development in Germany up to 1945.

Particular thanks are due to Messrs Theodor Mohr, Willy Radinger and Günter Sengfelder, who have selflessly sought to provide answers to often very difficult questions. To them goes my most sincere gratitude, in the hope that they will be prepared to offer similar invaluable service in the preparation of any future volumes in the series. I must also extend my heartfelt thanks and appreciation to my co-author Heinz Rode. Under the most difficult of conditions he has often made the impossible possible; for example, transforming fragmentary items of works drawings into realistic and lifelike illustrations, and thus providing the reader with vivid, pictorial impressions of the projects described.

In order to forestall any adverse criticism of the tactical codes, markings and camouflage schemes depicted: these should be regarded as pure artistic licence, used simply to enhance the image, provide that extra touch of realism, and add the 'feel' of an operational aircraft.

Introduction

A few months before the end of the war German heavy bomber development, after decades of neglect, was suddenly supposed to bring about a change in fortunes in the air war over Germany by the introduction of completely new bomber projects.

For it was only at that late stage, and against a background of total air war – which, by 1944/1945, had resulted in the destruction of over 90% of Germany's towns and industrial complexes – that Reichsmarschall Hermann Göring, the Luftwaffe Commander-in-Chief, and the high-ups in the Reichsluftfahrtministerium (RLM) began to turn their thoughts towards preparations for a strategic air war.

After the failure of the Heinkel He 177 – the Luftwaffe's only heavy bomber – there was not a single type with the performance necessary for waging strategic warfare. It was in this hopeless situation that Göring summoned key personnel of the industry and RLM to a Reichsmarschall's conference, convened at Dessau in the autumn of 1944, where he demanded the production of jet-powered heavy bombers.

Among the numerous proposals submitted to the RLM after the relevant specifications had been issued to the manufacturers were many heavy bomber projects which, in their conception and technology, were radically different from anything that had gone before.

Flying-wing bombers and bombers with negative and positive wing-sweep, with high-speed profiles and powered by anything up to eight jet engines came off the drawing boards. These aircraft, capable of flying long distances with heavy bomb loads, were intended to destroy airfields, industrial installations and other strategic targets deep in the enemy's hinterland. But, above all, they were meant to strike at his airfields and thus bring a halt to the Allied bombing offensive against the Reich.

After production at Junkers and the Bayerischen Motoren Werke (BMW), the major manufacturers of jet engines, was severely disrupted by Allied bombing attacks, deliveries sank to such a low level that only the most urgent requirements for fighter production could be met.

Only a few experimental examples of the He S 109-011 turbine, developed in conjunction by Heinkel and Hirth, had as yet been built and full series production could not have been initiated until 1948 at the earliest.

Such plans remained a pipe-dream. After the aviation industry's last production facilities were destroyed by enemy action, the Horten brothers, on Göring's personal orders, attempted in March 1945 to complete their Ho XVIII B-2 bomber in a crash programme at the underground Kahla site.

Hitler, Göring and the top Luftwaffe leaders had dreamed of bombing raids on US cities, which would 'bomb America out of the air war in Europe' – they already had visions of New York sinking in a sea of flames.

The end of the war wrote finis to these schemes, and also to any last, lingering hopes of a strategic jet bomber.

US bombers enter Reich airspace under heavy fighter escort.

Glossary

Abteilung 'L' – Department 'L', the Lippisch design department within the Messerschmitt company.

APZ Automatischer Peilzusatz – automatic supplementary direction finding equipment.

Arbeitsflugzeug Literally 'work-aircraft' – used for medium bomber

AVA Aerodynamische Versuchsanstalt – Aerodynamic Experimental Institute.

AWG Auswertegerät – plotting device.

BK Bordkanone – fixed aircraft cannon.

BMW Bayerische Motorenwerke – Bavarian Engine Works.

DFS Deutsches Forschungsinstitut für Segelflug – German Research Institute for Sailplanes.

Dipl-Ing Diplomingenieur – literally diploma-ed engineer, equivalent to Diploma of Engineering.

Doppelreiter Literally 'double-rider', wing fuel fairings.

DVL Deutsche Versuchsanstalt für Luftfahrt – German Aviation Experimental Institute.

E Entwurf – project.

EF Entwicklungsflugzeug – development aircraft.

EiV Eigenverständigungsanlage – crew intercom.

EHK Entwicklungshauptkommission – Main Development Commission.

ESK Entwicklungssonderkommission – Special Development Commission.

ETC Elektrische Trägervorrichtung für Cylinderbomben – electrically-operated carrier device for cylindrical bombs.

EZ Einheitszielvorrichtung – standard sightingdevice.

FDL Ferngerichtete Drehringlafette – remotely controlled barbette.

FHL Ferngerichtete Hecklafette – remotely controlled tail barbette.

Fl-E Flugzeugentwicklung – Aircraft Development Department within the TLR.

Flitzer Literally Dasher or Whizzer, single-seater jet fighter.

FuBl Funk-Blindlandeanlage – radio blind-landing equipment.

FuG Funkgerät – radio or radar set.

FZG Fernzielgerät – remote aiming device/bombsight.

General der Jagdflieger Air Officer Commanding fighters.

Generalleutnant Luftwaffe rank – equivalent to Air Vice Marshal (RAF) or Major General (USAAF).

Generalmajor Luftwaffe rank – equivalent to Air Commodore (RAF) or one-star General (USAAF).

Generalstab General Staff.

GM-1 Nitrous oxide.

Gruppe Luftwaffe equivalent to Wing (RAF) or Group (USAAF).

IFF Identification, friend or foe.

Jägerstab Fighter Staff.

Jumo Junkers Motorenbau

LFA Luftfahrtforschungsanstalt – Aviation Research Institute.

MG Maschinengewehr – machine gun; later also cannon.

MK Maschinenkanone – machine cannon.

MW 50 Methanol-water mixture.

NJG Nachtjagdgeschwader – night fighter group.

Obergruppenführer SS rank – equivalent to Lieutenant General.

Oberleutnant Luftwaffe rank – equivalent to Flying Officer (RAF) or 1st Lieutenant (USAAF).

Oberstleutnant Luftwaffe rank – equivalent to Wing Commander (RAF) or Lieutenant Colonel (USAAF).

OKL Oberkommando der Luftwaffe – Luftwaffe High Command.

OMW Otto Marder Works

'Otto-Jäger' Piston-engined fighter.

P Projekt – project.

PeilG Peilgerät – direction finding set.

Pulk Luftwaffe term for USAF bomber box.

Pulkzerstörer Heavily armed anti-bomber aircraft.

Rb Reihenbildkamera – automatic aerial camera.

RfRuK Reichsministerium für Rüstung und Kriegsproduktion – Reich's Ministry of Armament and War Production.

RLM Reichsluftfahrtministerium – Reich's Air Ministry.

Rüstsatz Field conversion set.

SC Splitterbombe — fragmentation bomb.

Schräge Musik Luftwaffe term for oblique upward-firing armament (literally oblique or jazz music).

SD Splitterbombe, Dickwand – fragmentation bomb, thick-walled.

Technisches Amt Technical Office (of the RLM).

TL Turbinenluftstrahl-Triebwerk – turbojet engine.

TLR Technische Luftrüstung – Technical Air Armaments Board.

UKW Ultrakurzwelle – VHF.

Volksflugzeug People's (ie the Nation-State) Aircraft.

Volksjäger People's Fighter.

Volkssturm Germany's equivalent to the British home guard.

WNF Wiener Neustädter Flugzeugwerke – aircraft works.

W/nr Werk nummer – construction (or airframe serial) number.

Zerstörer Heavy fighter, literally destroyer.

ZVG Zielflugvorsatzgerät – homer attachment device.

This glossary covers items mentioned in Luftwaffe Secret Projects: Fighters 1939-1945 (the first volume in this series) as well as in this present book.

Notes

Manufacturers

The Reichsluftfahrtministerium (RLM) adopted a series of (mostly) two-letter prefixes to act as design or manufacturer codes for aircraft. These mostly consisted of one upper and one lower case letter (eg Fw) but there were a handful of exceptions which used all capitals (eg BV):

Al	Albatros
Ao	AGO-Flugzeugwerke
Ar	Arado
Ba	Bachem
Bf	Bayerische Flugzeugwerke
Bü	Bücker
BV	Blohm und Voss
DFS	Deutsche Forschungsanstalt für Segelflug
Do	Dornier
FA	Focke-Achgelis
Fh	Flugzeugbau Halle
Fi	Fieseler
FK	Flugzeugbau Kiel
Fl	Flettner
Fw	Focke-Wulf
Go	Gothaer Waggonfabrik
Ha	Hamburger Flugzeugbau
He	Heinkel
Ho	Horten
Hs	Henschel
Hü	Hütter
Ju	Junkers
Ka	Kalkert
Kl	Klemm
Me	Messerschmitt
NR	Nagler-Rolz
Si	Siebel
Sk	Skoda-Kauba
Ta	Tank
WNF	Wiener-Neustädter-Flugzeugbau *
ZMe	Zeppelin/Messerschmitt
ZSO	Zeppelin/SNCASO

The RLM adopted a similar series of abbreviations for the design and/or manufacturers of engines:

As	Argus
BMW	Bayerische Motorenwerke
Bramo	Brandenburgische Motorenwerke
DB	Daimler-Benz
DZ	Deutz
HM	Heinkel/Hirth
Jumo	Junkers
Sh	Siemens
Z	Zündapp

Messerschmitt Aircraft Designations

This brings us to the inevitable 'chestnut' of 'Bf' or 'Me' for Messerschmitt's earlier designs. This work is very much a study of official documentation and RLM nomenclature has been adhered to.

For the RLM the transition from 'Bf' to 'Me' occurs between the unsuccessful Bf162 Jaguar (whose number was subsequently allocated to the He162 Volksjäger) and the Me163 Komet. The 'Me'155 avoids the issue by having been transferred at a very early stage to Blohm und Voss.

Then there is the 'grey area' of projected developments of 'Bf' types (eg the Bf109G) initiated after the change to 'Me'. This is tempting (eg Me109H) but since later operational variants of the '109 retained the 'Bf' prefix (Bf109K circa 1944-45) this work has standardised on all Messerschmitt types below the RLM number 162 being prefixed 'Bf' and all those from 163 and upwards being prefixed 'Me'.

Measurements

All German aircraft measurements etc are given in decimal (or SI – Système International d'Unités, established in 1960) units, with an Imperial (of British FPSR – foot, pound, second, Rankine) figure second. This is reversed in the few cases where UK or US-built aircraft are quoted.

The following information may help:

aspect ratio wingspan and chord – expressed as a ratio. Low aspect ratio, short, stubby wing; high aspect ratio, long, narrow wing.

ft feet – length, multiply by 0.305 to get metres (m). For height measurements involving service ceilings and cruise heights, the figure has been 'rounded'.

ft² square feet – area, multiply by 0.093 to get square metres (m²).

fuel measured in both litres/gallons and kilograms/pounds. The specific gravity (sg) of German fuel varied considerably during the war and conversions from volume to weight and vice versa are impossible without knowing the specific gravity of the fuel at the time.

gallon Imperial (or UK) gallon, multiply by 4.546 to get litres. (500 Imperial gallons equal 600 US gallons.)

hp horse power – power, measurement of power for piston and turboprop engines. Multiply by 0.746 to get kilowatts.

kg kilogram – weight, multiply by 2.205 to get pounds (lb). Fuel load frequently given in kilograms.

kg/m² kilograms per square metre – force, measurement of wing loading, multiply by 0.204 to get pounds per square foot.

km/h kilometres per hour – velocity, multiply by 0.621 to get miles per hour (mph).

kP kilopascal – force, for measuring thrust, effectively a kilogram of static thrust. Present day preferences are for the kilonewton (kN), one kN equalling 224.8lb or 101.96kg.

kW kilowatt – power, measurement of power for piston and turboprop engines. Multiply by 1.341 to get horse power.

lb pound – weight, multiply by 0.454 to get kilograms (kg). Also used for the force measurement of turbojet engines, with the same conversion factor, as pounds of static thrust.

lb/ft² pounds per square foot – force, measurement of wing loading, multiply by 4.882 to get kilograms per square metre.

litre volume, multiply by 0.219 to get Imperial (or UK) gallons.

m metre – length, multiply by 3.28 to get feet (ft).

m² square metre – area, multiply by 10.764 to get square feet (ft²).

mm millimetre – length, the bore of guns is traditionally a decimal measure (eg 30mm) and no Imperial conversion is given.

mph miles per hour – velocity, multiply by 1.609 to get kilometres per hour (km/h).

* – also Wn but WNF used in preference to avoid confusion with w/nr.

Chapter One

Heavy Bomber Development in Germany up until 1945

Generalluftzeugmeister Ernst Udet

Ernst Udet 1896-1941, was the first Generalluftzeugmeister Chief of Aircraft Procurement and Supply of the Luftwaffe.

With 62 victories Ernst Udet earned a reputation as one of the most successful fighter pilots of the First World War. A holder of the *Pour le Mérite*, he worked as a test pilot after the war and was also well-known as a daring stunt flyer; taking part in several films.

1935 Entered the newly formed Luftwaffe with the rank of Oberst (Colonel).

1936 Elevated to the post of Chief of the Technical Office of the RLM.

1938 Promoted to the position of Generalluftzeugmeister.

Udet concentrated on the development of single-engined fighters and dive-bombers, which reflected his own views but were not relevant to the concept of strategic air warfare.

Hitler and Göring blamed Udet, not without some justification, for the Luftwaffe's failure both in the Battle of Britain and on the eastern front. Personal intrigues, the lack of a proper aircraft development programme and a series of violent confrontations with Göring drove Udet to take his own life on 17th November 1941.

1926-1939

The first secret negotiations between the *Reichswehr* and the Junkers and Dornier works, whose aim was the development of a multi-engined bomber capable of transporting a strategic load over long distances, took place as early as 1926. For purposes of camouflage (dictated by the conditions imposed by the Treaty of Versailles), the interests of the *Reichswehr* were looked after by the *Reichsverkehrsministerium* (Ministry of Transport), which acted as the official negotiator.

In 1927 the aircraft procurement department of the *Heereswaffenamt* (Army Ordnance Directorate) formulated the 'technical requirements for the construction of a four-engined night bomber', which was referred to within the *Heereswaffenamt* under the title *Wa 6, Nr. 772/3/27 Gekados-Z*. Given the camouflage designation '*Gronabo*' (*Großer Nachtbomber* = large night bomber), this bomber project foresaw a cantilever-wing monoplane with four engines, capable of speeds of at least 320 km/h (200 mph) at an altitude of 5,000 metres (16,500 feet).

On 4th April 1932 the operations department of the *Truppenamt* (Armed Forces Directorate) informed the aircraft procurement department of the *Heereswaffenamt* that the Dornier company had already developed a four-engined bomber, designated the Do P, but that this did not meet the specifications as laid down.

With the advent of the newly created *Luftkommandoamt* – later to become the General Staff of the Luftwaffe – the supporters of the strategic heavy bomber concept believed the way was finally clear for them officially to put their ideas to the aviation industry.

Despite all the resistance that still remained against the production of a heavy bomber, the manufacturers Dornier, Junkers and Rohrbach were therefore invited to submit proposals to meet the technical specifications issued by the *Heereswaffenamt*.

Dornier put the plans for their *Projekt P 33*, the later Do19, before the Directorate at the end of 1933. Design proposals for the Junkers Ju 89 were presumably submitted by that company at about the same time.

But the spirit of 1914 - 1918 still dominated the minds and governed the actions of Udet, Milch and the majority of the old flyers who held the highest positions in the *Luftkommandoamt* (and later the General Staff) and whose word was law. They turned down the demands for a heavy bomber because of the 'limited strategic effect' of such a machine. To the non-flyers – the men of the Army High Command, who were convinced of the necessity for heavy and large bombers – the aviators' decision was beyond comprehension.

Meanwhile, design work on the Do19 and the Ju 89 continued apace. The then head of the *Technisches Amt* (Technical Office of the RLM), Oberst Wimmer, later described how Göring had 'reserved judgement' on a final decision regarding the continuation of work on the Ju 89 after viewing the mock-up at the beginning of 1935.

In contrast to Göring, the then *Reichswehrminister* (Defence Minister) Blomberg had no reservations whatsoever. Inspecting the Dornier Do19 mock-up, he declared his full support for the aircraft. Despite this, further work on the Do19 and Ju 89 prototypes was finally cancelled on Göring's orders on 29th April 1937. The probable reason for this cessation order was, ostensibly, the insufficient power output of existing German aero-engines and their inability to attain a minimum speed of 310 km/h (193 mph).

But this did not reflect the true facts, for at this time Germany's engine manufacturers were producing power plants of the most modern kind with ratings in excess of 800 hp.

Restricted by the allegedly too limited performance of available engines, the General Staff of the Luftwaffe felt itself obliged to opt instead for so-called *medium* bombers. This decision tallied exactly with the thinking of Milch, Kesselring and several other leading lights in the upper hierarchy of the Luftwaffe.

Albert Kesselring who, after the suicide of Udet, continued to propound his views with the General Staff, was firmly of the opinion that Germany required, first and foremost, a force of dive-bombers, backed up by large numbers of twin-engined medium bombers. To attain this end emphasis was laid upon the development and production of medium

Generalfeldmarschall Erhard Milch, Udet's successor in the office of Generalluftzeugmeister, was, like Generalfeldmarschall Albert Kesselring, for various reasons opposed to heavy bombers but a supporter of the medium bomber.

Generalfeldmarschall Albert Kesselring

Generalfeldmarschall Albert Kesselring 1885-1960, the Luftwaffe's one time Chief of Air Staff.

1914 Officer in a Bavarian artillery regiment, adjutant and officer of the General Staff. After the war an Oberstleutnant (Lieutenant-Colonel) in the Army Staff of the Reichswehr.

1935 Promoted Generalleutant and Chief of the Luftwaffe Administration Office.

1937 Elevated to Luftwaffe Chief of Air Staff with rank of General der Flieger, Kesselring was of the firm opinion that the Luftwaffe's primary need in any future war was for dive-bombers and twin-engined medium bombers.

1938 Assumed command of Luftflotte 1 (Air Fleet 1) headquarters in Berlin.

1939 Commanding Luftflotte 1 upon the outbreak of the Second World War.

1940 Promotion to Generalfeldmarschall.

1941-1945 Commander-in-Chief of southern and south-western fronts in Italy and the Mediterranean. Kesselring was highly regarded by the Allies as one of the ablest generals of the Second World War. Albert Kesselring died in 1960 in Bad Nauheim.

bombers: the Heinkel He 111, Dornier Do 215 and Junkers Ju 88.

In contrast to these purely practical bombers, heavy strategic bombers (such as were under development, or already being built, in the USA, Great Britain, and the then Soviet Union) were – in the event of war – tasked with long-range penetration deep into the enemy's hinterland, where they would destroy airfields, power stations, industrial and railway installations, and the like.

But this strategic concept was looked upon by the Luftwaffe leadership as something of an 'unnecessary luxury'. The German side did not believe in the possibility of a long drawn out war. Rather, they saw any future conflict as consisting of a series of short, sharp actions.

One of those who, despite everything, still championed the cause of the heavy bomber, was the very able Generalleutnant Walter Wever, the Luftwaffe's first Chief of Air Staff. He foresaw the urgent necessity of establishing a fleet of heavy bombers. But Walter Wever was killed in an aircraft crash in June 1936, and with him died any hope that Germany would ever possess a strategic bombing arm.

In 1936 G W Feuchter, a well-known aviation correspondent of the day who contributed to a number of newspapers and specialist magazines, wrote of a future air war and the Luftwaffe's operational options in any such conflict. In his piece he stressed the need for a strategic bomber, which, with a ceiling of 16,000 metres (52,500 feet) and a speed of 1,000 km/h (620 mph), would represent a weapon of decisive importance.

And these requirements were being quoted by G W Feuchter as early as 1936.

The development of heavy and long-range bombers, already neglected during the *Reichswehr* era, was now dismissed by Party, State and military leaders as unnecessary and not crucial in any forthcoming war. Up until 1938 there was not a single bomber type in Germany which came anywhere near fulfilling the requirements of a strategic role.

It was only after Junkers and Dornier had stopped work on their Ju 89 and Do 19, and the competition to build Germany's first large bomber was abandoned, that the Luftwaffe leadership again began to entertain the idea of a heavy bomber. Now, however, in place of the allegedly unsuitable Ju 89 and Do 19, a different type of bomber was envisaged.

The new machine was to be capable of carrying a 1,200 kg (2,650 lb) payload to a target over a distance of 2,500 kilometres (1,550 miles). The number of engines was left to the discretion of the manufacturers. Particular value was laid upon the maximum speed, which would dictate the equipment and

armament fitted. The minimum speed at an altitude of 6,000 metres (19,500 feet) was to be in the region of 500 km/h (310 mph). First flight was scheduled for January 1938.

After submitting plans, the Heinkel works at Rostock were awarded a development contract for their He P.1041 design. A mock-up was ready for inspection on 6th August 1937. The general arrangement of this mock-up was deemed satisfactory and the new type was given the official RLM designation He 177.

Dipl-Ing Heinrich Hertel, who had joined Heinkel from the *Deutschen Versuchsanstalt für Luftfahrt* (DVL: German Aviation Experimental Establishment) a few years earlier, was named technical director of the overall development programme. The project leader was Dipl-Ing Siegfried Günther.

As a fully operational long-range bomber a maximum loaded weight of 28,000 kg (62,000 lb) was specified, and great pains were taken not to exceed this figure. As there were no engines of sufficient power available for the He 177, trials were carried out, at the instigation of Dipl-Ing Siegfried Günther, with two side-by-side engines driving a single propeller. As a result, Daimler-Benz agreed to build two coupled DB 9-601 engines rated at 2,700 hp (see page 129).

This DB 9-606 twin power plant was exhaustively tested in the He 119, where it performed faultlessly. The maiden flight of the He 177 took place on 20th November 1939.

The low-drag surface evaporation cooling system, which Heinkel had fitted to, and tested on, the He 100 and He 119, proved a major problem on the He 177. The high temperatures caused the wing upper surface to distort to such an extent, and altered the aerofoil to such a degree, that test flying had to be halted on account of unairworthiness. Attempts to enlarge the cooling surface area brought no improvement.

The fitting of more orthodox, but higher drag, radiators resulted not only in an increase in weight, but also an attendant decrease in speed and range. In order to retain the necessary range, considerably more fuel had to be accommodated; this lead to yet another weight increase.

After the *Technisches Amt* and the Luftwaffe High Command had fully embraced the dive-bomber concept, it was decreed that the He 177 should also be capable of dive-bombing. The tragedy of this bomber was about to unfold. It would end in death and destruction – not of the enemy, but among its own.

As originally designed, the He 177 would – with a certain amount of structural strengthening – have been able to approach its target area in so-called 'inclined flight', a sort of shallow dive. But full dive-bombing capability necessitated a substantial strengthening of the wings and the fitting of large dive-brakes. Thus modified, the He 177 entered pre-production with a loaded weight of 31,000 kg (68,300 lb).

It is now common knowledge that, despite numerous improvements and modifications to the basic design, the He 177 never emerged as a reliable operational aircraft. The story of its inadequacies as a heavy bomber, which cost the lives of hundreds of its crew members – the vast majority, it must be said, not as the result of enemy action – is continued elsewhere (see page 23).

1943

The trials and tribulations described above, not least the irrational demand for dive-bombing capabilities, spelled the end for the piston-engined heavy bomber in Germany.

It was not until 1943 that the development of the jet engine began to promise the level of flight performance, in terms of speed, altitude and range, which would lead to the jet-powered bomber.

By the end of that year, after a lot of preliminary work, Junkers had come up with a project design for an aircraft fitted with forward-swept wings and powered by four jet engines; both features reflecting the very latest state of the art in aerodynamic and power plant technology. In order to be able to test the flight characteristics of such a radically new type of aircraft as quickly as possible, a machine was put together using components from other aircraft. This meant that, basically, only the wings and engine installation had to be designed and produced from scratch. In just a few months the prototype four-jet bomber ordered by the RLM had been built and given the designation Junkers Ju 287.

The fuselage was from a Heinkel He 177A-3, the tail surfaces were taken from the Junkers Ju 188 and the undercarriage – including the nosewheels – was adapted from a captured US Consolidated B-24 Liberator bomber.

Power was supplied by four Junkers Jumo 109-004 jet turbines which were arranged singly: one each side of the nose, and one under each wing.

As a safety precaution for the first flight of the Ju 287 on 16th August 1944, and for all other test flights, a Walter HWK 109-502 rocket pack was suspended beneath the nacelle of each wing turbojet. Producing 1,000 kp thrust to assist take-off, these Walter rockets were jettisoned as soon as their fuel was exhausted. (The -502 was a development of the 109-501, see page 134.)

Again, to undertake flight testing as quickly as possible, it was decided to dispense with a retractable undercarriage. The fixed main gear was attached directly to the wing and strut-braced. As the nosewheel of the Ju 287 had to support a heavier load than that of the B-24, two separate units were arranged side-by-side and slightly apart. To reduce drag, both main and nosewheels were fitted with oversized spats.

After a relatively short period of building and testing at the factory, the Ju 287 V1 was transferred to the Luftwaffe's test centre at Rechlin. The trials programme carried out there ran very smoothly and satisfactorily. But despite the test centre's good report, all further development work was abandoned after the second test flight upon the orders of the RLM. At the beginning of 1945 the RLM then returned to Junkers demanding that the company get the Ju 287 into series production as soon as possible.

Nearly all the projects worked on by Junkers in furtherance of the Ju 287 design featured the characteristic forward wing sweep. Although this arrangement offered undoubted aerodynamic and constructional advantages, it posed equally severe problems in terms of wing strength and stability. Subsequent projects, designated the EF 122, EF 125, EF 131 and EF 132, all featured an aerodynamically improved fuselage and more powerful engines. In these further developments of the Ju 287 Junkers were able to increase both the range and the weapon load and thus meet the RLM's requirements.

1944

In November 1944 the Messerschmitt design office put forward a proposal for a four-jet flying-wing bomber under the project number Me P 1107. Designed to carry a 4,000 kg (8,800 lb) bomb load over long distances at high speed, it far exceeded all of the RLM's conceptual requirements. Messerschmitt's designers based this bomber project on knowledge gained from prior work on a high-speed variant of the Me 262. At the same time, the circular cross-section of the fuselage could not disguise its similarity to the Me 264. The four jet engines were mounted in pairs beneath the wings and were easily accessible for maintenance. The horizontal tail surfaces, set high on the fin and rudder (T-tail), was taken over and used for the Me P 1106 fighter design, which was also on the drawing boards at the end of 1944.

A somewhat similar design submitted by Junkers, with the project designation EF-130, was intended to deliver a 4-ton bomb at speeds in excess of 1,000 km/h (620 mph) over a distance of 7,800 km (4,850 miles). With this project the Junkers' designers had reverted to an old tradition of Hugo Junkers,

Generalleutnant Walter Wever

Walter Wever was born in Berlin on 11th November 1887. He joined the 10th Grenadier Regiment in Schweidnitz as an officer-cadet in 1910. He took to the field upon the outbreak of war in 1914 as an Oberleutnant; 1916 to 1918 employed on General Staff duties. After the end of the war served with various General Staffs of the Reichswehr before promotion to General Staff Officer with VII. Division in Munich in 1921.

1926 Promoted to Major; entered Reichswehrministerium (MoD) in 1927.

1929 Appointed Battalion Commander in 12th Infantry Regiment, Wever was promoted to Oberstleutnant at the end of the year.

1931 Returned to the Reichswehrministerium.

1932 Became a Departmental Head with the rank of Oberst (Colonel). Upon the creation of the Luftfahrtministerium (Ministry of Aviation), Oberst Wever was appointed Director.

1935 As a Generalmajor, elevated to Chief of Air Staff of the newly established Luftwaffe.

20th April 1936 Promoted to Generalleutnant. Wever was the only member of the Air Staff to appreciate the importance of the long-range heavy bomber in any future air war.

1936 On 3rd June Walter Wever was killed when the aircraft he was piloting crashed.

Oberst Siegfried Knemeyer

Oberst Siegfried Knemeyer 1909-1979 was one of the most able men in the RLM. His ingenuity and perspicacity, his extensive technical knowledge and his experience as a pilot made him a natural choice, after the death of Udet, to take over the post of Chief of the Aircraft Development Office within the Technical Air Armament Department of the RLM.

He was a passionate and gifted flyer. Such was his mastery of the air that he – and he alone – could commence a loop from within a tight Staffel formation of nine machines and complete it by slotting back perfectly into his original position.

1933 Instructor with the Blind Flying School at Celle.

1935 Pilot of the RLM flight based at Staaken.

1936 The previously civilian Knemeyer donned Luftwaffe uniform. His lowly rank of Leutnant reflected his sparse knowledge of military ways – not his abilities in the air.

1940 Served in the *Sondergruppe* (Special Wing) *Rowehl*, where the most up-to-date aircraft and equipment for long-range reconnaissance were placed at his disposal. With a specially-equipped Focke-Wulf Fw 200 he carried out reconnaissance flights over the then USSR. Promoted to Hauptmann shortly afterwards, Knemeyer was awarded the Knight's Cross for his outstanding long-range reconnaissance activities. After Udet's death he became Chief of the Aircraft Development Office in the Technical Air Armament Department (TLR) of the RLM with the rank of Oberst. This position demanded not just extensive technical knowledge of aviation matters, but also great powers of persuasion and the ability to get things done. After 1945 Knemeyer made his way, via France and England, to the USA. There he worked at the USAF's test facility at Wright-Patterson AFB in Dayton, Ohio, which housed 'everything that could fly'. Knemeyer developed the basics of inertial navigation, which is today employed in both civil and military aviation alike. In June 1966, in recognition of his great contribution to aviation, Knemeyer was honoured with the United States' highest civil decoration, the Exceptional Civilian Service Award. He received the scroll from the hands of the Director of the Flight Dynamics Laboratory, Colonel G T Buck.

The innovations developed by Knemeyer in the field of flight navigation, his flight control equipment and flying instruments attest to his particular ability to find practical solutions to problems which other experts have at times regarded as insoluble. His name will forever be linked with the navigational calculator he invented: the 'Knemeyer'.

Siegfried Knemeyer died in the United States on 11th April 1979.

whose original flying-wing constructions had broken new ground back in the 'twenties.

At the end of October 1944 the Horten brothers, Walter and Reimar (see page 71), had also submitted a flying-wing long-range bomber project to the RLM. Powered either by two Junkers Jumo 109-018 turbojets, or by two 24-cylinder Argus As 9-413 piston engines, this was designed to carry a 2-ton bomb load at a maximum speed of 850 km/h (530 mph) and have a range of 7,800 km (4,850 miles). The Hortens' Ho VIII project was to be manned by a crew of four. With its simple but robust construction it was intended as a replacement for the more conventional types then in service.

During a visit to the Horten works, Oberst Siegfried Knemeyer of the *Amt für Technische Luftrüstung* (TLR = Directorate of Air Armament) personally flew the Horten Ho VII flying-wing aircraft. He was so impressed by the machine's flight characteristics that he declared the flying-wing to be *the* ideal layout for a long-range bomber. The Horten brothers saw in this a confirmation of their research and belief that the flying-wing was far superior to any conventional aircraft for flights over extreme distances. Before the end of 1944 the brothers had been awarded a development contract for the six-jet Ho XVIII-1 flying-wing, long-range bomber, which was intended for transatlantic service and operations against the USA.

On 26th January 1945 a committee of the *Deutschen Versuchsanstalt für Luftfahrt* (DVL = German Aviation Experimental Establishment) met under the leadership of the aerodynamicist Professor Bock to consider the bomber projects submitted by Arado, Blohm & Voss, Horten, Focke-Wulf and Messerschmitt, all of which promised near supersonic speeds and the ability to carry large bomb loads over ranges in excess of 10,000 km (6,200 miles).

A feature of all the designs was the inordinately high wing loading. It was clear that there was still a vast amount of work to be done in the drawing offices and the wind tunnels. But time was now slipping away. Messerschmitt's designers reacted quickly. On 31st January 1945 they laid before Karl-Otto Saur, chief of the Rüstungsstab (Armaments Staff), plans for an improved version of their Me P 1107 long-range bomber project. Designated the Me P 1108-1, this retained the overall dimensions of the earlier design, but now had the engines fully faired into the wing roots and the T-tail replaced by a V- or 'butterfly' tail.

The design specifications of the Me P 1108 included the following data: take-off weight 29,360 kg (64,700 lb), maximum speed

1,020 km/h (634 mph) with a range of 7,400 km (4,600 miles) as a bomber and 9,600 km (5,960 miles) as a reconnaissance machine.

It was also envisaged that, when fitted with the appropriate armament, the Me P 1108 could be employed in the fighter or Zerstörer roles, or even serve as an airborne command aircraft.

If the entire design staff was put on to the project, it was estimated that a full set of construction plans for the Me P 1108 could be produced in about eight weeks.

When Hitler was made aware of this Messerschmitt proposal he was filled with enthusiasm. The then Minister of Armaments and Munitions, Albert Speer, later gave a graphic description of the Führer's reaction in his '*Spandauer Tagebüchern*' (Spandau Diaries). He had never seen Hitler so excited as he was at that moment, imagining New York disappearing in a sea of flames. According to Speer, Hitler had visions of skyscrapers transformed into blazing torches. He pictured them crashing to the ground in ruins and the whole blazing inferno being reflected in the night sky.

As a result, Hitler instructed Saur that Messerschmitt was to transfer all its energies to the Me P 1108 design so that it could be used to wreak revenge on the United States for the destruction of Germany's cities.

The Junkers factory likewise upgraded their original Ju 287 project into a six-jet version under the designation EF 131 (EF = *Entwicklungs Flugzeug* – Experimental Aircraft). Influenced by the Horten and Messerschmitt designs, Junkers also proposed the EF 130, an all-wing project which, in dimensions and estimated performance, was very similar to the Me P 1108.

In order to compare all these proposed developments, representatives of the aircraft manufacturers concerned met up with top officials of the RLM for a second – and probably last – time at Dessau between 20th and 23rd February 1945. Reichsmarschall Hermann Göring was also present at these discussions.

Junkers presented their improved Ju 287 and the six-jet EF 130 project, Messerschmitt their Me P 1107/2, and the Horten brothers their Ho XVIII/I and Ho XVIII/II designs; the latter pair differing primarily in the bomb and fuel loads carried. Comparison lists undertaken by the DVL showed that the Junkers and Messerschmitt projects were inferior to the Horten proposals in range and bomb load.

In addition, the Hortens' method of construction – using tubular steel, wood and fabric – was not only simple in the extreme, it also produced a much smaller radar echo than an all-metal aircraft.

Göring was so convinced by the Horten Ho XVIII project that he ordered construction to begin immediately.

But even if the simplest methods and measurements were used – the smallest possible dimensions, rocket-assisted take-off, or a special take-off trolley to obviate the need for a complicated undercarriage – the chances of completing the Horten project in the foreseeable future were minimal.

But the designers did not give up. The Messerschmitt team, for example, continued work on the Me P 1108/II flying-wing project.

Junkers took a new line with their EF 130/II project, a scaled-down version of the basic EF concept. But in mid-March 1945 both Messerschmitt and Junkers abandoned all further work on their long-range bomber designs on the express orders of the RLM.

There are construction drawings from Messerschmitt's Oberammergau design department, dated 12th and 22nd March 1945 and relating to a further development of the Me P 1108/II long-range bomber, which indicate that the design of the jet engine intakes had not yet been fully resolved.

A passage in the war diary of the chief of the Air Armament Directorate (TLR) poses something of a mystery. The entry for 17th March 1945 reads: *'Above all, the Ju 287 is to be built in order to provide the front with a new type of fully operational bomber.'*

It must be remembered, however, that these words were written at the time of the final collapse when total confusion reigned, even in the RLM. Despite all the chaos, the Horten brothers were still striving to reduce the surface area of their Ho XVIII B-2 project in order to gain an increase in speed.

On 23rd March 1945 Reichsmarschall Göring by-passed official channels to give the Horten brothers a contract to build their long-range bomber, even though there were no tactical requirements for the machine and design work had not even been completed. Construction was to begin in the underground installation at Kahla in Thuringia on 1st April 1945.

As production of the Heinkel-Hirth 109-011 turbine, the engine intended to power the bomber, was suffering ever increasing delays, the Horten brothers tried to obtain examples of the experimental 3,000 kp thrust BMW 109-018 turbojet. When all efforts failed, the Hortens had no other choice but to revert to the Junkers Jumo 109-004, a few of which were still available.

But then the cessation of hostilities and the total collapse of the Reich brought a final end to the Luftwaffe's strategic heavy bomber.

Professor Dr-Ing Günther Bock

Professor Dr-Ing Günther Bock 1898-1970, Director of the German Aviation Experimental Establishment DVL, was Chairman of the commission convened on 16th January 1945 to consider the proposed long-range bomber projects.

1898 Born in Berlin.

1920 Commenced studies at Berlin's Technical University (TH).

1931 Appointed University Professor at the Danzig TH.

1935 Member of the Academy for Aviation Research, Chairman of the Committee of the Scientific Association for Aviation.

1936 Director and Head of the German Aviation Experimental Establishment (DVL) at Berlin-Adlershof

1937 Appointed University Professor in Service of the Reich.

1941 Assumed scientific leadership of the DVL Berlin.

1944 Appointed Director of the DVL.

1945 Leader of the committee appointed by Göring to examine and evaluate the proposals for long-range bomber projects submitted to the RLM. When the DVL facility in Berlin-Adlershof was occupied by Russian troops, Professor Dr Bock was taken into custody on 29th April 1945 and transported to the Soviet Union.

1954 Returned from captivity a very ill man. Appointed Professor at the Darmstadt TH.

1970 Professor Dr-Ing Bock dies in Munich.

Chapter Two

Bomber Projects of the Reichswehr 1926-1933

Rohrbach Ro XII 'Roska'

In 1926 the Rohrbach factory in Berlin developed a four-engined bomber, designated the Ro XII, to meet the specifications of the *Heereswaffenamt* (Army Ordnance Directorate). With a wingspan of 38.30 m (125 ft 7 in), a length of 20.50 m (67 ft 3 in), four separate engines, a fixed undercarriage and a bomb load of 700 kg (1,540 lbs), its range was to be 1,200 km (745 miles).

In layout the 'Roska' was a cantilever shoulder-wing monoplane of all-metal construction.

Due to the limited power output of the four engines, estimated speed was only 260 km/h (162 mph), which was below the specified requirements.

In all other respects the 'Roska' met the criteria of a standard heavy bomber of the period. But that alone did not suffice for the Air department of the *Heereswaffenamt* to recommend production.

The 'Roska' did not progress beyond the model stage, and in May 1927 the Reichswehr withdrew the development contract.

Other sources quote the wingspan as 43.05 m (141 ft 2 in) and the length as 21.60 m (70 ft 10 in). Power plant was to have been four 600 hp in-line engines.

Dornier Do P – A Four-engined Bomber for the Reichswehr

Dornier Do P – data

Dimensions

Span	30.00 m	98 ft 5 in
Length	23.40 m	76 ft 9 in
Height	7.30 m	23 ft 11 in

Weights

Loaded weight	12,000 kg	26,450 lb
Bomb load	1,000 kg	2,200 l

Performance

Max speed	210 km/h	130 mph
Range	1,000 km	620 miles
Ceiling	3,500 m	11,500 ft

Development of the Do P – a very large aircraft for its time – was begun in 1928 on behalf of the *Reichsverkehrsministerium* (Ministry of Transport).

The Do P was a strutted high-wing machine featuring an all-metal fuselage and wing structure; the latter being partially fabric-clad. Power was provided by four 500 hp Siemens-Jupiter radial engines arranged in tandem in two wing-mounted nacelles.

Only one example of the Do P was built. It was sent for trials to Lipezk, the *Reichwehr*'s test-centre in the Soviet Union.

As the Do P's flight characteristics proved unsatisfactory, it was rejected by the *Reichswehr* Command. No further examples were built.

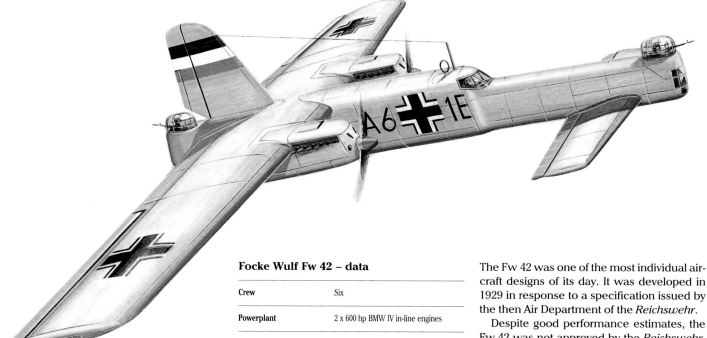

Focke Wulf Fw 42 – data

Crew	Six	
Powerplant	2 x 600 hp BMW IV in-line engines	
Dimensions		
Span	25.00 m	82 ft 0 in
Length	19.80 m	64 ft 11 in
Height	4.30 m	14 ft 1 in
Weights		
Bomb load	1,000 kg	2,200 lb
Performance		
Max speed	310 km/h	192 mph
Range	1,800 km	1,120 miles
Ceiling	6,000 m	19,680 ft

The Fw 42 was one of the most individual aircraft designs of its day. It was developed in 1929 in response to a specification issued by the then Air Department of the *Reichswehr*.

Despite good performance estimates, the Fw 42 was not approved by the *Reichswehr*. A contract to build a mock-up was issued by Dipl-Ing Roluf Lucht – later to become the RLM's *Generalstabsingenieur* and the Luftwaffe's senior engineer – who, for reasons of military secrecy and camouflage, was currently representing the *Reichswehr* within the Ministry of Transport. A production contract was not awarded, whereupon all work on the Fw 42 project was terminated.

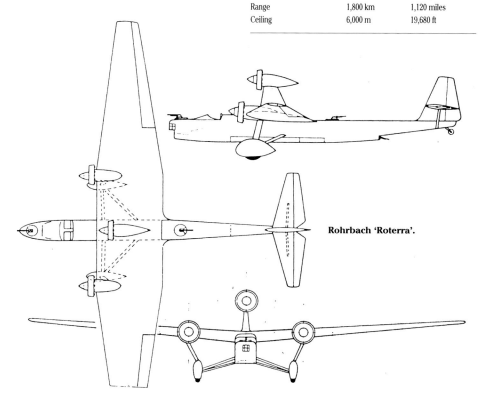

Rohrbach 'Roterra'.

Rohrbach 'Roterra'

One of the lesser-known Rohrbach designs is the 'Roterra' of 1930. This three-engined medium-range bomber failed to interest the *Reichswehr* on account of its insufficient engine power and consequent limited speed.

With a wingspan of 30.00 m (98 ft 5 in), a length of over 20.00 m (65 ft 7 in) and a wing area of 110 m² (1,185 ft²), the Rohrbach 'Roterra' was intended to attain a top speed of 250 km/h (155 mph).

Powered by three British 450 hp Bristol 'Aquilla' radial engines its estimated range exceeded 1,000 km (620 miles).

In 1932 Rohrbach granted licence manufacturing rights to Czechoslovakia where the 'Roterra', now known as the Avia 46, was produced in five different versions with bomb loads ranging from 700 to 1,000 kg (1,540 to 2,200 lbs).

Dornier Do Y – data

Crew	Four	
Powerplant	3 x 625 hp Gnome-Rhone radial engines	
Dimensions		
Span	36.62 m	120 ft 1 in
Length	18.20 m	59 ft 8 in
Height	7.30 m	23 ft 11 in
Wing area	108.8 m²	1,172 ft²
Weights		
Loaded weight	8,500 kg	18,734 lb
Performance		
Speed	310 km/h	192 mph
Range	1,500 km	932 miles

Dornier Do Y.

Dornier Do Y – An All-metal Bomber for the Reichswehr

The Do Y medium-range bomber, produced by Dornier's Swiss subsidiary in Zurich in 1930, was the first all-metal aircraft to be built. Its maiden flight took place on 17th October 1931. After extensive tests by the Air Directorate of the *Reichswehr*, the Do Y was rejected as being unsuitable for its intended role.

Dornier Do 23C – the Reichswehr's first production bomber.

Dornier Do F (Do 11) – data

Powerplant	2 x 550 hp Siemens-Jupiter radial engines	
Dimensions		
Span	28.00 m	91 ft 10 in
Length	18.70 m	61 ft 4 in
Height	5.60 m	18 ft 4 in
Loaded Weight	8,000 kg	17,630 lb
Performance		
Speed	250 km/h	155 mph
Ceiling	4,700 m	15,400 ft

Dornier Do F Do 11, the 'Flying Coffin'.

Dornier Do F (Do 11)

The Do F was developed as a freight and mail plane on behalf of the Reich's Ministry of Transport (RVM).

The maiden flight of this shoulder-wing aircraft, built by Dornier in Switzerland, took place on 7th May 1932.

After acceptance by the Association of the German Aviation Industry (RDL), which was the cover adopted by the *Reichswehr*, the Do F was sent for trials to the secret test and research centre of the *Reichswehr* at Lipezk, near Moscow, where it was modified as a night-bomber for the newly developed SC 500 bomb. Despite all the modifications and additions, the Do F failed to meet the specified requirements. A Do F equipped with more powerful engines entered series production at Dornier's Friedrichshafen works as the Do 11; 76 of these machines were built and delivered to the *Reichswehr*.

An improved version of the Do 11, the Do 13, underwent trials in mid-1932 but was rejected by the *Reichswehr*.

It was not until 1934, when the structurally modified and significantly improved Do 23 commenced flight testing, that the required specifications were finally met. A total of 237 Do 23s were delivered to the Luftwaffe.

Chapter Three

Heavy Bomber Projects 1933-1937

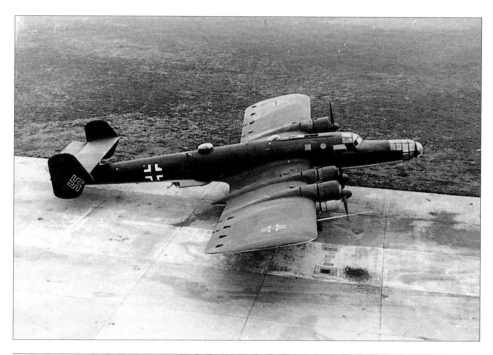

Immediately after the outbreak of war in 1939 the four available BV 142s, V1 to V4, which had been developed for service on the long-haul routes of Germany's civil airline Lufthansa, were ordered to be converted for military use by the Technical Office of the RLM.

The first prototype BV 142 V1/U2 (military code PC + BB) was modified similarly to the BV 142 V2/U1 with the addition of a lengthened, glazed nose and with improved armament allocated to Luftflotte 3 for special duties. The first fully converted multi-purpose aircraft, the BV 142 V2/U1 (military code PC + BC) was completed at the beginning of 1940. There followed the BV 142 V3/U1 (military code PC + PD) and the BV 142 V4/U1 (military code PC + BE), which were delivered directly to the Luftwaffe from the factory. A further conversion which had been envisaged for remotely controlled aircraft and glide bombs came to nothing, as the BV 142's performance and defensive deficiencies did not meet the proposed operational requirements. Following an RLM directive dated 27th September 1942, all four examples of the type were withdrawn from service and scrapped.

Blohm & Voss BV 142 V2/U1

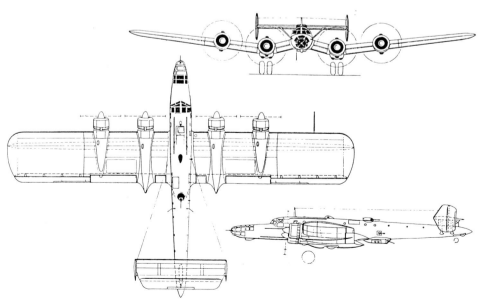

BV 142 V2/U1 – data

Crew	Four to Five	
Powerplant	4 x 1,000 hp BMW 9-132 H-1 radial engines	
Dimensions		
Span	29.50 m	96 ft 9 in
Length	20.45 m	67 ft 1 in
Height	5.05 m	16 ft 7 in
Wing area	130 m²	1,400 ft²
Weights		
Take-off weight	17,500 kg	38,500 lb
Performance		
Max speed	400 km/h	248 mph
Range	3,600 km	2,250 miles
Armament		
A-Stand:	1 x MG 15 or MG FF in Ikaria ball mounting	
B-Stand:	1 x MG 131 in HDL 131	
C-Stand:	1 x MG 15 or MG 81 Z in spherical mounting	
	2 x beam-mounted MG 15 or MG 81 Z in ball mtgs	

$$

$$

Junkers Ju 89 –
The Luftwaffe's First Heavy Bomber project

Junkers Ju 89 V1.

Junkers Ju 89 V2 – data

Dimensions

Span	35.27 m	115 ft 8 in
Length	26.50 m	86 ft 11 in
Height	7.61 m	24 ft 11 in
Wing area	184 m²	1,980 ft²
Undercarriage track	7.44 m	24 ft 5 in

Weights

Take-off weight	27,800 kg	61,275 lb
Empty weight	16,980 kg	37,425 lb
Bomb load	1,600-2,000 kg	3,525-4,408 lb

Performance

Max speed	386-410 km/h	240-255 mph
Service ceiling	7,000 m	22,950 ft
Range	2,980 km	1,850 miles

Armament   2 x MG 131 each in nose and tail turrets
1 x MG FF each in dorsal and ventral turrets

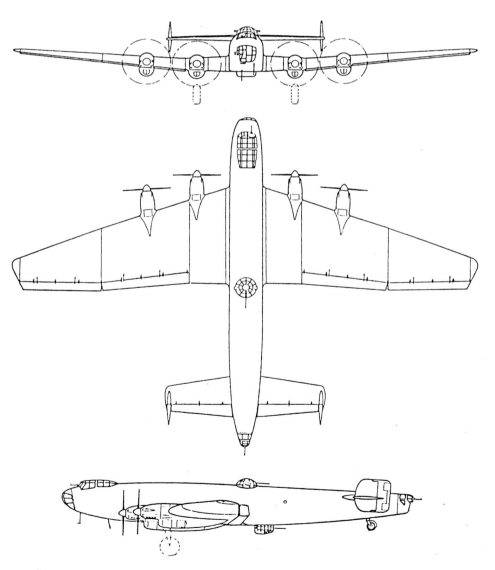

Junkers Ju 89 V1 – GA drawing.

From the moment he took power Hitler was determined to build up a strong and effective air force.

At the beginning of 1934 the Dornier and Junkers companies were requested to submit to the RLM suitable proposals for a bomber capable of carrying a bomb load in excess of two tons over a distance of 2,500 km (1,550 miles).

After the awarding of development and production contracts on 24th January 1935, work on the Junkers Ju 89 – construction of which had begun in 1933 under the leadership of Dipl-Ing E Zindel, then Junkers' chief designer (see page 31) – continued apace.

Despite severe problems, caused by the lack of sufficiently powerful engines, the Ju 89 V1 took off on its maiden flight on 7th December 1936. A few weeks later, early in 1937, the Ju 89 V2 took to the air for the first time.

Because of instability about the vertical axis, the rudders of the Ju 89 V2 required modification. At the same time assembly of the Ju 89 V3 was progressing rapidly.

Fitted with nose and tail armament the V3 was to have been the first armed prototype. But when it was in an advanced stage of assembly the RLM ordered work stopped on the Ju 89 V3. Instead, the components already completed were to be utilised, and further construction work redirected towards completing it as a heavy transport aircraft.

After a short period of development and construction, the new large capacity transport, designated the Ju 90 V1, took off for the first time on 28th August 1937. Despite a satisfactory performance the Luftwaffe leadership was losing interest in heavy bomber development.

On 29th April 1937 the RLM, without giving any further reasons, ordered an immediate halt to all construction and development work on both the Ju 89 and the Do 19.

The Ju 89 V1 and V2 were employed as trials aircraft in the Ju 90 programme. After the outbreak of war in 1939 they were taken over and used by the Luftwaffe as auxiliary transports.

Junkers Ju 89 V1 in flight.

Below: **Junkers Ju 89 V1.**

Dornier Do 19 –
A Bomber with a Future?

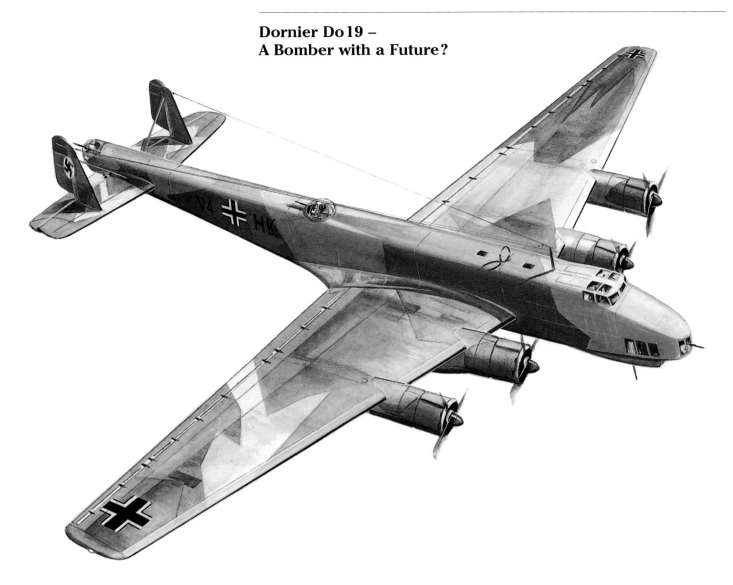

Dornier Do 19 – data

Dimensions

Span	35.00 m	114 ft 10 in
Length	24.45 m	80 ft 2 in
Height	5.77 m	18 ft 11 in
Wing area	162 m²	1,750 ft²

Weights

Loaded weight	18,500 kg	40,775 lb

Performance

Speed	315 km/h	196 mph
Range	1,500 km	932 miles

Dornier Do 19 in flight.

The Dornier Do 19 was an aircraft far in advance of its international contemporaries.

It was produced at a time when England was still drawing up its first specifications for a modern long-range bomber. The first project designs for the Do 19 were on the drawing boards by July 1933. On 24th February 1934 the Dornier company was awarded a contract to produce a mock-up of their Dornier P 30 project; the later Do 19. After inspecting the mock-up the RLM awarded a further contract for the production of three Do 19s. On 30th October 1936 the first prototype Do 19 V1 lifted off from the airfield at Löwental near Friedrichshafen on its maiden flight.

The Do 19 was a cantilever mid-wing design of light metal construction equipped with a fully retractable undercarriage. The square cross-section fuselage terminated in a twin tail unit with fabric covered rudders. The bomb bay, which accommodated a weapon load of more than 2,000 kg (4,408 lb), was situated in the middle of the fuselage.

Powered by four air-cooled BRAMO 9 322 J2 radial engines each rated at 715 hp, the Dornier Do 19 was able to achieve a speed of 315 km/h (195 mph).

In a communication dated 18th July 1936 the RLM ordered the cessation of all work on the Do 19 as there were no plans for the aircraft to enter series production. Despite this, trials at Rechlin continued. After 83 test flights the RLM finally decided to scrap the Do 19 prototypes and to remove long-range bomber development from the programme altogether. This decision, to delete the four-engined heavy bomber from its future plans, was one of the greatest mistakes made by the Luftwaffe during its formative years, as future years were to prove.

The then President of the Association of the German Aviation Industry, Admiral Lahs, wrote to Generalfeldmarschall Milch on 1st November 1942 regarding the Do 19 and Ju 89: *'had they been properly developed, both types would have been far superior to all American and English long-range bombers.'*

The Do 19 V1 was the first bomber to be equipped with an Askania-Sperry autopilot, which at this time was fitted to no other aircraft of any type, either at home or abroad.

Heinkel He 177 – A Bomber without a Chance

Following on from the specification for the Luftwaffe's Bomber-A programme issued by the RLM on 3rd June 1936, the Heinkel company received a contract to build a mock-up of the bomber project they had submitted under the designation P 1041. The He 177 was a cantilevered mid-wing aircraft of all-metal monocoque construction which was intended for use as a short-, medium- and long-range bomber depending upon weapon and equipment fit.

As there were no engines of sufficient power available at the time of development, Heinkel's chief engineer, Dipl-Ing S Günter, persuaded Daimler Benz to develop a compound power plant which consisted of two DB 9-601 engines coupled side-by-side. Designated the DB 209-606, this 2,700 hp power plant would attain series production. After exhaustive tests of the new 'double' engine in the Heinkel He 119, during which it performed admirably, it was fitted to the Heinkel He 177.

The first flight of the He 177 V1 was captained by Rechlin test pilot Dipl-Ing Carl Franke. Despite the premature cessation of the flight, brought about by excessively high oil temperatures, Franke praised the He 177's exceptionally good take-off and flight characteristics.

But all was not well. The first difficulties with the engine installations were already making themselves felt. Not enough attention was paid to these early warning signs, however. Attempts were made to prevent the frequent power plant fires by moving the engines forward and altering the oil and fuel feed lines. Heinkel's alternative remedy, to use four separate engines, was rejected by the RLM. Other serious problems, particularly the weakness of the wings under heavy load, also became apparent during the course of flight testing.

The dive-bombing capability required of the He 177, as laid down in the specification, necessitated a substantial strengthening of the airframe and wings. This, together with the fitting of dive brakes, led in turn to a marked increase in overall weight.

The He 177 that went into production thus had a take-off weight of 31,000 kg (68,000 lb) as opposed to the loaded weight of 28,000 kg (61,700 lb) which had been laid down in the original specification. And, as before, it was the coupled engine arrangement, with its associated high thermal overloading, which was the major cause of the unreliability and the accidents which would continue to plague the design until the end of the war.

Dornier Do 19 V

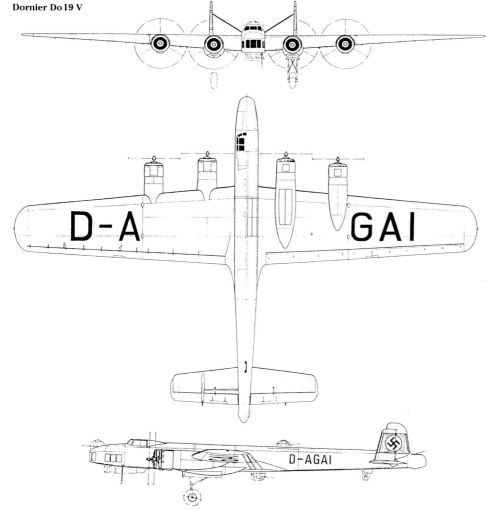

These problems, plus a large number of modifications to the He177, led at times to a complete halt in production.

Nevertheless the He177 was destined to become the best bomber available to the Luftwaffe during the war. In conception and design it was years ahead of contemporary bomber development. But it was also arguably the most controversial machine to enter Luftwaffe service. Aviation historians have found it difficult to do justice to the facts and deliver an unbiased opinion. The blinkered vision of bureaucracy, indecisiveness and ineptitude in the highest reaches of the RLM all conspired to prevent the He177 from becoming a potent and reliable weapon of war.

At the end of 1943 the RLM called a halt to the entire production programme and ordered the scrapping of all existing airframes. But industry and some front-line units were slow to comply with these instructions.

As the overall authority and final arbiter in such matters, the Ministry for Armaments and War Production therefore issued a similar edict on 8th July 1944 demanding the immediate cessation of production of the He177 and all its variants under threat of punishment. Despite these injunctions to stop production and scrap all completed machines, Heinkel continued design work on further developments of the He177 in secret.

Heinkel He 177 A-1 – data

Crew	Six	
Powerplant	2 x 2,700 hp DB 9-606A	
Dimensions		
Span	31.44 m	103 ft 1½ in
Length	21.80 m	71 ft 6 in
Height	6.70 m	21 ft 11½ in
Wing area	102 m²	1,098 ft²
Aspect ratio	9.72	
Weights		
Structural weight	8,500 kg	18,735 lb
Loaded weight	30,530 kg	67,280 lb
Wing loading	300 kg/m²	61 lb/ft²
Bomb load	4,800 kg	10,580 lb
Performance		
Max speed	545 km/h	338 mph
Service ceiling	8,800 m	28,850 ft
Range	3,700 km	2,300 miles

The Heinkel He177 V1 lands.

The Heinkel He177 V8 pictured at the Rechlin test centre.

Focke-Wulf's Transocean Project

In 1938 Germany's national airline, Deutsche Lufthansa, issued a requirement for a long-range aircraft capable of operating a non-stop service on their intended Frankfurt am Main to USA route.

Among the proposals submitted was one from Focke-Wulf. Their TO (Transocean) project came closest to meeting the specifications demanded by DLH and, at the same time, differed considerably in design layout from all the other proposals. With a range in excess of 7,750 km (4,800 miles) a speed of 700 km/h (435 mph) the *TO-Projekt* fulfilled the requirements laid down by the airline.

The technical specifications put forward on 14th February 1940 also included a proposed military variant, which met with the approval of the RLM. This Design 'B', a long-range bomber and reconnaissance aircraft, was intended as a replacement for the Fw 200 'Condor'.

By using four Daimler Benz DB 9-606 coupled engines, and transferring them from the wing edges into the fuselage, it was hoped to achieve an additional increase in speed at a higher wing loading. With a span of 35.80 m (117 ft 5 in) and a loaded weight of 42,000 kg (92,570 lb) the TO Project 'B' was intended to carry a 4,000 kg (8,816 lb) bomb load over a distance of 8,000 km (4,950 miles). The four coupled engines located in the fuselage would drive propellers mounted on the wing leading-edges via extension shafts.

A further study laid before the RLM was the Project 'F'. This proposal returned the coupled power plants to the wings in order to provide more space in the fuselage for military equipment.

Project 'L' envisaged a completely new form of fuselage construction. This comprised two arcs of a circle joined together; the lower arc, of smaller radius, forming the floor-frame and being connected to the larger cross-sectional segment above. Such an arrangement offered even more internal space, plus the possibility of pressurization. This method of fuselage construction is still in use today.

Nothing is known of those further developments of the basic TO design which were submitted to the RLM under the designations 'R' and 'S'. All project proposals did however feature a four-wheel main undercarriage; each wheel retracting into individual underwing bays.

Despite ongoing discussions between Lufthansa, the RLM and Focke-Wulf, involving Generalleutnant Udet, the Luftwaffe's Chief Engineer Lucht, *Fliegerstabsingenieur* (Engineer Major) Reidenbach and Focke-Wulf's chief designer Kurt Tank, the RLM – as the authority in overall charge of development – decided in the light of the current war situation not to go ahead with the TO project and cancelled the development contract in 1941.

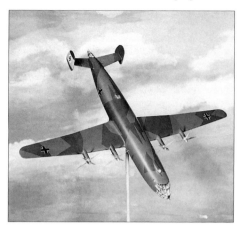

Model of the Focke-Wulf Transocean project.

Focke-Wulf TO projects – data

Powerplant	4 x 2,700 hp Daimler Benz 9-606 24-cylinder coupled engines	
Dimensions		
Span	35.80 m	117 ft 5 in
Length	28.10 m	92 ft 2 in
Wing area	128 m²	1,378 ft²
Weights		
Loaded weight	42,000 kg	92,570 lb
Load	3,960 kg	8,728 lb
Performance		
Speed	700 km/h	435 mph

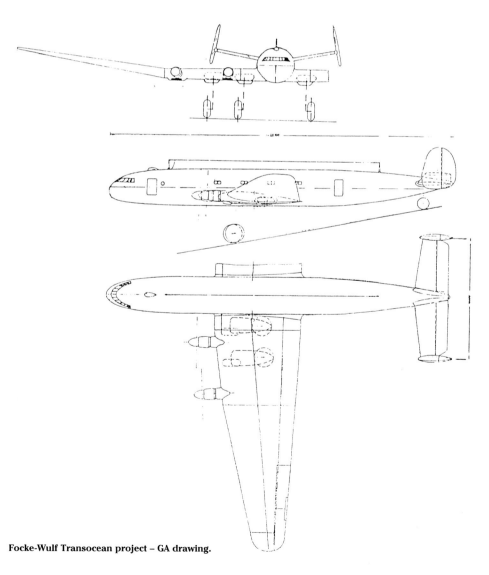

Focke-Wulf Transocean project – GA drawing.

Chapter Four

Prototypes and Projects in the Bomber-B Programme

At the beginning of July 1939 the Technical Office of the RLM issued a development contract for an aircraft of a type and purpose which broke entirely new ground.

Under the designation *Bomber-B* this was to be a twin-engined medium bomber capable of carrying a 4,000 kg (8,816 lb) bomb load to any point in the British Isles. Power would be supplied by either the Junkers Jumo 9-222 24-cylinder four-row radial or the 2,500 hp Daimler Benz DB 9-604, both currently under development. The requirement also included high-altitude and dive-bombing capabilities, which entailed the provision of a pressurised cabin for the four-man crew.

The specification was aimed primarily at the firms of Arado, Dornier, Junkers and Focke-Wulf, each of whom was invited to put forward development proposals.

The first manufacturer to respond was Arado. They submitted their E 340 design which, at the time the specification was issued, had already reached the mock-up stage. The Ar E 340 was a further study of the

Dornier Do 317(A) – data

Dimensions		
Span	20.64 m	67 ft 8½ in
Length	18.60 m	61 ft
Height	5.64 m	18 ft 6 in
Wing area	68 m²	732 ft²

Weights		
Take-off weight	18,600 kg	41,000 lb
Bomb load	4,000 kg	8,816 lb

Performance		
Max speed	560-600 km/h	348-372 miles
Range	3,980 km	2,472 miles

Dornier Do 317 V1.

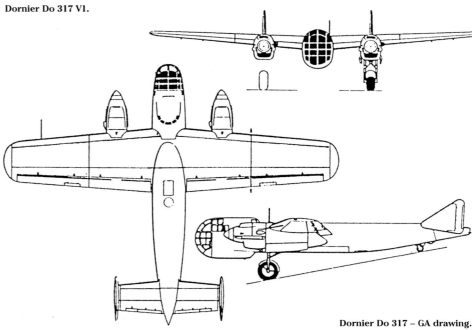

Dornier Do 317 – GA drawing.

earlier E 500 and differed from the latter only in a few minor structural details. The original layout, which featured a central gondola and two separate tailbooms, had been chosen in order to guarantee the rear gunner an unobstructed field of fire. But the finished design, supervised by Dipl-Ing Dr Blume, was rejected by the RLM on the very grounds of this unorthodoxy and all further work was abandoned. Dornier's Do 317, which was a further development of that company's Do 217, suffered likewise. This proposal also found little favour with the RLM. Only the Ju 288 of Junkers and Focke-Wulf's Fw 191 received the unequivocal backing of the authorities.

Towards the close of 1940 Dipl-Ing Kosel and his team at Focke-Wulf began detailed design work on the Fw 191, which would make its maiden flight at the beginning of April 1942.

The Jumo 9-222 engines, promised by Junkers and stipulated in the specification, could not be delivered on time and use had to be made of the less powerful BMW 9-801 instead. For technical reasons relating to the production process Daimler Benz had also been unable to deliver the promised DB 9-604 powerplant. And the RLM had, in the meantime, ordered work to cease on the DB 9-604, even though trial engines had achieved an output of 2,600 hp on the test rig. At Junkers, too, development of the Ju 288 continued apace under the leadership of Dipl-Ing Heinrich Hertel. But after months of effort and considerable expenditure this design was to suffer the same fate as the Fw 191; foundering on the lack of the intended Jumo 9-222 powerplant. Apart from the completion of a few prototypes, the RLM subsequently cancelled both the Fw 191 and the Ju 288.

Dornier Do 317

As their contribution to the Bomber-B programme Dornier proposed the Do 317, a further development of the Do 217. Despite the striking similarity between the two, hardly any component parts of the Do 217 were used in the new design.

The Do 317 was an all-metal, twin-engined shoulder wing machine with a twin fin and rudder assembly. Together with a fully-glazed pressure cabin for its crew of four, the Do 317 was to have been equipped with Jumo 9-222 24-cylinder engines.

The first prototype Do 317 V1 (VK+EY) was completed in September 1942 and trials began on an optimistic note.

During flight tests the (DB 603-powered) Do 317 displayed no appreciable improvement in performance over the Do 217E and P. However, the Do 317B currently under construction was to be fitted with two Daimler Benz DB 9-610 A/B engines in place of the absent Jumo 222s. Thus powered, a speed of some 600 km/h (372 mph) was achieved at an altitude of 6,000 m (19,680 ft).

Despite the good flying characteristics of both prototypes, the RLM decided against the Do 317 and ordered all further work to cease.

Arado Ar E 340

The Arado E 340 was envisaged as a high-performance, twin-engined medium bomber developed in response to the Bomber-B programme as a replacement for the Junkers Ju 88 and the Dornier Do 217.

Operational considerations dictated the required performance and the ability to dive-bomb. With a maximum speed of 600 km/h (372 mph) at an altitude of 7,000 m (23,000 ft) its range with a 4,000 kg (8,816 lb) bomb load was to be in the order of 3,600 km (2,235 miles).

The intended powerplant was to be either the Junkers Jumo 9-222 or the Daimler Benz DB 9-604.

The Arado designers elected to retain the same layout as proposed for the earlier E 500: a central fuselage gondola and two separate tailbooms. A fully-glazed pressure cabin would house the three-man crew.

The revolutionary new layout was rejected out of hand by the RLM and the design was dropped from the development programme – an incomprehensible decision for which no reason was ever given.

The same fate befell the Focke-Wulf Fw 191 and the Junkers Ju 288, both of which were likewise deleted from the development programme.

Arado Ar E 340

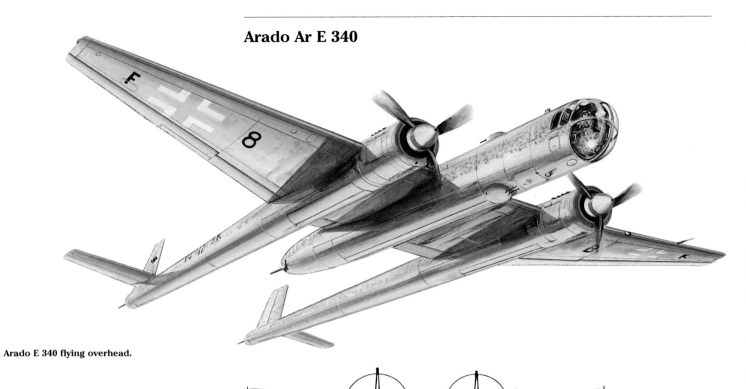

Arado E 340 flying overhead.

Arado E 340 – data

Dimensions

Span	23.00 m	75 ft 5½ in
Length	18.65 m	61 ft 2 in
Wing area	69 m²	743 ft²
Prop diameter	4.10 m	13 ft 5½ in

Weights

Loaded weight	19,300 kg	42,537 lb

Performance

Endurance	7.33 hrs	7 hrs 20 mins

Armament

Dorsal B-Stand:	FDL-131/7 barbette with 2 x MG 131 with FA 6 aiming
Ventral C-Stand:	FDL-131/7 barbette with 2 x MG 131
Fuselage tail:	FHL-151 barbette with remote control
Boom ends D-Stand:	2 x MG 131 with remote control

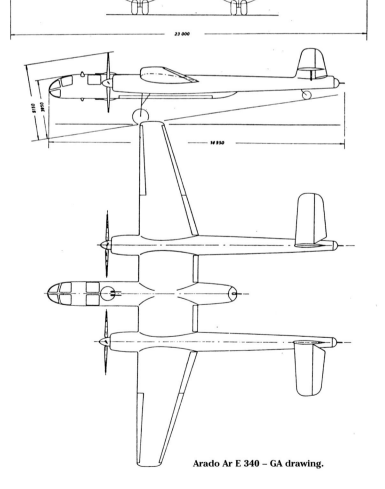

Arado Ar E 340 – GA drawing.

The Focke-Wulf Fw191 – An Aircraft of Superlatives

Design work on the Fw191 commenced in the spring of 1940. It was undertaken by a development team headed by Dipl-Ing Kosel. While a design group at Junkers, under the leadership of Professor Hertel, was developing the Ju 288 as a pattern aircraft in which every conceivable system was hydraulically powered, the Technical Office of the RLM demanded that the Fw191's systems be mechanical and powered by electric motors. The Focke-Wulf team were less than pleased at this stipulation. The incorporation of a large number of low-tension motors and their associated wiring led to an unnecessary increase in the weight of the Fw191. But the RLM overrode the objections raised by Focke-Wulf's designers.

By 1942 the first prototype Fw191 V1 was ready for flight. Despite all the promises, the expected Jumo 9-222 engines had not been forthcoming and, as an alternative, use had to be made of the less powerful BMW 9-801 powerplant.

The excessive electrification resulted in constant failures in many of the electric motors used for setting the flaps and rudders and caused untold problems during flight testing of the Fw191. Although already under construction, the Fw191 V3, V4 and V5 prototypes were never completed. Only the Fw191 V6 was allowed to convert to hydraulic power after grudging consent was given by the Technical Office.

Early in 1943 the Fw191 V6 commenced flight trials in the hands of Flugkapitän Sander, but a full test programme was never carried out.

After a ferry flight from Delmenhorst to the Wenzendorf experimental station on 26th July 1943, the construction of the Fw191 was finally halted. The Technical Office had abandoned the Bomber-B after it had become clear that the Jumo 9-222 would never enter series production due to a shortage of raw materials. The RLM rejected conversion to Daimler Benz DB 9-610 coupled engines without giving any reason. All other possible powerplants, such as the DB 9-605L, DB 9-614 and DB 9-628, were still undergoing trials.

After the demise of the Jumo 9-222 and the final production shutdown of the entire Bomber-B programme, Focke-Wulf submitted a proposal for a less refined version of the Fw191: the Fw191C. This project, featuring an increased wing span, was to be powered by four series production Jumo 9-211 engines. Although it could have been built in very short order, the RLM rejected the design.

Artist's impression of the four-engined Focke-Wulf Fw191C, which was also known within the company as the Fw 391 or Fw 491. The RLM did not recognize these designations, as no production contract had been awarded.

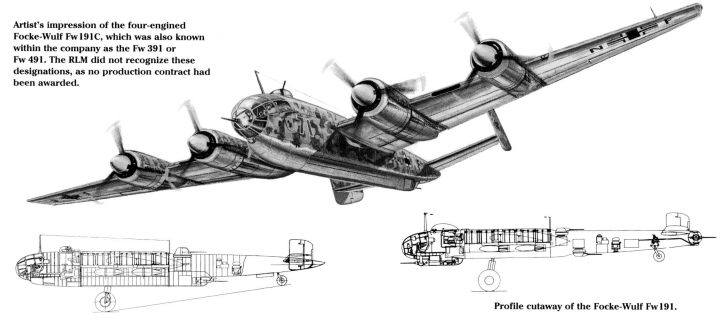

Profile cutaway of the Focke-Wulf Fw191.

Above: **Profile cutaway of the Focke-Wulf Fw191 with two DB 610 engines.**

Below: **Focke-Wulf Fw191 V1 front three quarter view.**

Focke-Wulf Fw191 – data

Dimensions

Span	26.00	85 ft 3½ in
Length	19.63 m	64 ft 4½ in
Height	5.60 m	18 ft 4½ in
Wing area	70.50 m²	759 ft²

Weights

Loaded weight	23,000 kg	50,700 lb
Bomb load	2,000 kg	4,408 lb

Performance

Range	2,500 km	1,552 miles
Speed	510 km/h	317 mph

Armament

	5 x MG 81 and 2 x MG 151

Junkers Ju 288

Under the generic project designation of Junkers EF 73 the Junkers design bureau under Dipl-Ing Heinrich Hertel had already developed a host of individual studies for a fast twin-engined bomber which, as it transpired, closely corresponded to the requirements specified by the RLM for the Bomber-B programme.

The EF 73 design selected for submission to the Technical Office was for a relatively small aircraft with a span of just 15.70 m (51 ft 6 in) and a length of 16.10 m (52 ft 9½ in) which, powered by two Jumo 9-222s, was to have a range of 2,700 km (1,677 miles) at a speed of 576 km/h (358 mph). The weapon load would be 3,000 kg (6,612 lb) and defensive armament comprised three remotely-controlled barbettes.

The maiden flight of the Ju 288 V1 was planned for October 1940 and series production was scheduled to begin early in 1942. But the failure of the Jumo 9-222 powerplant delayed prototype trials until mid-1942. These then had to be carried out with less powerful

Opposite page, top:
The Ju 288 V1 being prepared for flight at Dessau.

Opposite page, centre:
The Junkers Ju 288 V2 with BMW 9-801 engines.

Opposite page, bottom:
GA drawing of the Junkers Ju 288 V1.

Junkers Ju 288 V1 – data

Powerplant	2 x 1,250 hp BMW 9-801A	
Dimensions		
Span	15.70 m	51 ft 6 in
Length	16.10 m	52 ft 9½ in
Height	4.70 m	15 ft 5 in
Weights		
Bomb load	3,000 kg	6,612 lb
Performance		
Speed	576 km/h	358 mph
Range	2,700 km	1,677 miles

The Ju 288 V9 takes off from Dessau for a test-flight in 1943

BMW 9-801 twin-row radials, which only served to complicate the test programme even further.

On 11th June 1943 the RLM ordered the scrapping of the entire Bomber-B programme and with it any further work on the Ju 288. Flight testing nevertheless continued until mid-1944. By that time, of the 22 prototypes built, only five still survived; the remaining 17 having been damaged in accidents or scrapped. Those Ju 288s still intact were passed to the Luftwaffe, which reportedly used them individually on the eastern front.

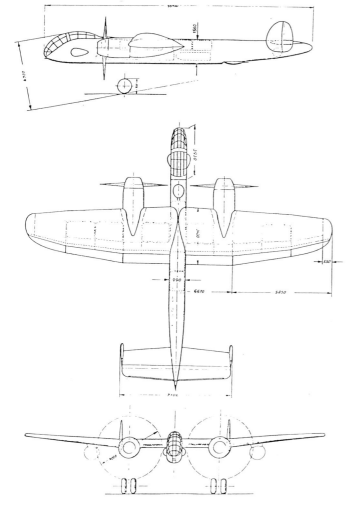

Dipl-Ing Ernst Zindel – Head of Overall Development

1897 Born 23rd January in Mistelbach, Upper Franconia.

1914 Volunteered for service with a Bavarian infantry regiment in Ingolstadt.

1916 After being severely wounded, studied shipbuilding at Charlottenburg TH.

1920 After graduation joined Junkers at Dessau as a designer.

1922 After the death of Chief Designer Dipl-Ing Otto Reuter, Ernst Zindel worked under Professor Dr Otto Marder, head of the research department. Ernst Zindel designed the Junkers G24, G31 and W 33/34 transport aircraft.

1927 Appointed head of Junkers' project development department.

1932 Took over as head of all development, design and flight-testing.

1933 Design director and deputy head of the Junkers Flugzeugwerke AG (Aircraft Co). Under his leadership the company produced the Junkers G 38, Ju 52, Ju 90, Ju 290, Ju 390, Ju 88 and Ju 388. Holder of various aircraft patents, including the Junkers pressurised cabin, which was first built into the Ju 49 high-altitude research aircraft. Until the war's end involved in the development of long-range jet bomber projects.

1945 After the war Ernst Zindel dedicated himself to the industrial reconstruction of West Germany. Design development of the infinitely variable gearbox while with Messrs. P.I.V. in Bad Homburg. Guest lecturer at the Technical Academy at Mülheim in the Ruhr.

1978 Ernst Zindel died, aged 81, on 10th October in Bad Homburg.

Dipl-Ing Ernst Zindel 1898-1978 was, from 1932 onwards, responsible for all development, design and flight-testing at Junkers.

Chapter Five

Strategic VLR Reconnaissance Aircraft & Guided Missile Carriers

Focke-Wulf Fw 300

The Focke-Wulf Fw 300 was developed in 1941 at the behest of Deutsche Lufthansa as a replacement for the Fw 200 'Condor' and was intended as a large transport for use on long-distance routes and for transocean services.

In 1942 the Reichsluftfahrtministerium ordered the conversion of the Fw 300 into a long-range reconnaissance machine and guided weapons carrier. An all-metal low wing design with a span of 46.20 m (151 ft 6½ in), length of 32.20 m (105 ft 7 in) and a wing area of 227 m² (2,443 ft²), the Fw 300 – powered by four 2,500 hp Junkers Jumo 9-222 engines – was to have a range of 8,800 km (5,465 miles) at 530 km/h (329 mph) in non-

stop flight. One notable feature of the Fw 300 was the proposed undercarriage, comprising four mainwheels, each with its own oleo leg, which retracted independently of each other into the undersurface of the wing. A pressure cabin was to be provided for the eight-man crew, from which all six weapon stations, each armed with two MG 151/20s, could be remotely controlled.

As well as being a long-range maritime reconnaissance aircraft, the Fw 300 was also intended for the anti-shipping role. With two additional waist gun positions the Fw 300 would have been a true 'Flying Fortress'. For service as an anti-shipping guided weapons carrier it was to have been additionally equipped with guided bombs.

Focke-Wulf Fw 300 – data

Crew	Eight	
Powerplant	4 x 2,500 hp Jumo 9-222 A/B or	
	4 x 1,850 hp Daimler-Benz DB 9-603E	
Dimensions		
Span	46.20 m	151 ft 6½ in
Length	32.20 m	105 ft 7 in
Height	5.60 m	18 ft 4½ in
Wing area	227 m²	2,443 ft²
Weights		
Loaded weight	47,500 kg	104,690 lb
Performance		
Range	9,000 km	5,590 miles
Speed	635 km/h	394 mph

Artist's impression of the Focke-Wulf Fw 300 as a large civil airliner.

Junkers EF 100 – Long-Range Maritime Reconnaissance Aircraft

Developed in 1940 for service on Deutsche Lufthansa's transocean routes, the EF 100 was to have been capable of transporting a 20,000 kg (44,080 lb) payload over a distance of 9,000 km (5,590 miles) non-stop.

In fact it never got that far. The Reichsluftfahrtministerium ordered its conversion for service as a long-range maritime reconnaissance aircraft and bomber. Of all-metal construction, the fuselage structure of the low-winged EF 100 closely resembled that of Focke-Wulf's *Transozeanprojekt* (see page 25); two cross-sectional arcs combining to provide ample freight and passenger space.

The militarized version could carry a 5,000 kg (11,020 lb) bomb load and a large amount of fuel.

At the same time the shape and structure of the fuselage was found to provide a lift effect which enhanced flight characteristics. Despite this, the Junkers design bureau abandoned further development work in 1941 upon the orders of the RLM, who had since come to regard the flying boat as providing greater possibilities for the way ahead.

In 1942 the RLM planned to order resumption of design work on the EF 100 as the Atlantic U-boats were then crying out for a long-range maritime reconnaissance aircraft. But for some inexplicable reason this decision was again overturned and all work on the EF 100 project was finally cancelled at the end of 1942.

Junkers EF 100 – data

Powerplant	6 x 2,500 hp Junkers Jumo 9-223 diesels	
Dimensions		
Span	65.00 m	213 ft 3 in
Length	49.80 m	163 ft 4 in
Height	9.00 m	29 ft 6½ in
Wing area	350 m²	3,767 ft²
Performance		
Range with military load	9,000 km	5,5990 miles

Colour impression of the Junkers EF 100.

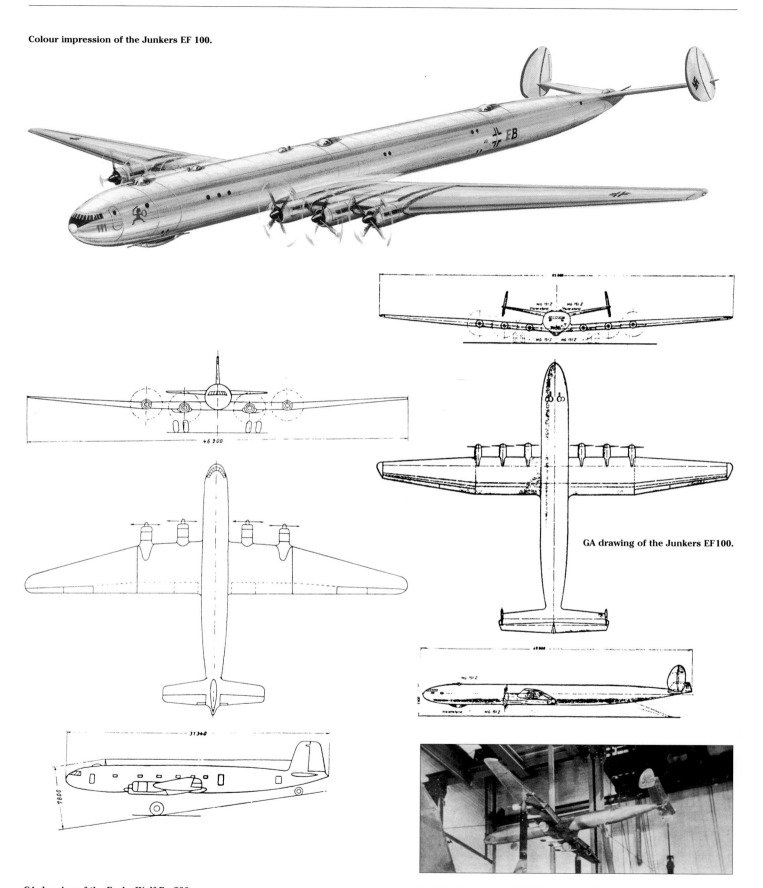

GA drawing of the Junkers EF 100.

GA drawing of the Focke-Wulf Fw 300.

Model of the Junkers EF 100 in the wind tunnel.

Junkers Ju 290A-7
Long-Range Bomber and Reconnaissance Aircraft

Colour impression of the Junkers Ju 290B-1 long-range bomber and reconnaissance aircraft.

Junkers Ju 290A-7 – data

Dimensions

Span	42.00 m	137 ft 9 in
Length	29.15 m	95 ft 7½ in
Height	6.83 m	22 ft 5 in
Wing area	204 m²	2,196 ft²

The Ju 290 long-range bomber was a military development of the Junkers Ju 90, a four-engined airliner which had been in regular service with Deutsche Lufthansa since 1938.

From the beginning of series manufacture of the Ju 290 and the maiden flight of the Ju 290 V1 prototype in July 1942, until production ceased in July 1944, a total of 48 machines had been built and delivered with a whole raft of various equipment fits depending upon each variant's intended operational role. The Junkers Ju 290A-7 was one of the most interesting versions of the A-series. Employed as a long-range bomber and reconnaissance machine against shipping targets, its most prominent external feature was the glazed gun position protruding from the nose. It also included significant improvements in the internal structure.

With its four 1,850 hp BMW 9-801 D-2 engines, the A-7 had a maximum speed of 445 km/h (276 mph) together with a range varying from 6,800 km (4,222 miles) as a bomber, to 11,500 km (7,140 miles) when employed in the long-range reconnaissance role and fitted with additional fuel tanks.

As a long-range anti-shipping weapon the A-7 was equipped with search radar and guidance systems. It was also fitted with ETC-2000 weapons racks beneath the fuselage and wing outer sections to enable it to carry three Henschel Hs 293 remotely-controlled glide bombs. Defensive armament comprised eight weapons stations, each operated manually by members of the eight- to ten-man crew.

A further development of A-7 was the Ju 290A-8. Also intended for the anti-shipping role, this too carried three Henschel Hs 293 glide bombs but featured increased defensive armament.

The Ju 290B-1 was to have been a long-range bomber version with a strengthened fuselage structure and a take-off weight of 49,500 kg (109,000 lb) when carrying a 4,500 kg (9,900 lb) bomb load. At an altitude of 5,500 m (18,000 ft) and a speed of 450 km/H (280 mph) the B-1's estimated range was in the order of 5,600 km (3,475 miles).

A planned further improvement of the Ju 290B-1 bomber was the Ju 290C. This would have had an even stronger fuselage and more powerful 1,850 hp BMW 9-801 engines. Additional projected versions of the Ju 290B-1 included a long-range reconnaissance variant and a heavy transport with a large, ventral loading ramp. The Ju 290D long-range bomber was an improved Ju 190C, as too was the Ju 290E night bomber project, which could carry an even heavier bomb load in its enlarged bomb-bay.

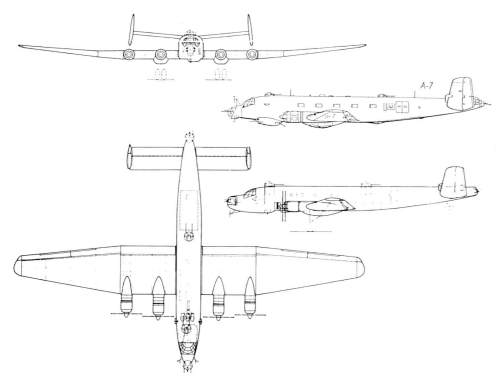

GA drawing of the Junkers Ju 290A-7.

An impression by Gerd Heumann of the Junkers Ju 290A-7 in flight.

The Junkers Ju 290A-7 as war booty in the United States.

Junkers EF101

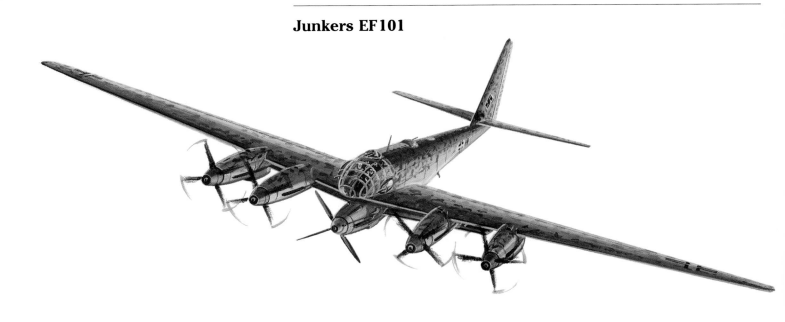

This Junkers project of 1942 was similar in conception to the Daimler Benz A and B projects (see page 77). It was a combination which consisted of a carrier aircraft and a high-altitude long-range reconnaissance machine – in this instance a further development of the Messerschmitt Me 109H – which was semi-recessed within the lower fuselage of the carrier.

The upper surfaces of the reconnaissance component were completely enclosed by the undersides of the carrier's wings and fuselage.

With a range in excess of 17,000 km (10,550 miles), the carrier's role was to transport the high-altitude reconnaissance aircraft deep into the operational area, where the latter – released from its 'mother ship' – would then carry out its designated task. Once this was completed it would return to the carrier aircraft which would recover it and transport it back to base. Recovery was achieved by means of a catch-and-lock device which had been developed by the DFS (German Glider Research Institute) and tested on a Heinkel He 177.

Junkers EF101 – data

Crew	Three – in a pressure cabin
Powerplant	4 x 2,700 hp Daimler Benz DB 9-613

Dimensions

Span	70.00 m	229 ft 7½ in
Length	26.50 m	86 ft 11 in
Height	9.60 m	31 ft 6 in
U/C track	18.50 m	60 ft 8 in

Performance

Range	17,000 km	10,550 miles
Ceiling	12,000 m	39,350 ft
Speed	760 km/h	472 mph

Armament	4 x remotely-controlled barbettes

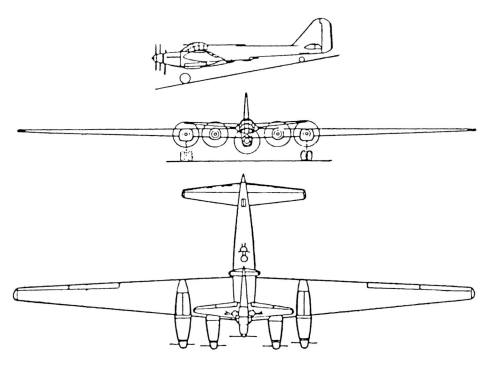

GA drawing of the Junkers EF 101.

Messerschmitt Me 261 –
Ultra Long-Range Reconnaissance Aircraft

The Messerschmitt Me 261 V1 long-range reconnaissance aircraft was powered by two DB 9-606 piston engines and was designed to fly 13,000 km (8,073 miles) non-stop.

Following an RLM decision of 18th March 1938, the Messerschmitt company received a contract for the development of a long-range aircraft which was to be capable of non-stop flight over routes in excess of 13,000 km (8,075 miles). It was at one point intended that the aircraft would carry the Olympic flame for the planned 1940 Olympic Games in Tokyo, non-stop from Berlin to Tokyo for prestige purposes.

The proposal, under the project designation P 1062, which Messerschmitt laid before the RLM was based upon the most up-to-date aerodynamic knowledge of the period. The first prototype, now bearing the official RLM designation Me 261 V1 and registered BJ+CP, took off on its maiden flight on 23rd December 1940. At the controls was the well known Messerschmitt test pilot Flugkapitän Karl Baur.

Further development work on the Me 261 was long and protracted, as the project did not have a priority rating, and powerplant deliveries were delayed until 1941. For some inexplicable reason the role specified for the aircraft by the RLM, that of long-range courier or ultra long-range reconnaissance machine, never materialized.

After a number of mostly satisfactory long-distance flights the Me 261 V1 was decommissioned on 8th July 1942. Little is known of the two other machines, the Me 261 V2 and V3, which had been completed in the meantime.

Despite a series of successful test flights, conducted primarily to prove the reliability of the engines, no military deployment was forthcoming. The Me 321 V2, BJ+CO, suffered damage in a bombing attack on Lechfeld in April 1945. An earlier landing accident, on 16th April 1943, had damaged the Me 261 V3, BJ+CR, so severely that it had been scrapped on the orders of the RLM. Only the Me 321 V2, repaired and almost back in flying condition, survived the war. After a partially successful attempt to destroy it had been made by Luftwaffe personnel, the machine fell into the hands of the Americans, who finally scrapped it a few weeks later.

Me 261 V1 – data

Crew	Six	
Powerplant	2 x 2,610 hp DB 9-606 A/B	
Dimensions		
Span	26.88 m	88 ft 2 in
Length	16.69 m	54 ft 9 in
Height	4.72 m	15 ft 5½ in
Wing area	85 m²	915 ft²
Prop diameter	4.50 m	14 ft 9 in
Performance		
Max speed	580-610 km/h	360-379 mph
Range	13,200 km	8,196 miles
Ceiling	12,500 m	41,000 ft
Endurance	24 hrs 36 mins at 5,000 m	16,400 ft

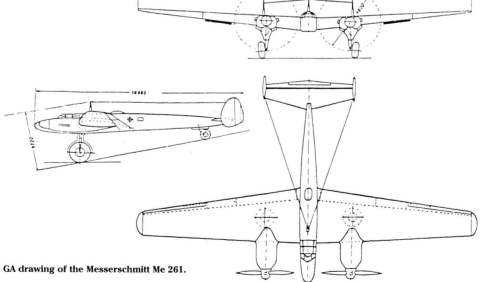

GA drawing of the Messerschmitt Me 261.

Far left: **Messerschmitt Me 261 V3 was damaged in a crash landing at Lechfeld on 16th April 1943 and subsequently scrapped by order of the Reichsluftfahrt-ministerium.**

Left: **This photo of the repaired Messerschmitt Me 261 V2 was taken at Lechfeld after the end of the war.**

Focke-Wulf Fw 261 –
A Very Long-Range Maritime Bomber

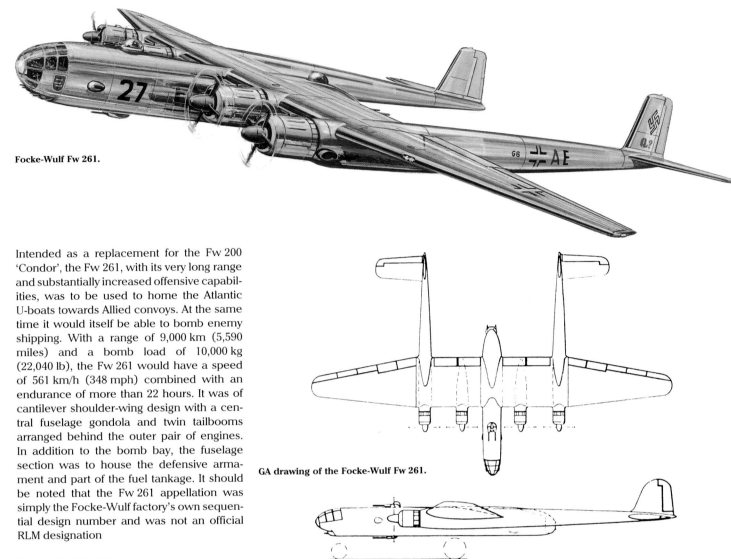

Focke-Wulf Fw 261.

Intended as a replacement for the Fw 200 'Condor', the Fw 261, with its very long range and substantially increased offensive capabilities, was to be used to home the Atlantic U-boats towards Allied convoys. At the same time it would itself be able to bomb enemy shipping. With a range of 9,000 km (5,590 miles) and a bomb load of 10,000 kg (22,040 lb), the Fw 261 would have a speed of 561 km/h (348 mph) combined with an endurance of more than 22 hours. It was of cantilever shoulder-wing design with a central fuselage gondola and twin tailbooms arranged behind the outer pair of engines. In addition to the bomb bay, the fuselage section was to house the defensive armament and part of the fuel tankage. It should be noted that the Fw 261 appellation was simply the Focke-Wulf factory's own sequential design number and was not an official RLM designation

GA drawing of the Focke-Wulf Fw 261.

Works cutaway drawing of the Focke-Wulf Fw 261 in profile.

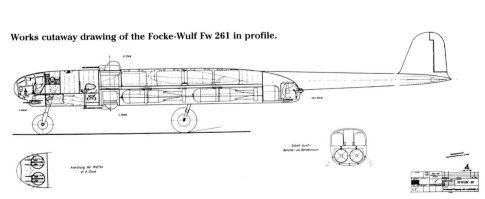

Focke-Wulf Fw 261 – data

Crew		Seven	
Powerplant		4 x 1,700 hp BMW 9-801D	
Dimensions			
Span		40 m	131 ft 2½ in
Length		26.10 m	85 ft 7½ in
Height		6.00 m	19 ft 8½ in
Wing area		187 m²	2,012 ft²
Weights			
Loaded weight		53,500 kg	117,900 lb
Bomb load		10,000 kg	22,040 lb
Armament			
Nose	A-Stand	2 x 2 MK 108	
Dorsal	B-Stand	HD 151Z	
Ventral	C-Stand	FDL 151Z	
Tail		4 x Mk 108	

Focke-Wulf's Large-Capacity Strategic Transport

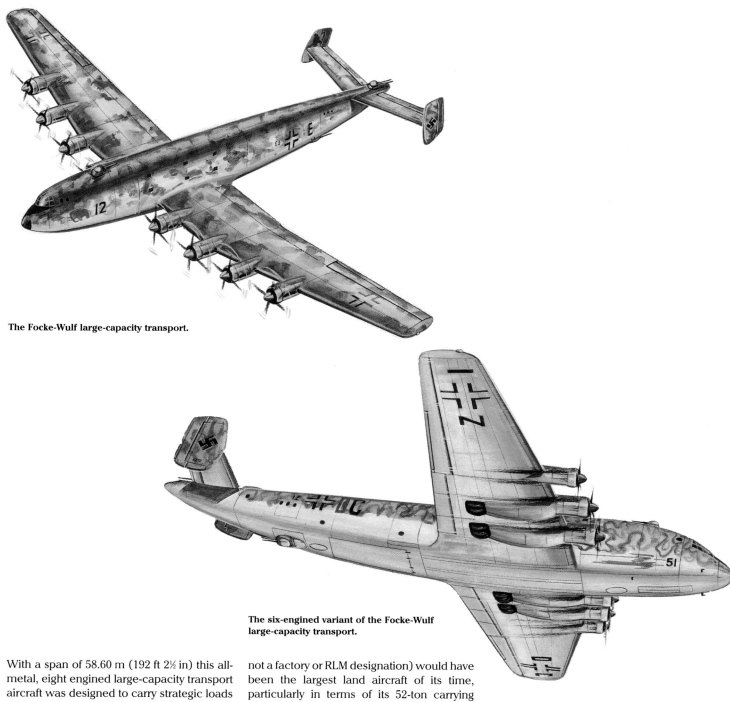

The Focke-Wulf large-capacity transport.

The six-engined variant of the Focke-Wulf large-capacity transport.

With a span of 58.60 m (192 ft 2½ in) this all-metal, eight engined large-capacity transport aircraft was designed to carry strategic loads of up to 52 tons (or 400 fully-equipped troops) over a distance of 2,100 km (1,305 miles).

The tricycle undercarriage of the low-wing transport would have facilitated the loading and unloading of bulky cargoes on a horizontal keel. To be powered by eight 2,500 hp Junkers Jumo 9-222 A/B engines, the Fw 195 project (another example of incorrect nomenclature; referring to the company's own internal sequential design number and not a factory or RLM designation) would have been the largest land aircraft of its time, particularly in terms of its 52-ton carrying capacity.

This project study, submitted to the RLM in August 1941 under drawing number 0310 221-15, did not progress any further due to the non-availability of the Junkers Jumo 9-222 engines. Plans for a scaled-down version, with just six Jumo 9-222s and a load capacity of 40 tons, were likewise abandoned for the lack of a suitable powerplant.

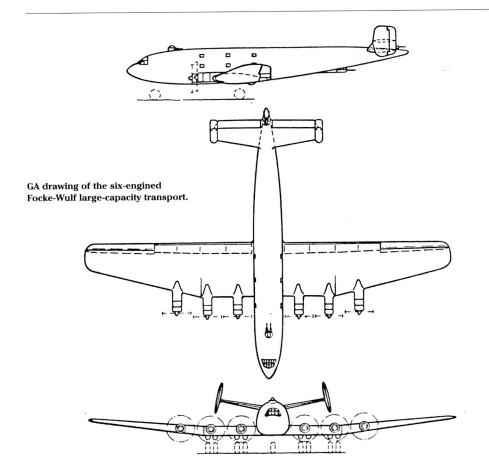

GA drawing of the six-engined
Focke-Wulf large-capacity transport.

Works impression of the Focke-Wulf large-capacity
transport being loaded with wheeled and tracked
vehicles.

Crew	Eight	
Powerplant	8 x 2,500 hp Jumo 109-222 A/B	
Dimensions		
Span	58.60 m	192 ft 2½ in
Length	47.00 m	154 ft 2 in
Height	11.80 m	38 ft 8½ in
Wing area	460 m²	4,950 ft²
Weights		
Loaded weight	112,000 kg	246,850 lb
Performance		
Speed	450 km/h	280 mph
Range	2,100 km	1,305 miles

Flugkapitän Dipl-Ing Karl Baur

1913 Karl Baur born on 13th November in
Laichingen/Württemberg.

1930 After completing his studies Karl Baur was an
early convert to gliding. Together with his friend Wolf
Hirth he was one of the pioneers of this sport.

1936 Engineer at the Aerodynamics Research
Institute (AVA) in Göttingen.

1940 Development engineer and test pilot with
Messerschmitt AG at Augsburg. Played a leading role
in the design and development of the Me 323 'Gigant'
large transport glider.

1942 Head of flight testing at Messerschmitt.
Undertook experimental and test flights with the
Me 261 long-range reconnaissance aircraft and the
four-engined Me 264 'Amerikabomber'. There was no
Messerschmitt design that he did not fly.

1945 After the war went to the United States; working as chief test engineer at the Vought aircraft company responsible for the development and testing of
carrier-based attack aircraft.

1963 Karl Baur died in the United States aged 50.

Flugkapitän Karl Baur 1913-1963 pictured in front
of the Me 264, the 'Amerikabomber'. There is no
Messerschmitt development that he did not fly.

Messerschmitt Me 264 –
Ultra Long-Range Reconnaissance Aircraft and Bomber

Colour impression of the Messerschmitt Me 264 powered by four BMW 109-028 turboprops.

In March 1941 the RLM awarded the Messerschmitt company an official development contract for a four-engined, long-distance aircraft which – with a load of some 2,000 kg (4,408 lb) and a range of 15,000 km (9,315 miles) – would be capable of carrying out so-called 'nuisance' flights over the USA; for example, dropping propaganda material on American towns and cities.* The RLM, then still under the leadership of Generalluftzeugmeister Ernst Udet, ordered three prototypes and 30 production aircraft.

But the scheme came to naught. After Udet's death the RLM displayed little further interest in the project, which slowly faded away, devoid of any priority rating, employing the minimum number of people in its continued development, and lacking a fixed timetable. Not even the encouraging projected flight performance, which would have made it suitable as a very long-range reconnaissance aircraft or bomber (as suggested by Messerschmitt) could rewaken the Reichsluftfahrtministerium's interest in the project. The Me 264 V1 nevertheless took off on its maiden flight in December 1942. Despite the relatively low powered engines it displayed good flight characteristics. Additional test flights confirmed the projected performance figures and gave the impetus to develop the Me 264 further. Among the variants under consideration was one powered by six piston engines plus additional jets, another with four powerful BMW 109-018 turbojets and third with a pair of BMW 109-028 turboprops.

But as for the actual Me 264 itself, and the proposed installation of higher-powered Jumo 109-213 engines, progress remained slow.

In May 1944 the Me 264 V1 was completely destroyed by incendiary bombs. The Me 264 V2 was also damaged in a bombing raid and the necessary repairs could no longer be undertaken due to the worsening war situation.

* At that time the United States was not yet officially at war, but as a 'neutral' state was already supporting Great Britain by supplying large amounts of war material (including 50 warships), as well as being guilty of infringements of international maritime law. Germany's official declaration of war on the USA followed in December 1941, when the Americans' neutrality effectively existed only on paper.

Messerschmitt Me 264 V1 – data

Powerplant	4 x 1,750 hp BMW 109-801D	
Dimensions		
Span	43.00 m	141 ft 0½ in
Length	20.90 m	68 ft 6½ in
Height	4.30 m	14 ft 1½ in
Wing area	127.7 m²	1,375 ft²
Aspect ratio	14.5	
Weights		
Loaded weight	56,000 kg	123,245 lb
Performance		
Speed	545 km/h	338 mph
Range	15,000 km	9,315 miles
Armament		
Nose A-Stand	1 x MG 131	
Fwd. dorsal B1-Stand	1 x MG 131	
Aft dorsal B2-Stand	1 x MG 151	
Ventral C-Stand	1 x MG 151	
Tail D-Stand	1 x MG 151	

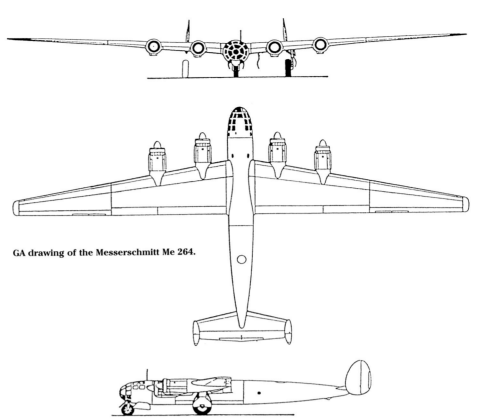

GA drawing of the Messerschmitt Me 264.

From the top: **The Messerschmitt Me 264 V1 with four Junkers Jumo 9-211 engines.**

Messerschmitt Me 264 V1: a close-up of the cockpit and the two starboard Jumo 9-211F engines.

Three-quarter frontal view of the Messerschmitt Me 264 V1 fitted with BMW 9-801s.

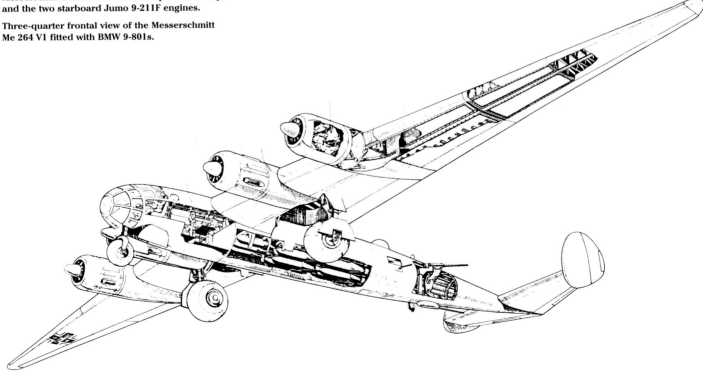

Partial cutaway of the Messerschmitt Me 264 in flight.

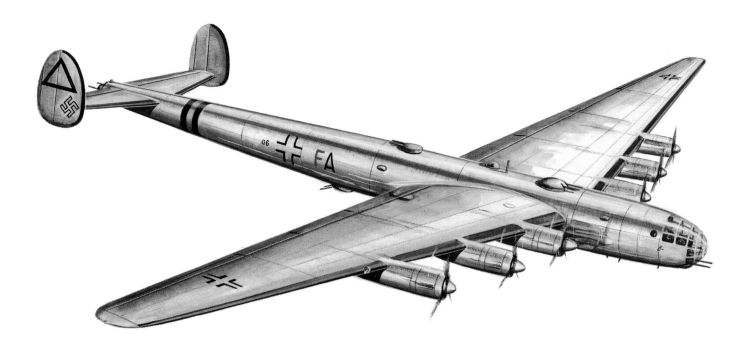

Its 15,000 km 9,315 miles range would have enabled the Me 264 ultra-long-distance reconnaissance aircraft – unofficially designated the Me 364 – to have carried out transocean operations.

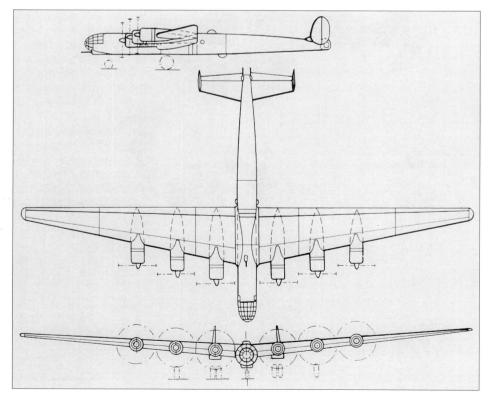

Above: **Model of the Messerschmitt Me 364.**

Left: **GA drawing of the six-engined Messerschmitt Me 364.**

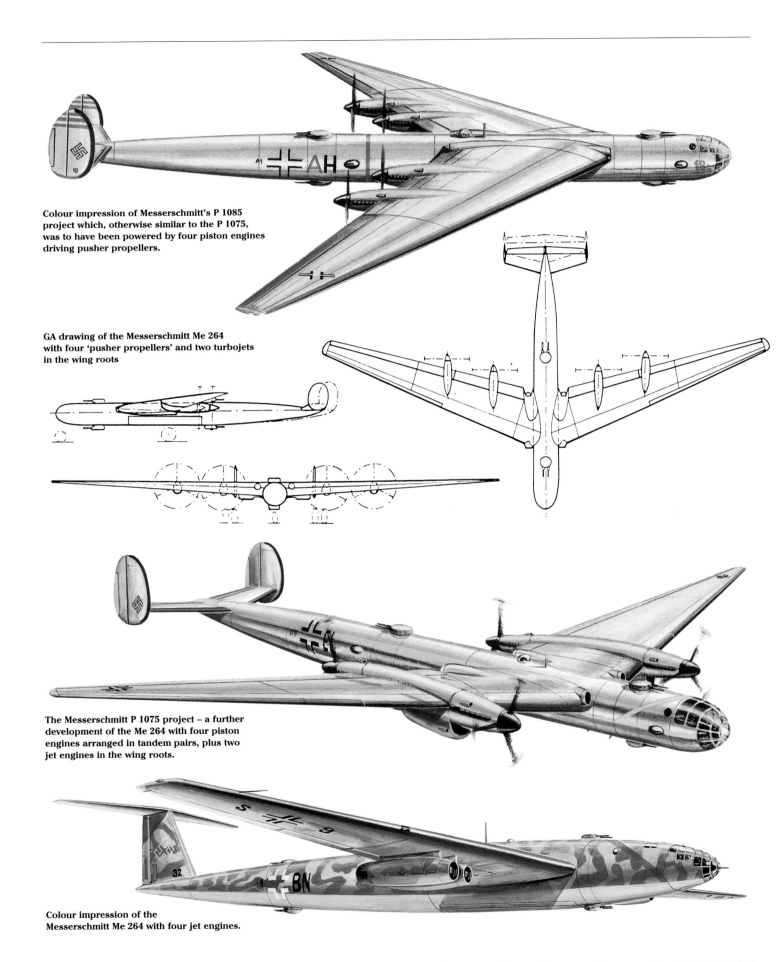

Colour impression of Messerschmitt's P 1085
project which, otherwise similar to the P 1075,
was to have been powered by four piston engines
driving pusher propellers.

GA drawing of the Messerschmitt Me 264
with four 'pusher propellers' and two turbojets
in the wing roots

The Messerschmitt P 1075 project – a further
development of the Me 264 with four piston
engines arranged in tandem pairs, plus two
jet engines in the wing roots.

Colour impression of the
Messerschmitt Me 264 with four jet engines.

Heinkel He 111Z –
The Luftwaffe's First Twin-Fuselage Bomber

Three-quarter frontal colour impression of the Heinkel He 111Z-1 in flight.

By mating two He 111H-6 fuselages together, joined by a new wing centre-section, Heinkel created the He 111Z, the first twin-fuselage long-range bomber, which was also intended to serve as a cargo-glider tug. A further development, designated the Z-3, was projected which would be able to carry a bomb load in excess of 7,000 kg (15,428 lb) over a distance of 1,900 km (1,180 miles).

With a loaded weight of 28,400 kg (62,595 lb) and a span measuring 35.20 m (115 ft 5½ in), the He 111Z was powered by five 1,200 hp Jumo 9-211F engines. A crew of from eight to ten was envisaged, whose primary duty – apart from the pilot and bombaimer – would be to man the defensive armament. Only the flight and engines controls had to be altered; the He 111Z being piloted from the left-hand cockpit.

Eleven examples of the He 111Z were built under licence at the Mitteldeutsche Metallwerke Erfurt for delivery to the Luftwaffe as glider tugs. No Z-2 (long-range reconnaissance) or Z-3 (bomber) variants were ever produced.

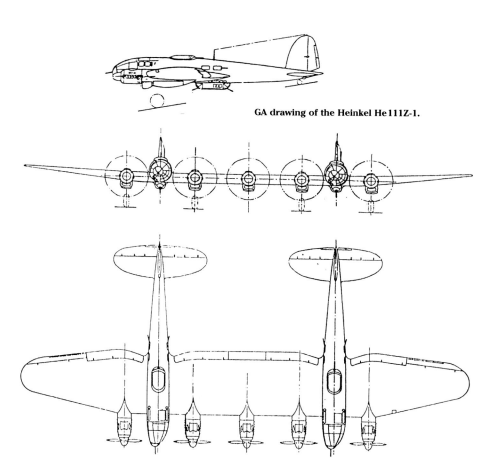

GA drawing of the Heinkel He 111Z-1.

Heinkel He 111Z-1 – data

Powerplant	5 x 1,200 hp Jumo 9-211F
A BMW 9-801 was sometimes fitted in the fifth central position	

Dimensions		
Span	35.20 m	115 ft 5½ in
Length	16.69 m	54 ft 9 in
Undercarriage track	10.00 m	32 ft 9½ in

Weights		
Empty weight	14,970 kg	32,994 lb
Loaded weight with overload	21,400-28,400 kg	47,165 – 62,595 lb

Performance		
Speed without bomb load	420-480 km/h	260-298 mph

Frontal view of the Heinkel He 111Z-1.

Chapter Six

Target New York –
Strategic Heavy & Long-Range
Bomber Projects 1942-1944

As the war situation worsened, the design bureaus of Focke-Wulf, Junkers and Messerschmitt all sought to develop long-range bombers which would be able to carry a 4,000 kg (8,816 lb) bomb load into US airspace, where they could mount harassment and bombing raids against towns and other targets along America's eastern seaboard. The main target for such attacks was to have been New York.

At a conference at the OKL (Luftwaffe GHQ) on 16th May 1942, attended by Reichsmarschall Göring and leading figures of the German aviation industry and the RLM, the possibility of carrying out raids on American cities was thoroughly discussed. New York was at the forefront of these deliberations as the primary target. The Luftwaffe upper hierarchy was united in its belief that such air attacks could be instrumental in 'knocking' the Americans out of the European theatre of war, and, above all, in dissuading the US bomber fleets from continuing their raids on Germany's towns and cities.

German aircraft manufacturers subsequently submitted proposals to both the RLM and the Luftwaffe leadership for suitable long-range bomber projects, worked out to the smallest detail. But the idea of mounting air strikes against the USA, as discussed during the conference of 16th May 1942, was, only weeks later, ruled out as 'inopportune'.

The industry attempted to influence and overturn this decision by continuing to submit plans for four- and six-engined long-range bomber projects.

But on 14th March 1943 the RLM issued a decree forbidding all further work on heavy bomber projects under the threat of the severest penalties. Ignoring this injunction, the industry continued to develop long-range bomber projects in secret. Projects which at this time envisaged the use of high-performance piston engines, and which would have been quite capable of reaching the USA, failed to get the approval of the RLM.

The Me 264, two prototypes of which had been built and flown, and which had officially been christened the 'Amerikabomber', only progressed as far as it did because of the close personal relationship between Messerschmitt and Hitler and the highest Party circles. But not even the Me 264 had received any form of priority rating which would have speeded up production. Allied bombing raids on Messerschmitt's factories and assembly shops, and the lack of a suitable powerplant, were the main reasons for the Me 264's foundering before an order finally put a stop to work altogether.

It was not until Germany's towns and industrial centres had been bombed into rubble that political and military leaders finally realised their mistake in failing to create a strategic bombing arm. A few weeks before the end of the war desperate attempts were then made to develop jet-powered long-range bombers. Despite the hopelessness of Germany's situation, design teams from Junkers, Messerschmitt and Focke-Wulf – as well as the Horten brothers (who were rank outsiders) – continued untiringly to submit new projects which were far in advance of anything that had gone before. According to expert opinion, these remarkable projects could well have had a direct influence on the course of the war if only – yes, if only – the RLM had seen fit to award them development contracts just a few months earlier.

Target New York: a map showing the point of aim and probable radii of damage which would have been caused by an area bombing raid by German long-range bombers. An original OKL map dating from 1943.

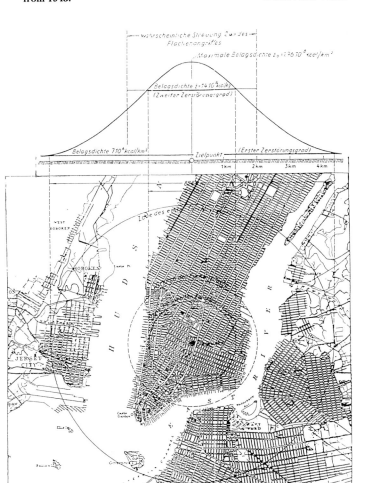

Junkers Ju 488 –
Long-Range Bomber

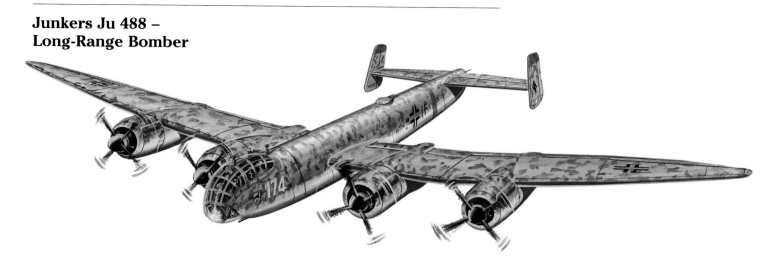

In September 1943 the Technical Office of the RLM awarded Junkers a contract for a bomber with good high-altitude performance. As their starting point Junkers chose their proven Ju 188T-1, the airframe of which offered the most promise. By utilising components from each of the Ju 88, 188, 288 and 388 models, the wings, fuselage, undercarriage and powerplant for the Ju 488 could all be produced and unit-assembled without undue technical expenditure.

The only parts needing to be designed and constructed from scratch were the wing centre-section and certain fuselage components.

Assembly of the first two prototypes, the Ju 488 V401 and V402, commenced in September 1944. The RLM also gave the go-ahead for four further machines of the projected A-series. Unlike the two initial prototypes, the Ju 488 V3 to V6 would have an entirely new fuselage.

Due to a combination of enemy action and sabotage, the first two prototypes were never completed. And although production of the remaining four aircraft had reached an advanced stage, the RLM called a halt to the entire Ju 488 programme in November 1944.

Junkers Ju 488 – data

Crew	Three	
Powerplant	4 x 2,500 hp Junkers Jumo 9-222 A/B-3	
Dimensions		
Span	31.29 m	102 ft 8½ in
Length	23.24 m	76 ft 2½ in
Height	7.10 m	23 ft 2½ in
Wing area	88 m²	947 ft²
Weights		
Take-off weight	36,000 kg	79,350 lb
Wing loading	409 kg/m²	84 lb/ft²
Bomb load	5,000 kg	11,020 lb
Performance		
Max speed	690 km/h	428 mph
Service ceiling	11,350 m	37,230 ft
Range	4,500 km	2,795 miles
Armament		
Dorsal B-Stand	1 x FDL 151Z	
Tail	1 x FDL 151Z	

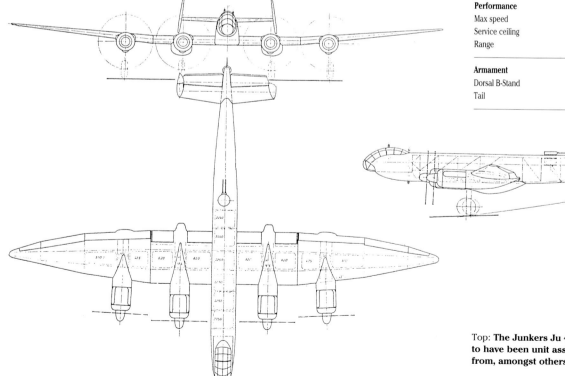

Top: **The Junkers Ju 488 long-range bomber was to have been unit assembled using components from, amongst others, the Ju 88 and the Ju 188.**

Left: **GA drawing of the Junkers Ju 488.**

Junkers Ju 290Z

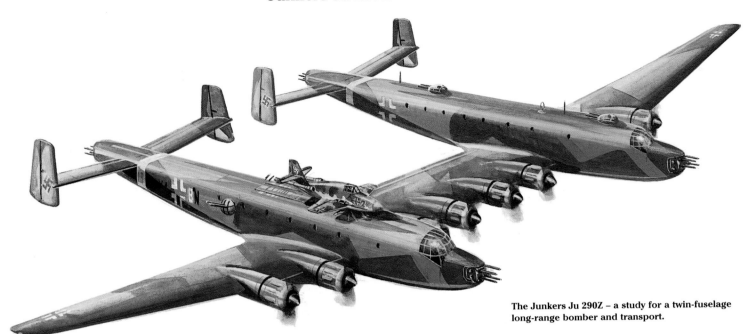

The Junkers Ju 290Z – a study for a twin-fuselage long-range bomber and transport.

Project documentation from Junkers' Dessau works in the years 1942 to 1944 make reference to a project which was described as a long-range reconnaissance aircraft, bomber and transport equipped with parasite fighter. Drawings of this aircraft were produced by project engineer P Schmidt-Stiebitz, a member of the Junkers design team.

It was to be a twin-fuselage machine, similar in layout to the He 111Z, with a span of 60.00 m (196 ft 9½ in) and powered by eight BMW 9-801 engines. Unit assembled from the fuselages and outer wings of two Junkers Ju 290s, a new constant chord central wing fillet would join the inboard wing sections carrying the four inner engines.

This project related back to an earlier specification which the RLM had issued to a number of manufacturers. Along with Junkers, Heinkel had also submitted a design for a six-engined large-capacity transport 'for glider-towing and long-range reconnaissance' (to quote the project description). The original specification had stipulated, among other things, the ability to fly long stretches, in excess of 11,000 km (6,830 miles), and that development costs should be kept to the barest possible minimum. These requirements would ultimately result in the later Ju 390.

The parasite aircraft – a Messerschmitt Me 328 – was to have been carried atop the Ju 290Z's right-hand fuselage. Take-off and landing during flight was to have been accomplished by means of a 'slip-coupling'. But development of this eight-engined machine was abandoned in favour of the Ju 390.

Ju 290 – data

Powerplant	8 x BMW 9-801D	
Dimensions		
Span	60.00 m	196 ft 9½ in
Length	28.0 m	91 ft 10 in
Height	6.90 m	22 ft 8½ in
U/c track	2 x 7.30 m	2 x 23 ft 11½ in
Weights		
Loaded weight	c 90,000 kg	c. 198.360 lb

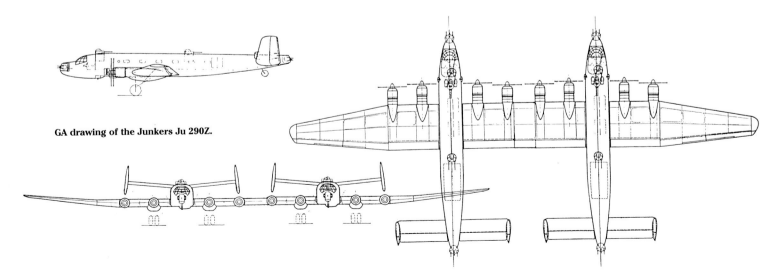

GA drawing of the Junkers Ju 290Z.

LUFTWAFFE SECRET PROJECTS: STRATEGIC BOMBERS 1935-1945

Messerschmitt Me P 08.01 – A Heavy Long-Range Strategic Bomber

The Messerschmitt Me P 08.01 was arguably the acme of strategic heavy bomber design. The original project description of 1st September 1941 portrays a long-range bomber which, operationally and in its variety of roles, far exceeded all tactical and strategic demands of the period. It was so designed that it could be adapted for the most varied of operational tasks in the shortest of time:

1. As a long-range bomber with a bomb load of more than 20,000 kg (44,080 lb) and a range of 15,000 km (9,315 miles).

2. For maritime deployment carrying a 20,000 kg (44,080 lb) weapon load of glide-bombs, mines or aerial torpedoes.

3. As a tactical bomber with 50,000 kg (110,200 lb) of bombs or other offensive stores and a range of 2,500 km (1,550 miles).

4. As an ultra long-range reconnaissance machine capable of flying 27,000 km (16,767 miles).

5. As a tactical or strategic large-capacity transport carrying a 22-ton tank or an equivalent weight in anti-tank weapons.

6. As a tug for towing gliders of up to 100,000 kg (220,400 lb) loaded weight.

7. As an airborne anti-aircraft platform armed with four 88 mm anti-aircraft guns.

Combined with this wide variety of roles, the proposed flying wing configuration – used here for the first time in heavy bomber design – would offer a good climb and combat performance. Restricted by the pusher propellers, bombs could only be released when the aircraft was in a nose down attitude, but this was possible at any dive angle up to 90°. Fuel tanks, radiators and engines were all protected by extremely thick armour, in addition to which there was to be a defensive armament comprising remotely controlled guns in nose and tail positions. The fuselage and crew cabin were faired almost completely into the centre-section of the wing. The P 08.01 was to be of all-metal construction; the pilot and crew positions being pres-

surised. The nosewheel and twin-wheel main undercarriage members retracted hydraulically into the fuselage. The triple-section wing was metal skinned. The wing centre-section formed the main structural component. Powerplants, fuel tanks and weapons bays were located between the wing's solid ribs. The sweep of the wing leading-edge made it possible for the aircraft to fly through barrage-balloon defences. Hydraulically operated split flaps served both as dive brakes and to assist landing. The proposed powerplant consisted of four Daimler Benz DB 9-615 coupled engines. The extension shaft and radiator housings were integral components of the wing structure. Large calibre bombs could, in addition, be carried externally below the wing sections.

Messerschmitt Me P 08.01 – data

Powerplant	4 x 4,000 hp Daimler Benz DB 9-615	
Dimensions		
Span	50.60 m	165 ft 11½ in
Length	15.35 m	50 ft 4 in
Wing area	300 m²	3,230 ft²
Weights		
Take-off weight	90,000 kg	198,360 lb
Bomb load or other stores	20,000-50,000 kg	44,080-110,200 lb
Performance		
Range with 20,000 kg 44,080 lb load	17,630 km	10,948 miles
Range as long-range reconnaissance aircraft	27,150 km	17,023 miles
Speed at 8,500 m 27,880 ft	645 km/h	400 mph
Fuel capacity	40,000 kg	88,160 lb

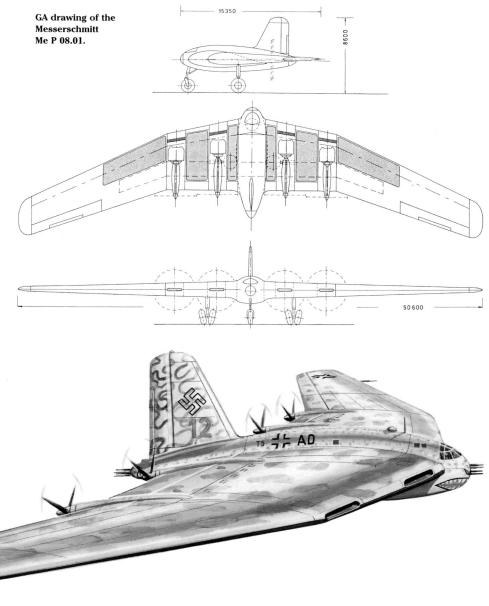

GA drawing of the Messerschmitt Me P 08.01.

Messerschmitt Me P 08.01 – project for a heavy long-range strategic bomber.

Junkers Ju 287 – The Luftwaffe's First Jet Bomber

In 1942 the RLM placed an order with Junkers for the design and construction of a jet-powered heavy bomber. Design work began immediately under the leadership of Dipl-Ing Hans Wocke who, for aerodynamic reasons, elected to produce an aircraft with forward-swept wings. Extensive wind tunnel tests had shown that with a wing of negative sweep the disruptive boundary layer airflow tended to move inwards to the centre of the wing and there combine with the boundary layer of the fuselage. Recognition of this fact led to a marked improvement in general flight behaviour at both low and high speeds – and to the construction of the first Ju 287 V1.

Assembly was completed at the beginning of 1944. The maiden flight took place on 16th August 1944 and was followed by flight testing. In building the first prototype Ju 287 V1 the fullest use possible was made of components from other, proven aircraft types. Thus, for example, part of the fuselage was that of a Heinkel He 177, the tail unit was taken from the Junkers Ju 188G-2, and the undercarriage was adapted from a captured American B-24 Liberator bomber. Only the wing was of completely new design.

Work had begun on the two prototypes, the first of which, the Ju 287 V1, was ferried to Rechlin for further tests. After a lengthy series of trials, development of the Ju 287 was halt-ed temporarily as the RLM needed all production capacity for the manufacture of fighter aircraft. At the beginning of 1945 the Ministry resuscitated the Ju 287 V1 project and ordered series production. The operational version was a great improvement on the original V1, featuring a new fuselage somewhat resembling that of the Ju 388. Only the wing design remained the same. A pressure cabin for the three-man crew was introduced, behind which were located the bomb bay and the fuel tanks. A remotely-controlled turret in the tail was aimed by a periscope at the rear of the cabin. The projected power-plant, the 3,500 kg (7,700 lb) thrust BMW 109-018 turbojet, was still undergoing tests and was not yet available. The Heinkel-Hirth HeS 109-011 turbine could not be fitted either, as this too had still to receive service clearance. Junkers thus had no other option but to fall back on the BMW 109-003 turbojet. In order to provide the necessary power, six of these engines had to be used – mounted in clusters of three under each wing. The machine so equipped was designated the Ju 287 V3.

A further variant, known as the Ju 287S and powered by two 2,900 kg (6,390 lb) thrust Jumo 109-012 jets under each wing, was the final type of the proposed development series, none of which were built due to the deteriorating war situation.

Below left: **The Junkers Ju 287 V1 pictured at Rechlin early in 1944.**

Bottom left: **The Junkers Ju 287 V1 at Brandis near Leipzig in 1944.**

Below right: **Four Walter 109-500 take-off assistance rockets help get the Junkers Ju 287 V1 into the air.**

Bottom right: **The Junkers Ju 287 V1 being readied for flight at Dessau. The undercarriage units came from a captured US B-24 Liberator bomber. Note the dynamo trolley used to start the turbojets.**

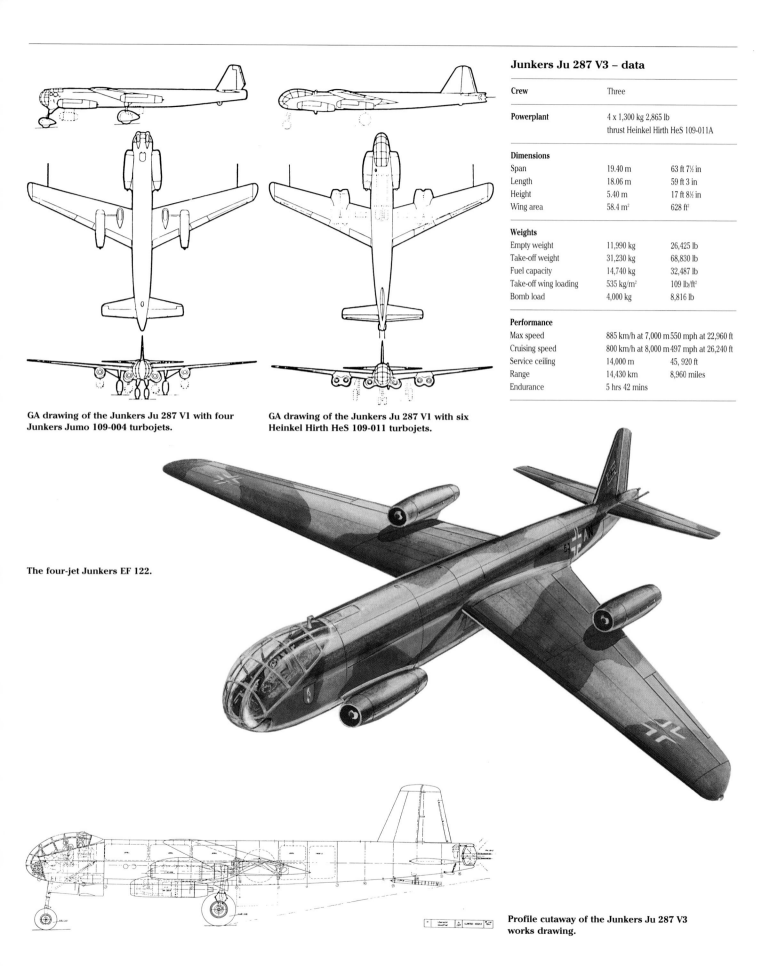

Junkers Ju 287 V3 – data

Crew	Three	
Powerplant	4 x 1,300 kg 2,865 lb thrust Heinkel Hirth HeS 109-011A	

Dimensions		
Span	19.40 m	63 ft 7½ in
Length	18.06 m	59 ft 3 in
Height	5.40 m	17 ft 8½ in
Wing area	58.4 m²	628 ft²

Weights		
Empty weight	11,990 kg	26,425 lb
Take-off weight	31,230 kg	68,830 lb
Fuel capacity	14,740 kg	32,487 lb
Take-off wing loading	535 kg/m²	109 lb/ft²
Bomb load	4,000 kg	8,816 lb

Performance		
Max speed	885 km/h at 7,000 m	550 mph at 22,960 ft
Cruising speed	800 km/h at 8,000 m	497 mph at 26,240 ft
Service ceiling	14,000 m	45, 920 ft
Range	14,430 km	8,960 miles
Endurance	5 hrs 42 mins	

GA drawing of the Junkers Ju 287 V1 with four Junkers Jumo 109-004 turbojets.

GA drawing of the Junkers Ju 287 V1 with six Heinkel Hirth HeS 109-011 turbojets.

The four-jet Junkers EF 122.

Profile cutaway of the Junkers Ju 287 V3 works drawing.

Flying test-bed for the underwing triple-cluster
arrangement of the six Junkers Jumo 109-004 A1
jet engines.

Junkers Ju 287 V3 in the proposed series production configuration. Note the characteristic canopy
frame of the pressure cabin housing the three-
man crew.

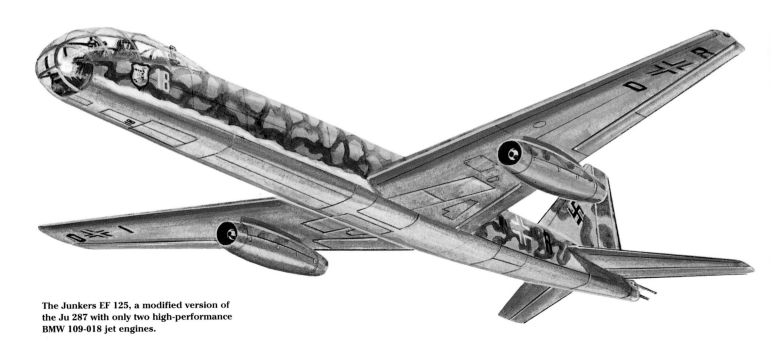

The Junkers EF 125, a modified version of
the Ju 287 with only two high-performance
BMW 109-018 jet engines.

Focke-Wulf's Long-Range Bomber Projects

Between 1942 and 1944 the Focke-Wulf design team submitted to the RLM a number of project proposals for long-range bombers, all of which complied with the specifications laid down by the Technical Office.

Despite their incorporating the most modern of design features and possessing excellent projected performance figures, the RLM regarded these proposals as little more than 'interesting design studies for which there is no foreseeable use', for by that time the planned harassment raids and air strikes on the United States had been deemed inappropriate and were no longer regarded as a priority.

The proposed bomber projects, which had been drawn up in remarkably short time by a Focke-Wulf planning group headed by Dipl-Ings. Bansemier, Tank and Kosel, had been designed to make the round trip to the USA and back to base non-stop. Any problems in range reduction caused by increased bomb loads could be overcome by in-flight refuelling.

Representatives from Focke-Wulf had already submitted their first proposals for long-range bombers to the RLM before the end of 1942. Had development and production contracts been forthcoming, these could well have been operational by 1944, but all attempts by the aviation industry to persuade the Luftwaffe leadership to change its mind regarding strategic bombing by constantly submitting new bomber proposals proved fruitless. Finally, in an edict dated 14th February 1943, the RLM specifically ordered that all further design work on heavy bomber projects should cease.

The project proposals bearing the drawing number 03.10206-20, which had been put forward to the RLM on 16th July 1942, was for an all-metal, four-engined long-range heavy bomber. Three different powerplants had been proposed:

Variant A: with four 4,000 hp BMW 9-803 28-cylinder radial engines;

Variant B: with four 3,000 hp Junkers Jumo 9-222 engines;

Variant C: with six Junkers Jumo 9-213s or six 1,950 hp Daimler-Benz DB 9-603s.

With a bomb load of 10,000 kg (22,040 lb) range would have been in the order of 8,500 km (5,278 miles), and with a 5,000 kg (11,020 lb) load approximately 10,300 km (6,396 miles). The crew was housed in pressurised compartments. The 35,000 ltr (7,700 gal) fuel load was carried in protected wing and fuselage tanks. Power-assisted controls and a triaxial autopilot were also to have been fitted.

The Focke-Wulf project, drawing number 03.10206-20, Variant A with four BMW 109-803 engines, was often erroneously referred to as the Fw 238.

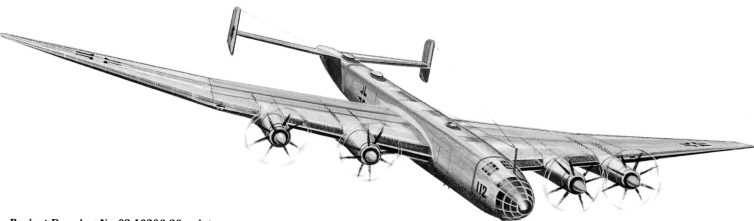

Project Drawing No 03.10206-20 – data

Crew	Ten	

Dimensions		
Span	50.00 m	164 ft 0 in
Length	29.70 m	97 ft 5 in
Height	5.60 m	18 ft 4½ in
Wing area	250 m²	2,690 ft²
Wing loading	350 kg/m²	72 lb/ft²

Weights		
Loaded weight	80,500 kg	177,422 lb

Performance		
Speed	550 km/h at 9,500 m	341 mph at 31,160 ft
Range	8,500-10,300 km	5,278-6,396 miles

Armament

Defensive armament was to comprise three hydraulically operated turrets each with 2 x MG 151/20, plus 4 x MG 151/20 in the tail turret.
For the anti-shipping role an additional ventral gondola containing 4 x MK 108 cannon could be fitted.

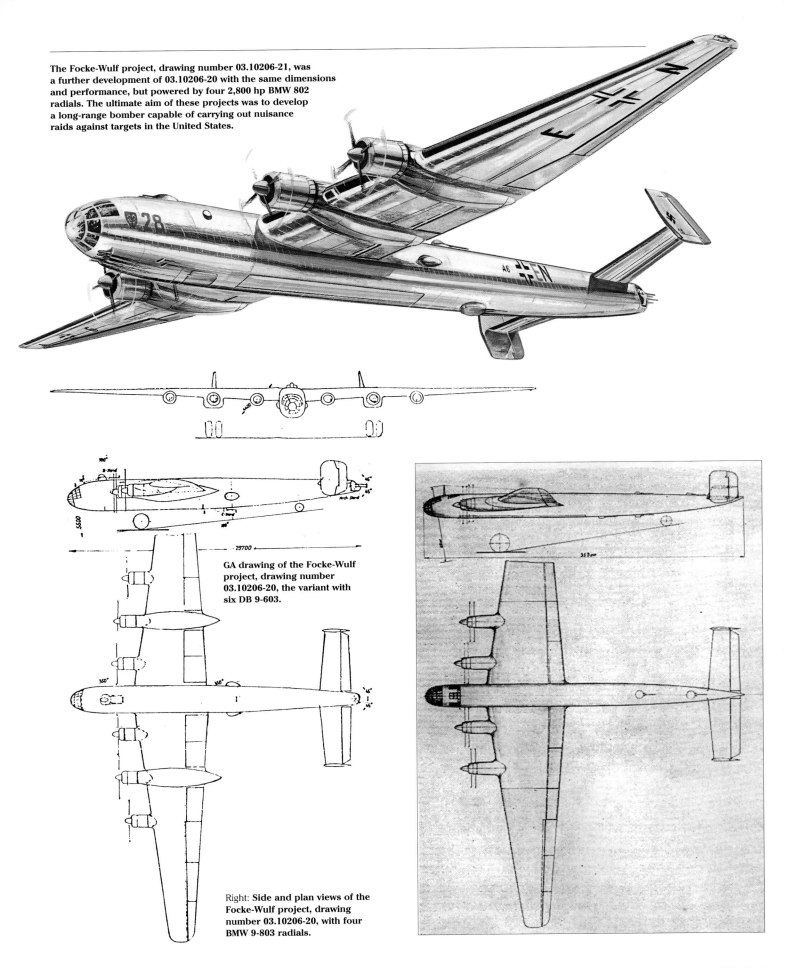

The Focke-Wulf project, drawing number 03.10206-21, was a further development of 03.10206-20 with the same dimensions and performance, but powered by four 2,800 hp BMW 802 radials. The ultimate aim of these projects was to develop a long-range bomber capable of carrying out nuisance raids against targets in the United States.

GA drawing of the Focke-Wulf project, drawing number 03.10206-20, the variant with six DB 9-603.

Right: Side and plan views of the Focke-Wulf project, drawing number 03.10206-20, with four BMW 9-803 radials.

Project Drawing Number 03.10206-22

With a span of 63m (206 ft 8 in) and a fuselage length of 35.40 m (116 ft 2½ in) this design had a loaded weight of 126,500 kg (278,806 lb).

A scaled-up version of drawing number 03.10206-20, the projected range with a 4,000 kg (8,816 lb) bomb load was 13,000 km (8,073 miles). With a 24,000 kg (52,896 lb) bomb load range was reduced to 8,000 km (4,968 miles). The proposed powerplant was to have been either four BMW 9-803s, or six Jumo 9-222s.

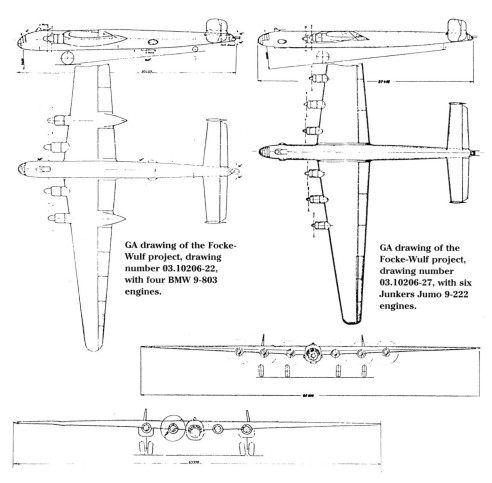

GA drawing of the Focke-Wulf project, drawing number 03.10206-22, with four BMW 9-803 engines.

GA drawing of the Focke-Wulf project, drawing number 03.10206-27, with six Junkers Jumo 9-222 engines.

Project Drawing No 03.10206-22 – data

Crew	Twelve	
Powerplant	4 x BMW 9-803	
Dimensions		
Span	63.00 m	206 ft 8 in
Length	35.40 m	116 ft 2½ in
Height	6.20 m	20 ft 4 in
Wing area	360 m²	3,875 ft²
Wing loading	350 kg/m²	72 lb/ft²
Weights		
Loaded weight	126,000 kg	277,703 lb
Performance		
Speed	550 km/h	342 mph
Range dependent upon load	8,000-13,000 km	4,9688-8,073 miles

Project Drawing Number 03.10206-27

This was a proposal for a six-engined long-range bomber with the same 63.00 m (206 ft 8 in) span as 03.10206-22, but with a lengthened fuselage and increased loaded weight. With a 4,000 kg (8,816 lb) bomb load the range was again 13,000 km (8,073 miles).

Power was to have been supplied by six Junkers Jumo 9-222 four-row radials equipped with exhaust gas turbochargers.

Structurally identical to the earlier proposals, the only major difference was in the main undercarriage, which was to consist of four individual members retracting into the inner pair of engine nacelles on each wing.

Project Drawing No 03.10206-27 – data

Crew	Twelve	
Powerplant	6 x 3,000 hp Junkers Jumo 9-222	
Dimensions		
Span	63.00 m	206 ft 8 in
Length	37.40 m	122 ft 8 in
Height	5.40 m	17 ft 8½ in
Wing area	360 m²	3,875 ft²
Wing loading	329 kg/m²	67 lb/ft²
Weights		
Loaded weight	118,500 kg	261,175 lb
Performance		
Speed	510 km/h at 6,000 m	317 mph at 19,680 ft
Armament		
5 x hydraulically operated turrets each with 2 x MG 151/20		

Project Drawing Number 03.10206-27 continued.

Colour impressions of the Focke-Wulf project, drawing number 03.10206-27, with six Junkers Jumo 9-222 engines.

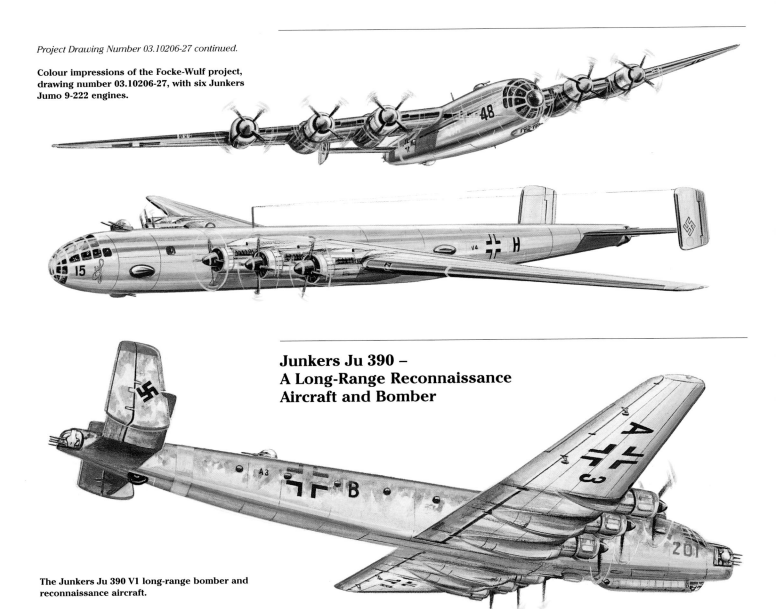

Junkers Ju 390 –
A Long-Range Reconnaissance
Aircraft and Bomber

The Junkers Ju 390 V1 long-range bomber and reconnaissance aircraft.

In March 1942 the RLM awarded Junkers a development contract for a long-range reconnaissance aircraft, transport and guided-weapons carrier which, with a range of 12,000 km (7,452 miles), would be capable of reaching the American coast.

Under the leadership of Dipl-Ing Heinz Kraft, the Junkers design team in Prague began work on a six-engined variant of the Ju 290C. By adding additional fuselage bays and wing sections to the airframe of the latter, a greatly scaled-up model was produced.

In addition to Junkers, Heinkel and Focke-Wulf also submitted proposals in response to the RLM specifications. But the solution suggested by Junkers was by far the simplest and least costly; leading to the maiden flight of the first prototype Ju 390 V1 on 21st October 1943.

Powered by six 1,970 hp BMW 9-801E engines and with a loaded weight of 75,010 kg (165, 322 lb), the Ju 390 V1 was capable of a speed of 473 km/h (294 mph). Range varied from 5,860 km (3,639 miles) up to 12,000 km (7,452 miles) depending upon operational role.

In addition to its other tasks, the Ju 390 was also intended for service as a tanker for the in-flight refuelling of strategic bombers. In the light of its good flight characteristics plans were drawn up for series manufacture, but these failed to materialize as a result of the introduction of the fighter emergency-production programme. All further development work on the Ju 390 and the proposed production run were cancelled in mid-May 1944 on the orders of the RLM. At the end of 1944 the sole Ju 390 V1 was laid up, minus propellers, at Junkers' works field at Dessau, where it was destroyed in 1945.

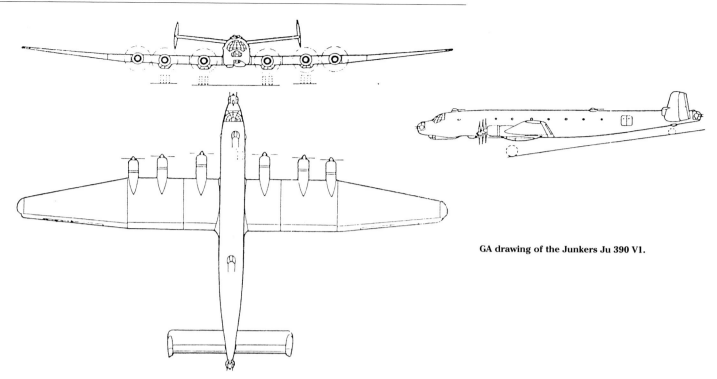

GA drawing of the Junkers Ju 390 V1.

Right: **The Junkers Ju 390 V1 in flight.**

Lower right: **Frontal view of the Junkers Ju 390 V1.**

Junkers Ju 390 V1 – data

Powerplant	6 x 1,970 hp BMW 9-801E	
Dimensions		
Span	50.32 m	165 ft 0½ in
Length	33. 40 m	109 ft 6½ in
Height	6.10 m	20 ft 0 in
Wing area	254.30 m²	2,737 ft²
Weights		
Payload	35,910 kg	79,146 lb
Performance		
Speed	473 km/h	294 mph
Ceiling	8,900 m	29,192 ft
Range	5,860-12,000 km	3,639-7,452 miles

Heinkel He 274 – A High-Altitude Heavy Bomber

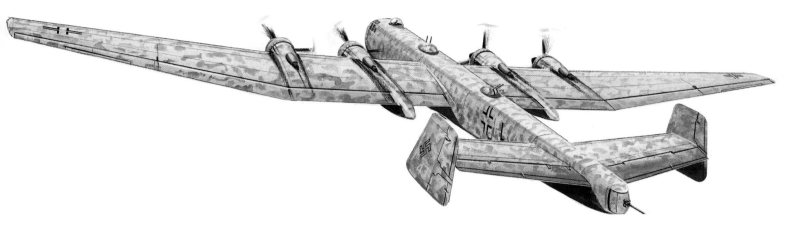

Heinkel He 274 heavy high-altitude bomber.

In July 1941 the Heinkel design team in Vienna began work on a four-engined bomber, based upon the Heinkel He 177, which was intended specifically as a high-altitude bomber powered by four separate engines.

They first tried increasing the wing area of a He 177A-3. But the resulting design, known as the He 177H, did not deliver the required high-altitude performance. By redesigning the fuselage and wings they then created an entirely new machine. Designated the He 274 by the RLM, this aircraft, powered by four individual engines, met the specified high-altitude requirements.

The four-man crew were grouped together in a pressure cabin in the nose, from where the defensive armament was remotely controlled.

Sabotage at the start of construction delayed the completion of the He 274 V1 and the He 274 V2. It was not until after their surrender to the Allies that the two aircraft were made ready for flight. They were then employed as test-beds for high-altitude pressure cabins by the French aviation industry.

At the close of these trials both He 274s were unceremoniously scrapped.

Heinkel He 274 – data

Crew	Four	
Powerplant	4 x 1,750 hp Daimler Benz DB 9-603 with high-altitude supercharging	
Dimensions		
Span	44.10 m	144 ft 8 in
Length	22.30 m	73 ft 2 in
Height	5.20 m	17 ft 0½ in
Weights		
Loaded weight	36,100 kg	79,564 lb
Bomb load	3,000 kg	6,612 lb
Performance		
Range	5,800 km	3,602 miles
Service ceiling	14,300 m	46,905 ft
Speed	585 km/h	363 mph
	at 11,000 m	at 36,080 ft

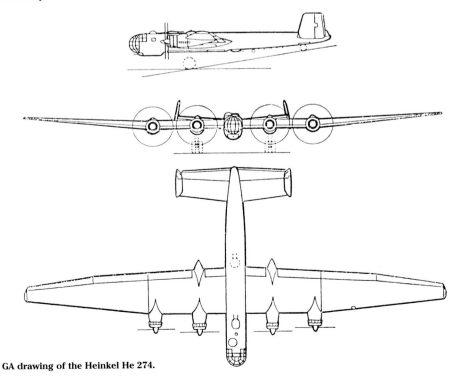

GA drawing of the Heinkel He 274.

LUFTWAFFE SECRET PROJECTS: STRATEGIC BOMBERS 1935-1945

Heinkel He 274 preparatory to take-off at a French test centre in 1945.

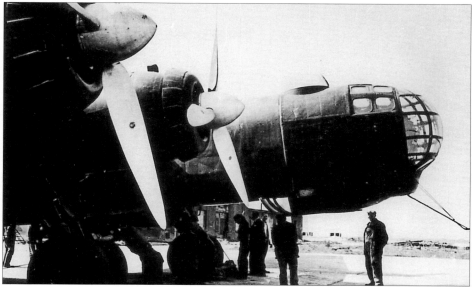

Heinkel He 274 – close-up of the crew cabin.

The Heinkel He 274 in flight- an imposing sight.

Heinkel He 277 – An Unpopular Project

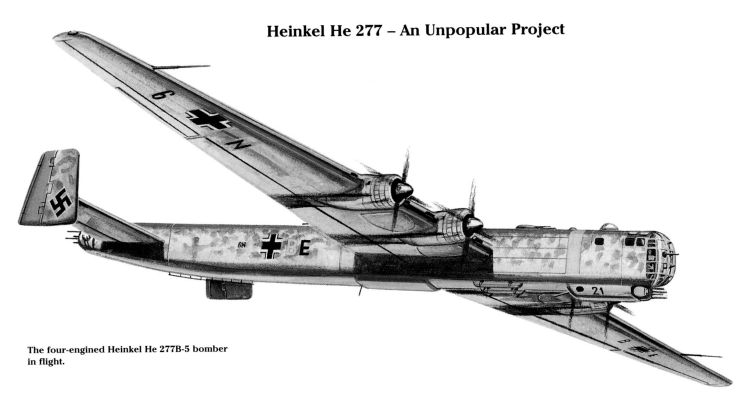

The four-engined Heinkel He 277B-5 bomber in flight.

Heinkel He 277 – data

Crew	Five to Six	
Powerplant	4 x 1,750 hp Daimler Benz DB 9-603E	
Dimensions		
Span	40.00 m	131 ft 2½ in
Length	23.00 m	75 ft 5½ in
Height	3.10 m	10 ft 2 in
U/c track	6.40 m	20 ft 11½ in
Fuselage width	1.90 m	6 ft 3 in
Weights		
Loaded weight	44,000 kg	96,976 lb
Weapon load	6,000 kg	13,224 lb
Performance		
Range	8,000 km	4,968 miles

After it became apparent that the problems with the Heinkel He 177's coupled power-plants could not be resolved, Heinkel put before the RLM a proposal for a new design powered by four separate engines.

This suggestion was turned down as there was still a distinct antipathy in official circles towards heavy four-engined bombers. Ignoring this rejection, Heinkel went ahead with the conversion of a He 177A-5 to four-engine layout without the knowledge or acquiescence of the RLM. But the machine so modified, which was known as the He 177B (the designation He 277 could not be used in dealings with the RLM), did not come up to the designers' expectations in terms of either performance or handling. The increased torque of the four propellers caused instability about the vertical axis. To overcome this, various tail unit configurations were tested, from single to triple fins. In the end, a twin fin arrangement was decided upon.

In the summer of 1943 the RLM finally and grudgingly agreed to Heinkel's use of the designation He 277 – and promptly demanded immediate development to the series production stage. The prototype, built as the He 177B-5 but now officially recognized as the He 277, had been produced by utilizing as many A-series components as possible. Only the extreme nose and tail had been re-designed to include pressurization. The second prototype was fitted with a completely new crew cabin. Armament was upgraded

and divided between four remotely controlled stations. Flight testing began at Rechlin in April 1944.

Despite the test-centre's excellent report, an RLM decree of 3rd July 1944 ordered the He 277's removal from the production list and the scrapping of all completed and semi-completed airframes.

The Heinkel He 277B-5 after modification with the new powerplant arrangement. Representing the pinnacle of series development, the four-engined Heinkel He 277B-5 was in every respect comparable to the American B-29.

The Heinkel He 277B-5 fitted with a third, central tailfin. This experimental installation was not a success.

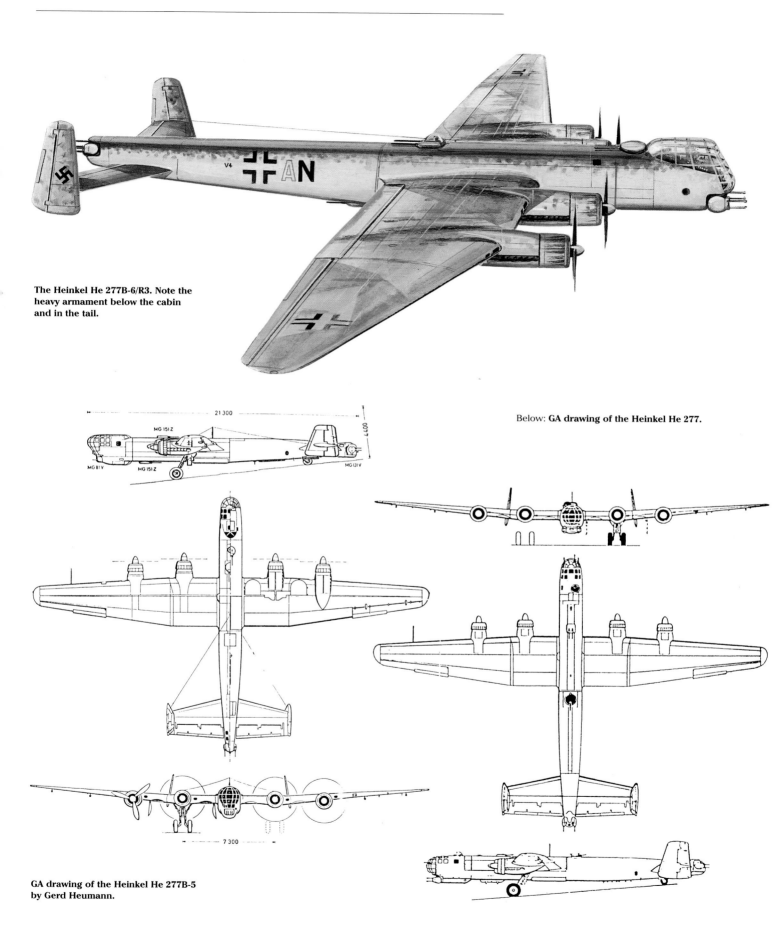

The Heinkel He 277B-6/R3. Note the heavy armament below the cabin and in the tail.

Below: **GA drawing of the Heinkel He 277.**

21 300

MG 151 Z

MG 81 V   MG 151 Z   MG 131 V

4 400

7 300

GA drawing of the Heinkel He 277B-5 by Gerd Heumann.

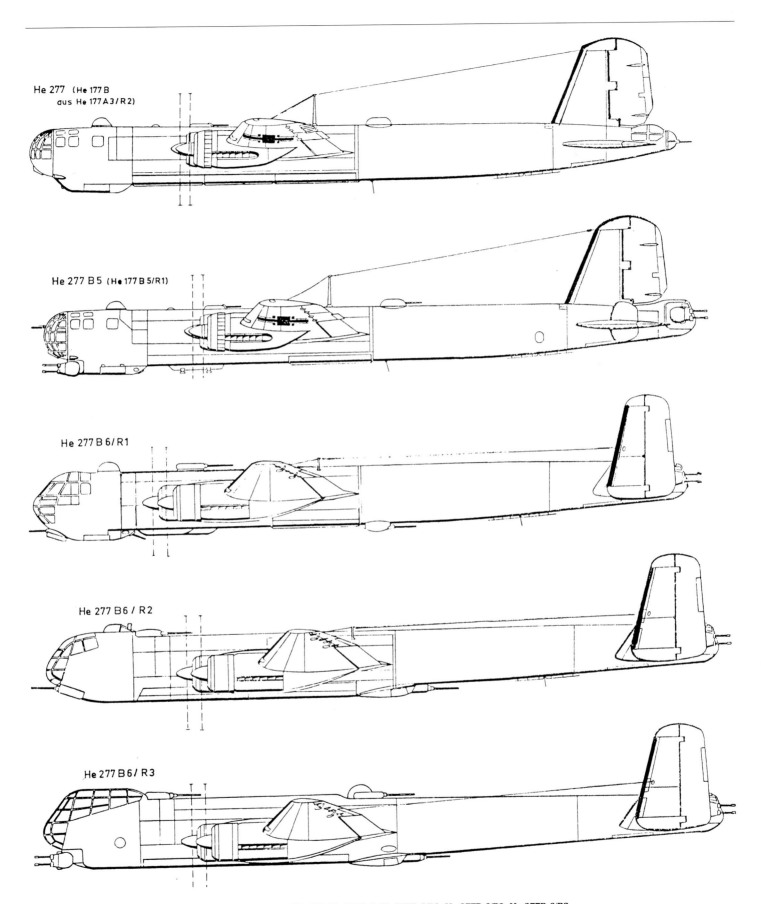

He 277 (He 177 B
aus He 177 A 3/R 2)

He 277 B 5 (He 177 B 5/R1)

He 277 B 6/R1

He 277 B 6/R2

He 277 B 6/R3

Series overview of the Heinkel He 277: From top to bottom: **He 277, He 277B-5, He 277B-6/R1, He 277B-6/R2, He 277B-6/R3.**

Chapter Seven

Long- and Very Long-Range Jet Bomber Projects 1944-1945

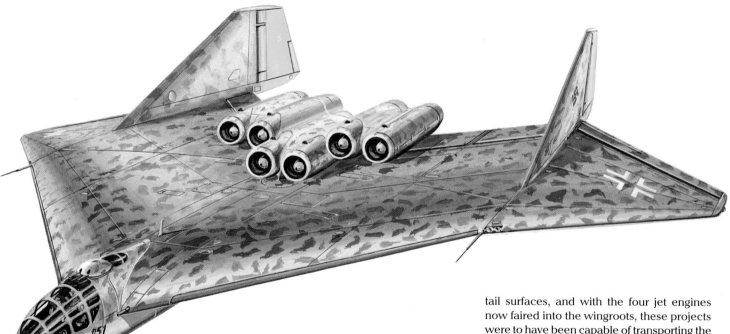

The Arado E 555-1 long-distance flying-wing bomber, the first design in the E 555 development series.

In the autumn of 1944 Reichsmarschall Göring instructed the Junkers and Messerschmitt works to design and produce very long-range bombers which would be capable of delivering a 4,000 kg (8,816 lb) bomb load, at high speeds and over extreme distances, on to a target and then returning safely to base. The object of the exercise was to attack distant convoys and to mount strategic air strikes against the USA and the Soviet Union.

By November 1944 Messerschmitt had already submitted to the RLM a design for a four-jet bomber with the project number P 1107. This featured sharply swept wings, beneath which the four engines were mounted in pairs. In order not to obstruct the exhaust gas efflux from the jet engines, the Messerschmitt designers placed the horizontal tail surfaces above the tailfin and rudder, an arrangement – commonly known as the T-tail – still to be found in today's world of international aviation.

Parallel to their work on the P 1107, the designers also began to develop flying-wing bomber projects under the designations P 1107/I and P 1107/II. Both with and without

tail surfaces, and with the four jet engines now faired into the wingroots, these projects were to have been capable of transporting the required 4,000 kg (8,816 lb) bomb load over distances of 7,800 km (4,844 miles) at speeds of up to 900 km/h (559 mph).

The accompanying project description also included a take-off weight of 29,000 kg (69,916 lb) and a speed of 980 km/h (608 mph). The 7,800 km (4,844 miles) range as a bomber would be increased to 9,600 km (5,961 miles) for the reconnaissance role.

In the meantime Junkers were improving upon their Ju 287 by incorporating a new fuselage and utilizing more powerful engines. The resulting design, the Ju 287S, was a forward-swept-wing bomber intended to be ready for operational service within the shortest possible time. Although this new configuration promised advantages in terms of aerodynamics and construction, it did raise considerable problems in relation to stability and strength.

In collaboration with the German Gliding Research Institute (DFS), Junkers were also developing a four-jet flying-wing bomber. Under the project designation EF 130, this design combined a speed of 950 km/h (590 mph) with a range of 4,000 km (2,484 miles).

At the beginning of December 1944 Oberst Siegfried Knemeyer of the Technical Air Armaments Branch (TLR), who was responsible for the development of new aircraft types, visited the Horten brothers, Walter and Reimar, at their Oranienburg works. The purpose of the visit was for Knemeyer to test-fly their Horten VII flying-wing design (see also page 13). Completely won over, Knemeyer declared the flying-wing to be the ideal configuration for a long-distance bomber. The Horten brothers regarded Knemeyer's words as vindication of their research work and, in particular, confirmation that the flying-wing they had developed was far superior to conventional aircraft designs for use over very long distances. Their subsequent proposal, under the project designation Ho XVIII B-2, had a span of 42.80 m (140 ft 4½ in) with a length of 19 m (62 ft 4 in) and a height of 5.75 m (18 ft 10½ in). Powered by six Junkers Jumo 109-004H turbojets each delivering

1,200 kg (2,645 lb) thrust, the Ho XVIII B-2 would be capable of a speed of 990 km/h (615 mph). Service ceiling was 16,000 m (52,480 ft) and the range with a normal fuel load would be 9,000 km (5,590 miles); increasing to 12,000 km (7,452 miles) with the use of auxiliary tanks.

In January 1945 a committee from the German Aviation Experimental Establishment (DVL) examined the bomber proposals submitted to the RLM. In their closing report the committee confirmed that Messerschmitt's P 1107/I and II projects offered the highest speeds. But in the all-important matter of range, both Messerschmitt's and Junkers' proposals were markedly inferior to the Horten designs. In addition to their simple construction, the use of tubular steel and wood in the manufacture of the Horten projects was a decisive factor in their being awarded a licence to build.

Despite the increasingly severe damage

being inflicted upon aircraft manufacturing and assembly plants by Allied bombing raids, the Messerschmitt design bureau pressed ahead with a new variant of the P 1107. But this latest project, a flying-wing bomber bearing the designation P 1108, stood not the slightest chance of coming to fruition.

At the end of March 1945 Junkers and Messerschmitt ceased all further development work on long-range bomber projects by order of the RLM. Only the Horten brothers continued work on their Ho XVIII B-2 upon the personal instructions of Reichsmarschall Göring.

Certain unconfirmed RLM reports suggest that production of the Ho XVIII B-2 was begun on 1st April 1945 in the underground plant at Kahla in Thuringia. But this was probably somebody's idea of an April Fool's joke, as no documentation to support these claims has ever been found.

Arado Long-Range Flying-Wing Bomber Projects of the E 555 Development Series

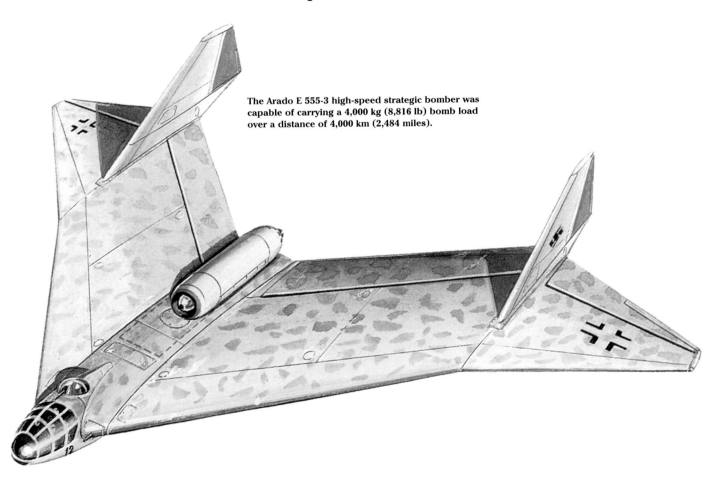

The Arado E 555-3 high-speed strategic bomber was capable of carrying a 4,000 kg (8,816 lb) bomb load over a distance of 4,000 km (2,484 miles).

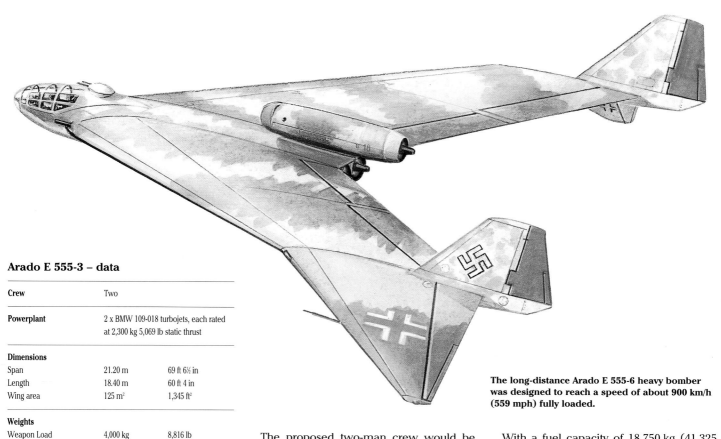

Arado E 555-3 – data

Crew	Two	
Powerplant	2 x BMW 109-018 turbojets, each rated at 2,300 kg 5,069 lb static thrust	
Dimensions		
Span	21.20 m	69 ft 6½ in
Length	18.40 m	60 ft 4 in
Wing area	125 m²	1,345 ft²
Weights		
Weapon Load	4,000 kg	8,816 lb
Take-off weight	25,200 kg	55,540 lb
Fuel capacity	10,000 kg	22,040 lb
Performance		
Speed	875-915km/h	543-568 mph
Range	4,000 km	2,484 miles

The long-distance Arado E 555-6 heavy bomber was designed to reach a speed of about 900 km/h (559 mph) fully loaded.

The proposed two-man crew would be housed in a pressurised cabin. The twin-wheeled main undercarriage members would retract into the wings, the nosewheel into the centre-section aft of the crew cabin. The bomb load could be carried either internally or on external racks.

With a fuel capacity of 18,750 kg (41,325 lb), range was 5,400 km (3,353 miles); but this could be increased to 7,500 km (4,657 miles) by fitting an additional tank.

As well as a dorsal barbette, two fixed forward-firing MK 103 cannon were to be installed either side of the cabin. Fully loaded, the calculated speed was in the order of 875 to 900 km/h (543-559 mph).

Arado E 555-3 – Strategic High-Speed Bomber

The stated aim of the E 555 project series was the creation of a bomber which combined a high speed with long range, and which would be capable of transporting a four-ton bomb load over a distance of 4,000 km (2,484 miles). In the view of the Arado design team, these requirements could best be met by a flying-wing configuration featuring 45° sweep and an extremely thin laminar profile; similar in construction and wing planform, in fact, to the E 555-3 project.

The use of just two high-powered BMW 109-018 turbojets, mounted above and below the wing, would permit much higher speeds to be reached than could be attained with a larger number of less powerful jet engines. The former's arrangement above and below the wing centre-section would also help improve the equalization of thrust.

Arado E 555-6 – Long-Range Heavy Bomber

Like almost all the designs in the E 555 project series, the E 555-6 was also of flying-wing configuration; albeit differing from the E 555-1, -2, -3, -4 and -7 projects in having a wing of considerably greater span. The two outer sections featured some 20° anhedral; their trailing edges forming a straight line. The cabin and other components remained basically the same. But power was provided by three BMW 109-018 jet engines – one above and two below the wing centre section – so that balanced thrust could be ensured in the event of a single engine failure. Although the wing span was increased to 28.40 m (93 ft 2 in), wing area remained at 160 m² (1,722 ft²). This was achieved by reducing the chord and bringing the aspect ratio down to 5. External stores could be carried beneath the wings.

Arado E 555-6 – data

Crew	Three	
Powerplant	3 x BMW 109-018 turbojets, each rated at 2,300 kg 5,069 lb static thrust	
Dimensions		
Span	28,40 m	93 ft 2 in
Length	12,35 m	40 ft 6 in
Height	3,74 m	12 ft 3 in
Wing area	160 m²	1,722 ft²
Aspect ratio	5	
Weights		
Fuel capacity	18,750 kg	41,325 lb
Weapon load	4,000 kg	8,816 lb
Performance		
Speed	875-920 km/h	543-571 mph
Range	5,400-7,500 km	3,353-4,657 miles

Arado E 555-7 –
A Long-Range Reconnaissance Aircraft and Bomber

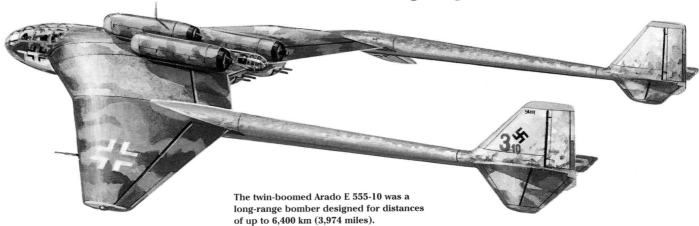

The Arado E 555-7 was conceived as a long-range reconnaissance aircraft and bomber. With a fuel capacity of 15,700 l (3,454 gals) it was to have carried a 4,000 kg (8,816 lb) bomb load over a distance of 5,000 km (3,105 miles) at 950 km/h (590 mph).

Project E 555-7 was very similar to the E 555-1, -2, -3, -4 and -6 designs of this development series both structurally and in terms of intended use, but in engine arrangement it more closely approximated projects E 555-8, -9 and -10.

The lengthening of the fuselage gondola to accommodate the aft weapon station meant that the upper pair of engines had to be set further apart. Of the three BMW 109-018s, two were now on top of the wings, situated above the undercarriage bays, while the third was attached below the wing centre-section.

Defensive armament again included the two fixed forward-firing MK 103 either side of the cabin, but these were now augmented by a quartet of rearward-firing MG 151s to right and left of, and controlled by, the manned aft centre-line station. This additional trailing-edge armament provided a much greater fire power than would have been possible from a standard aircraft fuselage. Carrying a 4,000 kg

(8,816 lb) bomb load and with 15,700 kg (34,602 lb) of fuel, the E 555-7 could fly some 5,000 km (3,105 miles) at a speed of 950 km/h (590 mph)

Arado E 555-7 – data

Dimensions

Span	25.20 m	82 ft 8 in
Length	8.80 m	28 ft 10½ in
Height	3.65 m	11 ft 11½ in
Wing area	160 m²	1,722 ft²

Weights

Fuel capacity	5,700 kg	12,563 lb
Weapon load	4,000 kg	8,816 lb
Loaded weight	41,300 kg	91,025 lb

Performance

Ceiling	14,700 m	48,216 ft
Range	4,500 km	2,794 miles

Arado E 555-10 – A Long-Range Bomber

The twin-boomed Arado E 555-10 was a long-range bomber designed for distances of up to 6,400 km (3,974 miles).

Apart from its twin tailbooms, this project was also similar in structure and wing plan form to the other designs in the E 555 development series. In mid-1944 the TE Development Group of the Arado works in Landeshut / Silesia received a contract from the RLM for design studies for a high-speed jet bomber capable of carrying a 4,000 kg (8,816 lb) bomb load to a target over a distance of more than 4,000 km (2,484 miles).

As previous studies had already provided sufficient data to work from, it was now a matter of selecting the optimum design. To this end a conference had been convened at the RLM on 20th April 1944. Chaired by *Flug-baumeister* Scheibe and Ing Haspe, and attended by Arado representatives, its purpose was to draw up definitive requirements for the E 555 jet-bomber project series.

Arado had almost no experience relating to the flight characteristics of flying-wing designs, which meant that lengthy periods of testing and trials could be expected. It was therefore decided that, starting from project E 555-9 and E 555-10, tailbooms would be attached to the wing trailing-edges (each 4.80 m (15 ft 9 in) from the fuselage centre-line). As with the E 555-7, power would be provided by three BMW 109-018s; the only difference being that the third engine was moved from below the wing to the upper surface, where it was now located between the cabin and the aft weapon station.

The twin mainwheel members retracted into the wings; the nosewheel bay was under the crew cabin.

The 4,000 kg (8,816 lb) bomb load was carried part internally in the centre-section and partly on external underwing fairings. The crew of three was divided between the pressurised nose cabin and aft weapon station.

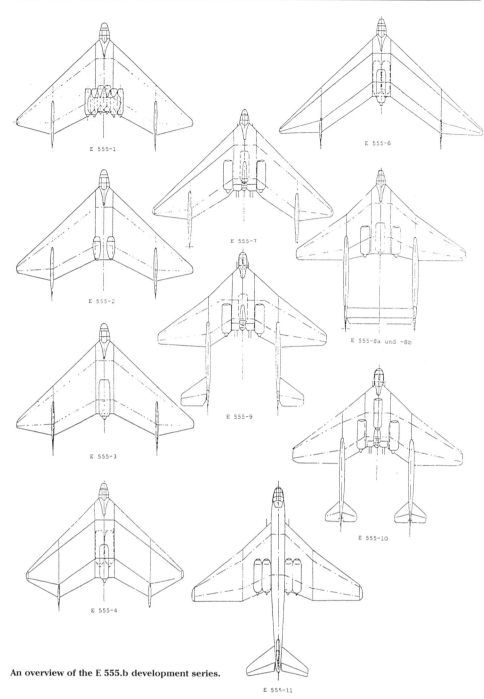

An overview of the E 555.b development series.

Arado E 555-10 – data

Dimensions

Span	23.66 m	77 ft 7½ in
Length	9.20 m	30 ft 2 in
Wing area	140 m²	1,507 ft²
Aspect ratio	4	

Weights

Loaded weight	47,845 kg	105,450 lb
Weapon load	4,000 kg	8,816 lb

Performance

Ceiling	14,500 m	47,560 ft
Range	6,400 km	3,974 miles
Speed	920 km/h	571 mph

Arado E 555-11 – A Long-Range Bomber for both Strategic and Tactical Operations

Arado E 555-11 – data

Crew	Two	
Dimensions		
Span	23.66 m	77 ft 7½ in
Length	25.10 m	82 ft 4 in
Height	4.10 m	13 ft 5½ in
Wing area	140 m²	1,507 ft²
Weights		
Loaded weight	47,000 kg	103,588 lb
Weapon load	4,000-6,000 kg	8,816-13,224 lb
Performance		
Speed	950-1,020 km/h	590-633 mph
Range	7,000-8,000 km	4,347-4,968 miles

At the end of 1944 the Arado design department submitted to the RLM a proposal for a four-jet bomber under the project designation E 555-11. Unlike all the other proposals in the E 555 development series, however, this was not a flying-wing, but had been conceived as a 'fuselage aircraft'. An unusual feature was the four high-powered Jumo 109-012 jet engines, each delivering 2,100 kg (4,628 lb) thrust, which were positioned in pairs on the wing upper surfaces either side of the fuselage. This arrangement was also intended to improve equalization of thrust. Incorporating the laminar wing developed by Arado, this all-metal mid-wing design was capable of speeds up to 950 km/h (590 mph) carrying a 4,000 kg (8,816 lb) weapon load. Range was to have been 7,000-8,000 km (4,347-4,968 miles).

Because of its high speed, there were no plans to provide the E 555-11 with defensive armament. But a further proposal for use as a guided-weapons carrier would have seen it equipped with air-to-air and air-to-ground missiles.

Heinkel Projects for a Four-Jet Long-Range Bomber

The 60-ton Flying-Wing Bomber – data

Crew	Two	
Powerplant	4 x Heinkel-Hirth HeS 109-011 turbojets each rated at 1,300 kg (2,865 lb) static thrust	
Dimensions		
Span	31.50 m	103 ft 4 in
Length	19.85 m	65 ft 1½ in
Weights		
Weapon load	3,000 kg	6,612 lb
Performance		
Range	28,000 km	17,388 miles

According to a report which Dipl-Ing Siegfried Günter – who had been head of Heinkel's Project and Design Department in Vienna – was required to write for the US Technical Service on 1st October 1945, Heinkel engineers had been engaged on designs for four-jet long-range bombers right up until May 1945. These designs included not only aircraft of standard 'fuselage and tail' configuration, but also of flying-wing layout.

Work was concentrated particularly on one flying-wing bomber which was powered by four HeS 109-011 jet engines, each developing 1,300 kg (2,865 lb) static thrust, and which weighed 26 tons.

Another flying-wing bomber was to have been fitted with either four BMW 109-018s, each of 3,000 kg (6,612 lb) static thrust, or six Junkers Jumo 004 jet engines, each of 1,300 kg (2,865 lb) static thrust. This machine which possessed a very high wing loading, would have weighed 60 tons.

One specific innovation mentioned by Siegfried Günter in his report was that the 60-ton project was to have been the first aircraft to feature wings incorporating a two-stage sweep, transitioning from 45° to 35°, which would have resulted in a new 'biconvex profile' with a 10% relative thickness.

These developments harked back to a specification which had been drawn up on 22nd February 1945 in the wake of a 'Reichsmarschall Conference' held at Dessau. Again according to Günter's report, the 60-ton flying-wing project was to have combined a 3,000 kg (6,612 lb) bomb load with a range of 28,000 km (17,388 miles).

Dipl-Ing Günter also described more orthodox bomber projects, with fuselages and tails, which had performance figures comparable to the designs of Junkers, Messerschmitt and Horten.

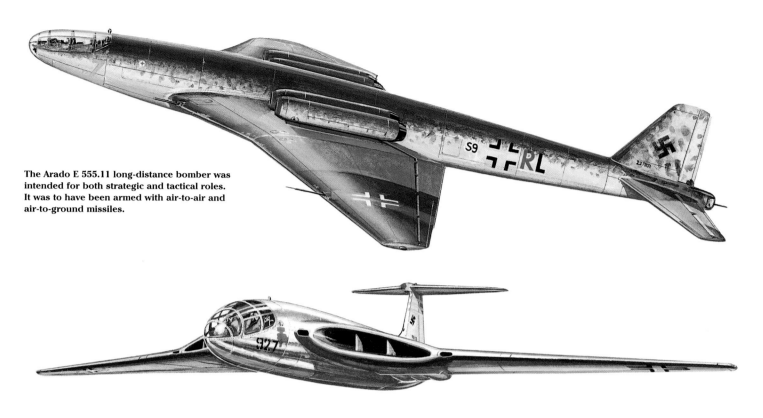

The Arado E 555.11 long-distance bomber was intended for both strategic and tactical roles. It was to have been armed with air-to-air and air-to-ground missiles.

Heinkel's four-jet long-range bomber of 1945 was designed to carry a 3,000 kg (6,612 lb) bomb load over a range of 28,000 km (17,388 miles).

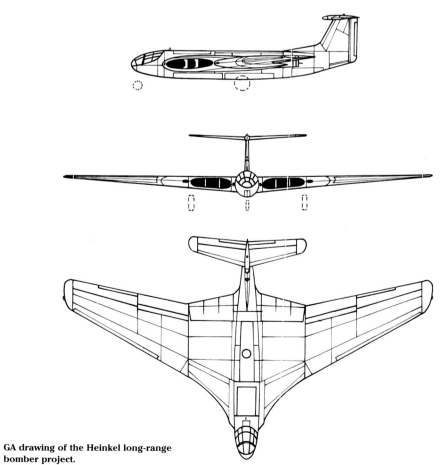

GA drawing of the Heinkel long-range bomber project.

Dr-Ing Siegfried Günter 1899-1969 was chief designer and head of the project bureau at the Heinkel Aircraft Company. Under his leadership was produced the world's first jet-propelled aircraft, the Heinkel He 178 – as well as the Heinkel He 177 bomber, together with numerous long-range bomber projects.

Dr-Ing Siegfried Günter

1899 Siegfried Günter born on 8th December in Kaula/Thuringia.

1910 Received a classical education at the Weimar grammar school.

1916 Designed the first high-performance aircraft propeller.

1917 Entered military service.

1920 Studied mechanical engineering, specialist subject aircraft manufacture, at Hannover TH; sat engineering examinations.

1923 Built gliders.

1926 Sat main diploma examination; subsequently employed as designer with Bäumer-Aero Aircraft Manufacturing Company. Contributed to design of Bäumer 'Sausewind' high-speed aircraft.

1931 Designer with Heinkel. Development and design of the He 49 and He 51.

1932 Oversaw construction of Heinkel company's own wind tunnel.

1933 Together with twin brother Walter, Siegfried Günter took over as head of the Heinkel company's projects department.

1937 Became member of the Lilienthal Society for Aviation Research.

1939 Construction and maiden flight of the world's first rocket-powered aircraft,the Heinkel He 176, as well as the first jet-propelled aircraft, the Heinkel He 178. Until 1945 head of project design and development at Heinkel's Vienna works.

1945 Post-war, occupied for many months writing up his activities (technical descriptions of e.g. tail-mounted jet powerplants and his high-speed designs) for the US Technical Service.

1947 Appointed Honorary Dr of Munich University.

1948 Siegfried Günter taken to the USSR by Soviet agents. Played a leading part in the design of the MiG-15 jet fighter.

1954 Siegfried Günter returned from USSR and takes over as head of development department at the newly re-established Heinkel Works. Responsible for Germany's first jet airliner, the Heinkel He 211, and the vertical take-off VJ-101.

1969 Siegfried Günter dies in Munich aged 70.

The Horten brothers, Walter left and Reimar, designed the strategic Horten Ho XVIII B-2 heavy bomber, which was to fly to America with a 1-ton bomb load and back without refuelling.

Horten Ho XVIII B-2 –
The Luftwaffe's Last Jet Bomber Project

The Ho XVIII B-2 was the last project undertaken by the Horten brothers. It was developed with the assistance of Dipl-Ing K Nickel and was the result of an appeal made to the German aviation industry by Göring in the autumn of 1944 for a long-distance bomber which, with a range of 9,000 km (5,589 miles), would be in a position to carry a 4-ton bomb load to the American continent.

In March 1945, after various studies and preliminary projects, the Horten brothers laid before Göring and the highest government circles a study for a flying-wing bomber which could be constructed of the most basic items – so-called 'salvage' material, such as tubular steel, wood and fabric.

After all the project documentation had been submitted, Göring awarded a production contract on 23rd March 1945. Assembly was reportedly to have commenced on 1st April 1945 in the underground workshops of the Kahla complex in Thuringia.

The Horten Ho XVIII B-2 – The Luftwaffe's last jet bomber project.

Horten Ho XVIII B-2 – data

Powerplant	6 x Junkers Jumo 109-004 H jet engines each rated at 1,160 kg (2,557 lb) static thrust	
Dimensions		
Span	42.50 m	139 ft 5 in
Length	19.00 m	62 ft 4 in
Height	5.80 m	19 ft 0½ in
Wing sweep	35°	
Weights		
Weapon load	4,000 kg	8,816 lb
Loaded weight	41,800 kg	92,127 lb
Performance		
Max speed	910 km/h	565 mph
Range	9,000-12,000 km	5,589-7,452 miles, aerial refuelling was to be provided
Armament	2 x remotely-controlled weapon stations in nose and tail	

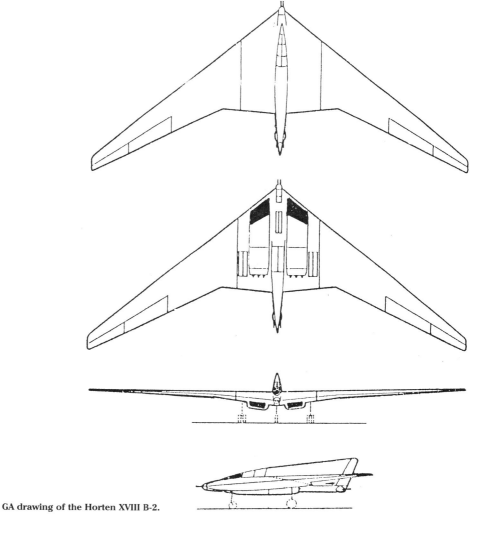

GA drawing of the Horten XVIII B-2.

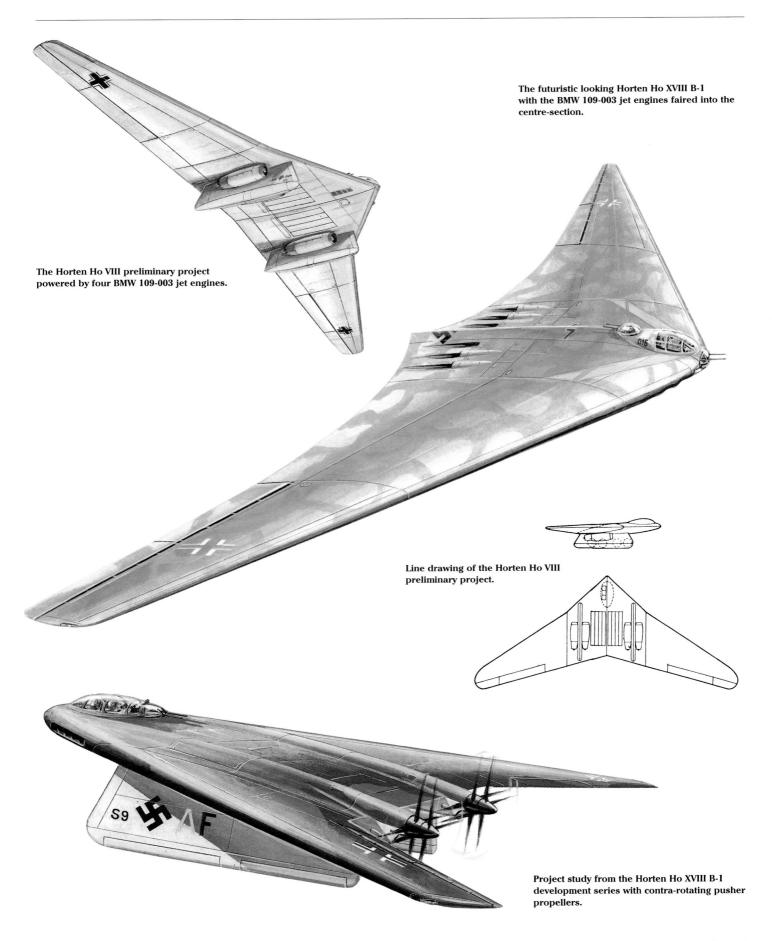

The futuristic looking Horten Ho XVIII B-1
with the BMW 109-003 jet engines faired into the
centre-section.

The Horten Ho VIII preliminary project
powered by four BMW 109-003 jet engines.

Line drawing of the Horten Ho VIII
preliminary project.

Project study from the Horten Ho XVIII B-1
development series with contra-rotating pusher
propellers.

The BMW High-Speed Bomber Project I

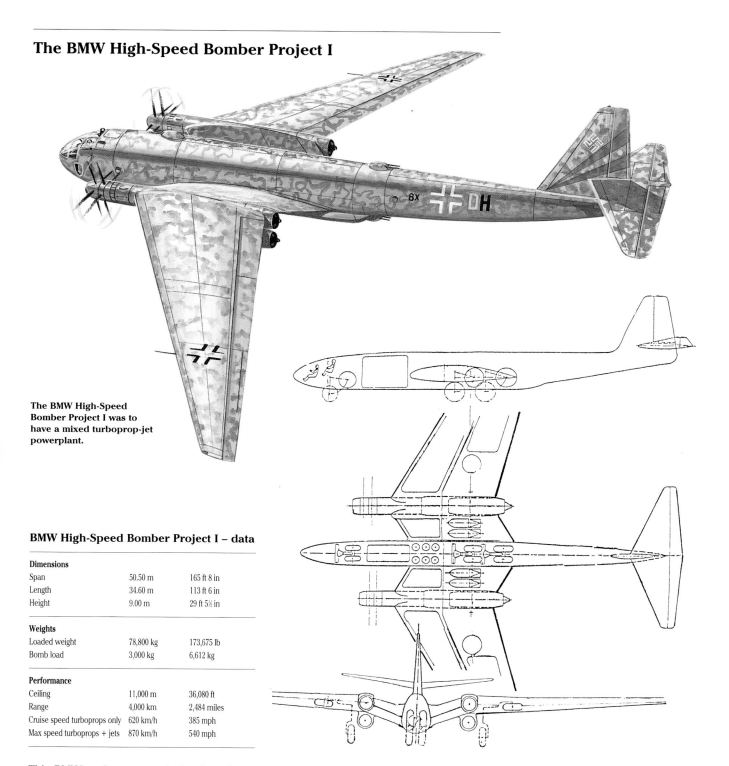

The BMW High-Speed Bomber Project I was to have a mixed turboprop-jet powerplant.

BMW High-Speed Bomber Project I – data

Dimensions		
Span	50.50 m	165 ft 8 in
Length	34.60 m	113 ft 6 in
Height	9.00 m	29 ft 5½ in
Weights		
Loaded weight	78,800 kg	173,675 lb
Bomb load	3,000 kg	6,612 kg
Performance		
Ceiling	11,000 m	36,080 ft
Range	4,000 km	2,484 miles
Cruise speed turboprops only	620 km/h	385 mph
Max speed turboprops + jets	870 km/h	540 mph

This BMW project was a design for a large mixed-powerplant bomber. Two BMW 109-028 turboprops and two BMW 109-018 jet engines were to be mounted in the cranked wings between the forward-swept inner sections and the rear-swept outer sections.

The jet engines positioned below the turboprops were intended for use at take-off, as well as to provide additional speed in the event of interception by the enemy. The two turboprops allowed for cruise speed while the High-Speed Bomber I was en route to the target area.

Tandem pairs of mainwheels retracted into the mid-fuselage section. Twin nosewheels were located beneath the crew cabin. Two outrigger wheels in the outer wing sections stabilized the machine during take-off and landing. The three-man crew cabin in the nose was fully pressurised and it was from here that the defensive armament was remotely-controlled.

GA drawing of the BMW High-Speed Bomber Project I.

BMW High-Speed Bomber Project II

Two propjet engines lent the BMW High-Speed Bomber Project II a distinctly bizarre appearance – but they would give the cantilevered low-wing design a top speed in excess of 870 km/h 540 mph.

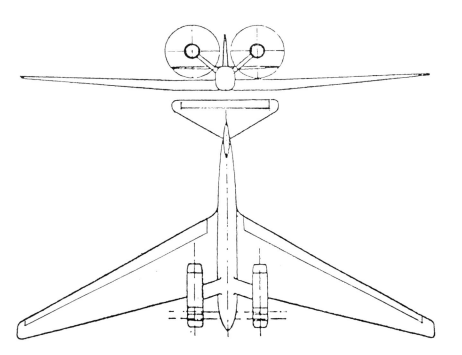

GA drawing of the BMW High-Speed Bomber Project II.

BMW High-Speed Bomber Project II – data

Crew	Two to Three	
Powerplant	2 x BMW 109-028 turboprops	
Dimensions		
Span	32.50 m	106 ft 7 in
Length	28.00 m	91 ft 10 in
Height	6.50 m	21 ft 4 in
Prop diameter	4.10 m	13 ft 5½ in
Weights		
Bomb load	2,000 kg	4,408 lb
Performance		
Range	2,800 km	1,739 miles

This rather bizarre looking bomber was designed in 1943 by the BMW project department headed by *Flugbaumeister* Dipl-Ing Kappus.

Two BMW 109-028 turboprop engines, each with a shaft output of 6,570 hp and additional residual thrust of some 600 kg (1,322 lb), were to give the High-Speed Bomber II a speed in excess of 870 km/h (540 mph). The engines were mounted on two sponsons projecting at an angle of 45° above the fuselage; this arrangement being chosen to keep the exhaust gases and turbulent airflow from the propellers well away from the tail control surfaces. At the same time, the height of the engines above the ground meant that the tricycle undercarriage required only the minimum of clearance.

The cantilevered low-wing design featured forward-swept wings – similar to the Junkers Ju 287 – with a negative sweep of 28.5°, combined with swept horizontal tail surface leading edges. Development work was carried out in the autumn of 1944, without a contract from the RLM, to test installation arrangements for turboprop engines.

The BMW Jet Bomber Project I

The BMW Jet Bomber Project I was based upon an almost tail-less design. Powered by six BMW 109-003 jet engines, a speed of 820 km/h (509 mph) was predicted.

To ensure sufficient stability about the vertical axis, a fin and rudder was attached to the end of a narrow fuselage-like boom.

Of the six engines, two were mounted in each wing; the remaining pair being located below and to either side of the crew cabin. As in the High-Speed Bomber II, the cabin, accommodating a crew of two, was fully pressurised. It was from here, too, that the heavy defensive armament was remotely controlled.

BMW Jet Bomber Project I – data

Dimensions		
Span	26.50 m	86 ft 11 in
Length	18.00 m	59 ft 0½ in
Height	4.35 m	14 ft 3 in
Wing area	100 m²	1,076 ft²
Wing loading	250 kg/m²	51 lb/ft²
Weights		
Loaded weight	25,000 kg	55,100 lb
Bomb load	5,000 kg	11,020 lb
Performance		
Range	2,600 km	1,615 miles

The BMW Jet Bomber Project I. Two of the engines can be seen below the cockpit, the other four were buried in the wings.

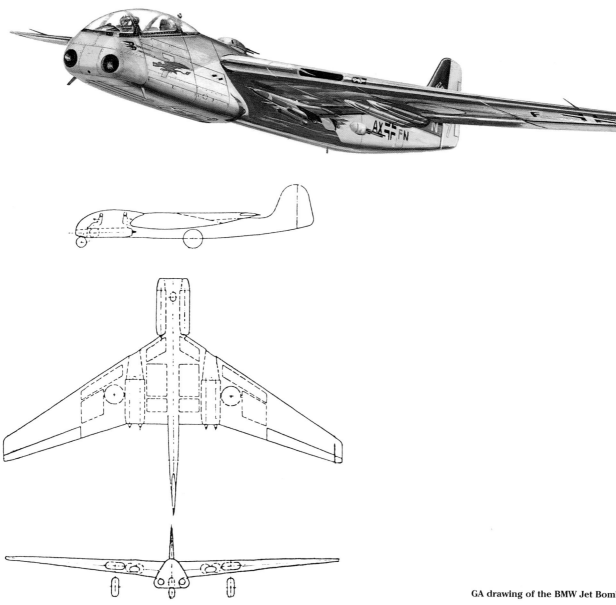

GA drawing of the BMW Jet Bomber Project I.

The BMW Jet Bomber Project II

The BMW Jet Bomber Project II was to have combined a range of 4,000 km (2,484 miles) with the ability to carry a 5-ton bomb load.

The Messerschmitt designers broke fresh ground in the layout of this flying-wing bomber. In order to retain directional stability together with the inherent stability of the swept wing, the two BMW 109-018 jet engines were located in the middle of the fuselage. This arrangement would provide sufficient inherent stability should one engine fail. Engine air was delivered via bifurcated trunking from the nose intake. A ventral bath below this trunking offered ample space and visibility for the bomb-aimer and obviated the need for a fully glazed nose.

BMW Bomber Project II – data

Dimensions

Span	35.50 m	116 ft 5½ in
Length	18.00 m	59 ft 0½ in
Height	4.50 m	14 ft 9 in
Wing area	115.70 m²	1,245 ft²

Weights

Loaded weight	31,500 kg	69,426 lb
Bomb load	5,000 kg	11,020 lb

Performance

Speed	950 km/h	590 mph
Range	4,000 km	2,484 miles

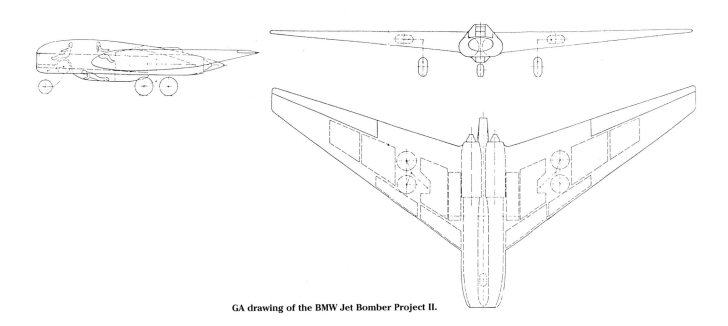

GA drawing of the BMW Jet Bomber Project II.

The Daimler Benz A and B Projects

Project Numbers 310 256-02 and -03

By the time BMW entered the field of aviation design with their innovatory bomber projects, the Planning and Development Department at Daimler Benz AG, under the leadership of Dipl-Ing Nallinger and Chief Engineer Übelacker, were already at a very advanced stage in their designs for long-range composite-carrier aircraft. It was in 1942/43 that Daimler Benz had combined with Focke-Wulf to form a joint study group for the development of ultra long-range aircraft capable of attacking strategic targets in the USA and Soviet industrial plants far beyond the Urals. These strikes were to be carried out in non-stop flight and without recourse to aerial refuel-ling.

The two designs, simply referred to as Projects 'A' and 'B', were to have been built shortly before the war's end. The aerodynamic and technical side of the Daimler Benz-inspired projects was in the hands of Prof Dr-Ing Kurt Tank, Focke-Wulf's chief designer, who, together with his design team, formed part of the joint study group.

Project 'A' was a carrier aircraft designed to transport a jet bomber between its tall, fixed undercarriage. This combination was to have been capable of delivering a 30,000 kg (66,120 lb) bomb load over a distance of 17,000 km (10,557 miles).

Project 'B' was an improved and expanded version of Project 'A' able to carry five manned, or remotely-controlled, explosive delivery systems to distant target areas. These flying-bombs, whether piloted manually or equipped with radio-guidance, were to be armed with heavy 2,500 kg (5,510 lb) hollow-charge warheads, whose destructive effect was far greater than that of conventional bombs. Power for both 'A' and 'B' carrier components was to have been provided by either six 2,700 hp Daimler Benz DB 9-603 E or N piston engines, or by four Daimler Benz DB 109-021 turboprops each of 6,800 hp shaft output plus additional thrust of 600 kg (1,322 lb). Illustrated on page 78 is a project study of the type powered by four DB-Hirth 109-022 jet engines, a more powerful development of the Heinkel-Hirth 109-011.

The Very Fast Bomber Project (Project Number 310 256-05) and the Expendable Flying-Bomb (Project Number 310 256-04) were the designations given to the weapon-delivery components of the 'A' and 'B' projects described above. The manned Flying-Bomb was intended for suicide missions against shipping or other pin-point targets; the pilot being expected to aim his aircraft, with its hollow-charge warhead in the nose, at the target by hand.

Professor Dr-Ing Kurt Tank

1898 Born in Bromberg-Schwedenhöhe.

1914 Lieutenant – later Squadron-Commander – in a cavalry regiment.

1918 Returns from the war seriously wounded and with high awards for bravery.

1920 Begins studies at Berlin TH.

1924 Development designer with *Rohrbach-Metallflugzeugbau* (Rohrbach Metal Aircraft Manufacturing Co). Designer of such types as the Rohrbach Ro IX Rofix single-seat fighter.

1930 Head of the project bureau at BMW in Augsburg.

1931 Takes over as head of design and flight-testing at Focke-Wulf in Bremen.

1936 Designs the Focke-Wulf Fw Condor.

1938 Appointed Flugkapitän.

1943 Appointed Professor in recognition of his work in the field of design. Further honoured late in 1943 with permission to designate all aircraft produced under his design leadership with prefix Ta (for Tank).

1944 In the course of flight-testing the Ta 152H, Kurt Tank achieves a speed of 746 km/h (463 mph) at an altitude of 14,000 m (45,920 ft). Occupied until end of war with the Ta 400 long-distance bomber and other bomber projects such as the Tank Ta 183.

1945 Tank accepts an invitation to go to Argentina, where he continues work on the Ta 183 in the aircraft factory of the Argentine Army.

1950 Design and construction of Argentina's first jet fighter, the Instituto Aerotecnico IAe33 Pulqúi II.

1954 Discontinues development work in Argentina.

1955 Summoned to India. Design and construction of the Indian HF 24 interceptor fighter.

1970 Returns to Germany.

1983 Kurt Tank dies in Munich.

Professor Dr-Ing Kurt Tank 1898-1983, Focke-Wulf's chief designer, was responsible not only for such well-known aircraft as the Fw 44 Stieglitz, Fw 190 and Fw 200 Condor, but also for the Ta 400 long-distance bomber project. He also test-flew the aircraft he and his colleagues constructed.

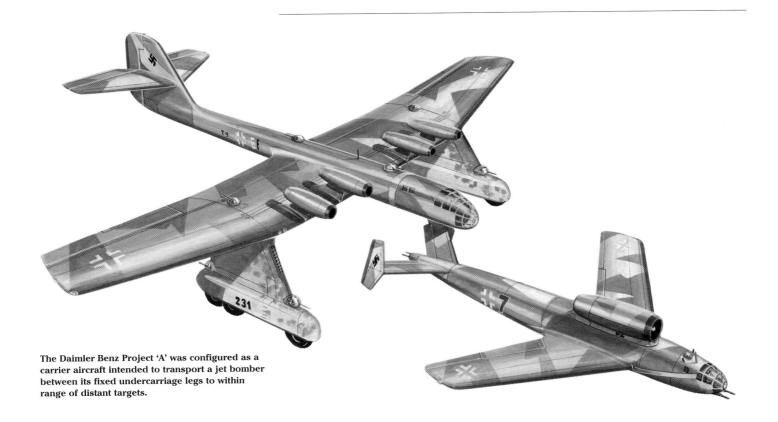

The Daimler Benz Project 'A' was configured as a carrier aircraft intended to transport a jet bomber between its fixed undercarriage legs to within range of distant targets.

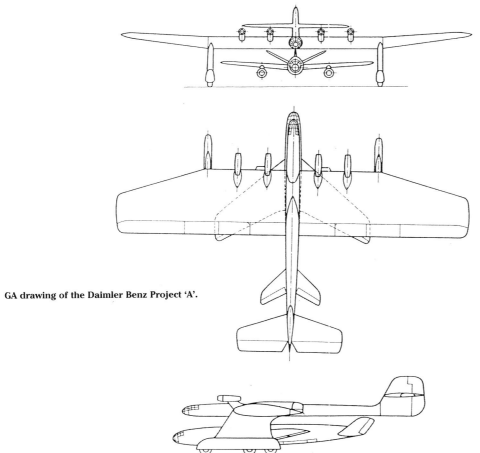

GA drawing of the Daimler Benz Project 'A'.

Daimler Benz A and B Projects – data (Carrier Components)

Crew	Three to Four	
Powerplant	6 x 2,700 hp Daimler Benz DB 9-609E or N piston engines, or 4 x Daimler Benz DB 109-021 turboprops each of 6,800 hp shaft output plus 600 kg (1,322 lb) additional thrust	
Dimensions		
Span	54.00 m	177 ft 1½ in
Wing area	500 m²	5,382 ft²
Length	35.00 m	114 ft 10 in
Height	11.20 m	36 ft 9 in
Wing Chord	11.0 m	36 ft 1 in
U/c track	24.40 m	80 ft 0½ in
Propellers	4 or 6 x 5.00 m	16 ft 5 in
	diameter four-blade variable pitch	
Undercarriage	2 sets of 3 paired wheels	
Weights		
Weight empty equipped	48,500 kg	106,894 lb
Load	73,500 kg	161,994 lb
Loaded weight	122,000 kg	268,888 lb
Performance		
Range	17,000 km	10,557 miles

Daimler Benz Very Fast Bomber Project

Crew	Two
Powerplant	1 x Daimler Benz DB 109-016 turbojet rated at 12,000 kg (26,448 lb) static thrust

Dimensions		
Span	22.00 m	72 ft 2 in
Length	30.75 m	100 ft 10½ in
Height	8.50 m	27 ft 10½ in
U/c track	7.80 m	25 ft 7 in

Weights		
Loaded weight	70,000 kg	154,280 lb

Performance		
Approach height	10,000 m	32,800 ft

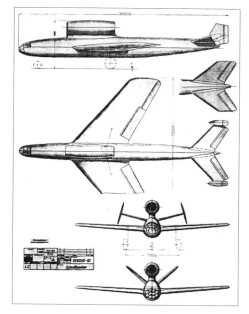

The Daimler Benz high-speed bomber, drawing number 310 256-05, which formed the lower component of Project 'A' and was to be transported to within striking distance of the target area. After separation from the carrier, the bomber could deliver a 30,000 kg 66,120 lb weapon load of i.e. sixty SC 500 bombs in clusters of ten, or thirty SB 1000 bombs in clusters of five.

Daimler Piloted Flying-Bomb – data

Crew	One
Powerplant	1 x Heinkel-Hirth HeS 109-011 turbojet rated at 1,300 kg (2,865 lb) static thrust

Dimensions		
Span	8.50 m	27 ft 10½ in
Length	9.20 m	30 ft 2 in
Height	3.20 m	10 ft 6 in

Armament		
Warhead	2,500 kg hollow charge	5,510 lb

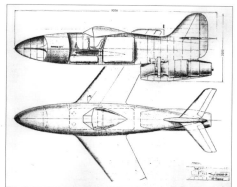

Project drawing of a manned flying-bomb, drawing number 310 256-04, five of which could be transported by the Project 'B' carrier component. Armed with a 2,500 kg 5,510 lb hollow-charge explosive warhead, these bombs would be aimed by hand at shipping and other pin-point targets in the manner of Japanese Kamikaze attacks.

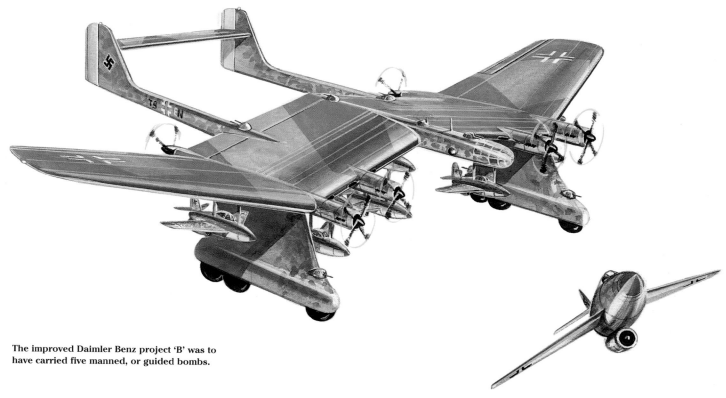

The improved Daimler Benz project 'B' was to have carried five manned, or guided bombs.

Tank Ta 400 –
A Long-Distance Bomber

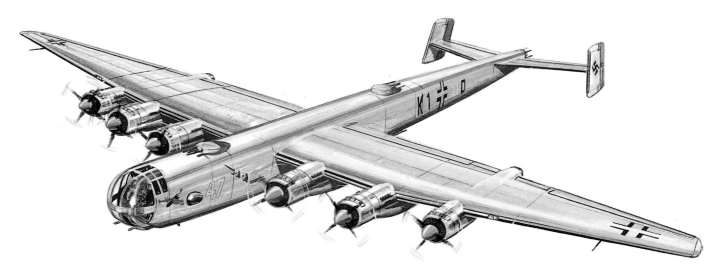

Focke-Wulf Tank Ta 400, a cantilevered mid-wing bomber with six engines.

Model of the Tank Ta 400 in the wind tunnel.

In the middle of 1943 the RLM awarded contracts to Junkers, Messerschmitt and Focke-Wulf for the development of long-distance bombers capable of reaching the American continent carrying a 10,000 kg (22,040 lb) bomb load.

Under the designation Tank Ta 400, the Focke-Wulf project bureau at Bad Eilsen, headed by chief designer Dr Kurt Tank, developed a six-engined cantilevered mid-wing bomber which would be able to transport the required 10,000 kg (22,040 lb) warload at a speed of 720 km/h (447 mph). The proposed powerplant comprised six 1,750 hp BMW 9-801D piston engines; the outboard engine on each wing being supplemented by a Junkers Jumo 109-004 turbojet.

Tank Ta 400 – data

Crew	Six	
Powerplant	6 x 1,750 hp BMW 9-801D piston engines, plus 2 x Junkers Jumo 109-004B turbojets each rated at 1,050 kg (2,314 lb) static thrust	
Dimensions		
Span	45.80 m	150 ft 3 in
Length	28.70 m	94 ft 1½ in
Weights		
Loaded weight	60,000 kg	132,240 lb
Performance		
Range	9,000 km	5,589 miles

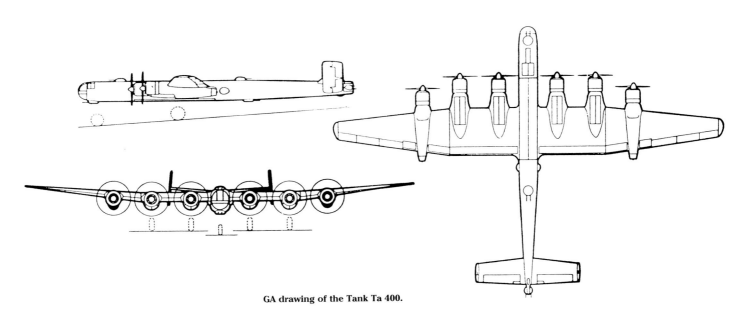

GA drawing of the Tank Ta 400.

Heinkel He 343 – A Four-Jet High-Speed Bomber

In June 1943 the Technical Office of the RLM issued a specification for a two-seat bomber capable of carrying a 2,000 kg (4,408 lb) bomb load over a distance of 2,500 km (1,552 miles) at speeds of up to 800 km/h (497 mph). In response, Heinkel's design bureau in Vienna came up with a project late in 1943, designated the P 1068, which would form the basis for a number of subsequent comparison studies. Among these was the P 1068.01-80, a six-jet bomber project which was abandoned when the calculated loaded weight proved to be excessive.

Another project in this development series was the P 1068.01-84 four-jet bomber, a striking and unusual design combining a novel powerplant arrangement with a wing featuring 35° sweep. The four jet engines were located on the sides of the fuselage: two ahead of, and below, the wingroot leading-edges and two aft of, and above, the wingroot trailing-edges. This cantilevered mid-wing design had a tricycle undercarriage and a pressurised cabin for the crew of two.

The various project studies were later added to the official register of aircraft types under the generic RLM designation of Heinkel He 343.

The Heinkel He 343A-1, for example, was a medium bomber of 18.00 m (59 ft 0½ in) span, which could carry a bomb load of 3,000 kg (6,612 lb). Powered by four Heinkel-Hirth HeS 109-011 jet engines, it weighed 119,550 kg (43,088 lb) and had a projected speed of 910 km/h (565 mph).

Other variants of the Heinkel He 343 were developed, including the He 343B-1. This latter differed from the earlier He 343A-1, A-2 and A-3 versions by having a twin fin and rudder and incorporating remotely-controlled tail armament.

Professor Dr-Ing Ernst Heinkel, industrialist and pioneer of high-speed flight, built the world's first jet-propelled aircraft – the Heinkel He 178.

Heinkel He 343A-1 – data

Crew	Two	
Powerplant	4 x Heinkel-Hirth HeS 109-011 turbojets each rated at 1,300 kg (2,865 lb) st. thrust	
Dimensions		
Span	18.00 m	59 ft 0½ in
Length	16.50 m	54 ft 1½ in
Height	5.35 m	17 ft 6½ in
Wing area	42.45 m²	457 ft²
Weights		
Loaded weight	19,550 kg	43,088 lb
Bomb load	3,000 kg	6,612 lb
Performance		
Speed	910 km/h	565 mph
Range	2,800 km	1,739 miles

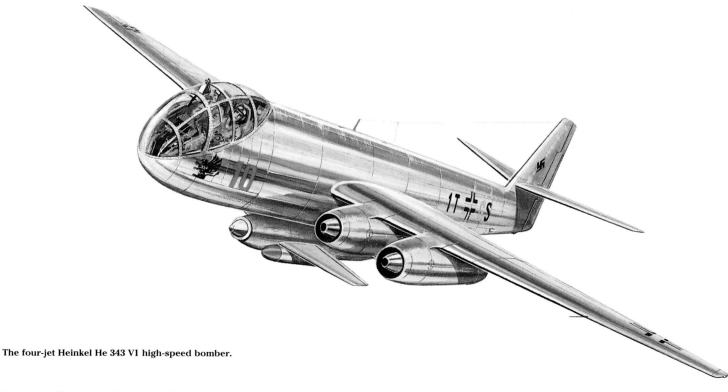

The four-jet Heinkel He 343 V1 high-speed bomber.

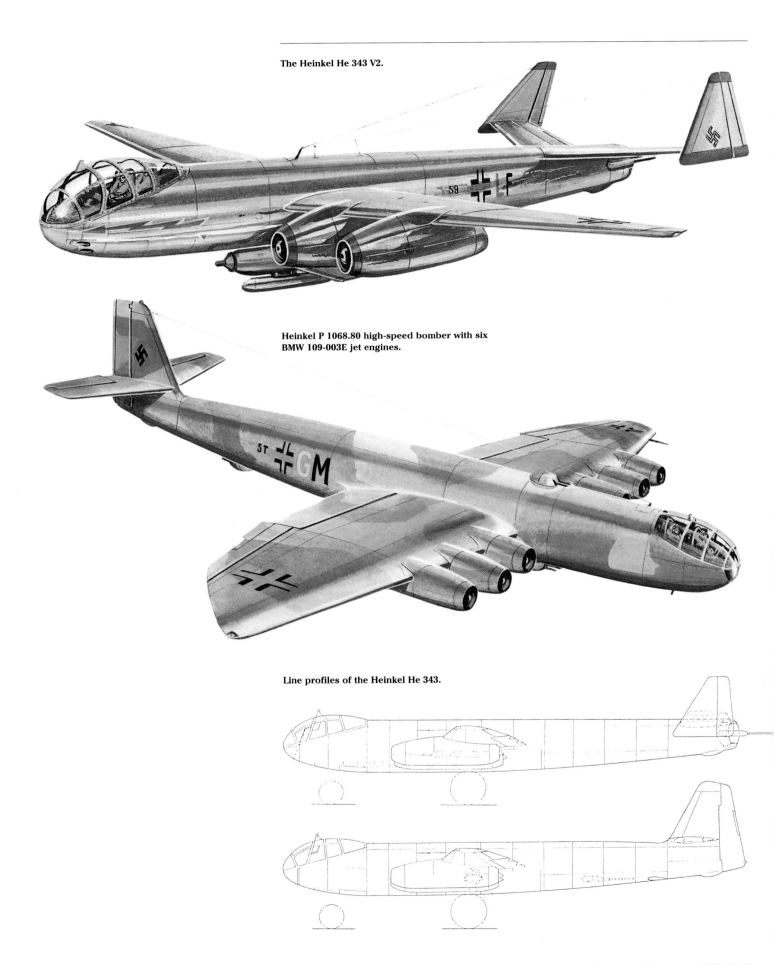

The Heinkel He 343 V2.

Heinkel P 1068.80 high-speed bomber with six
BMW 109-003E jet engines.

Line profiles of the Heinkel He 343.

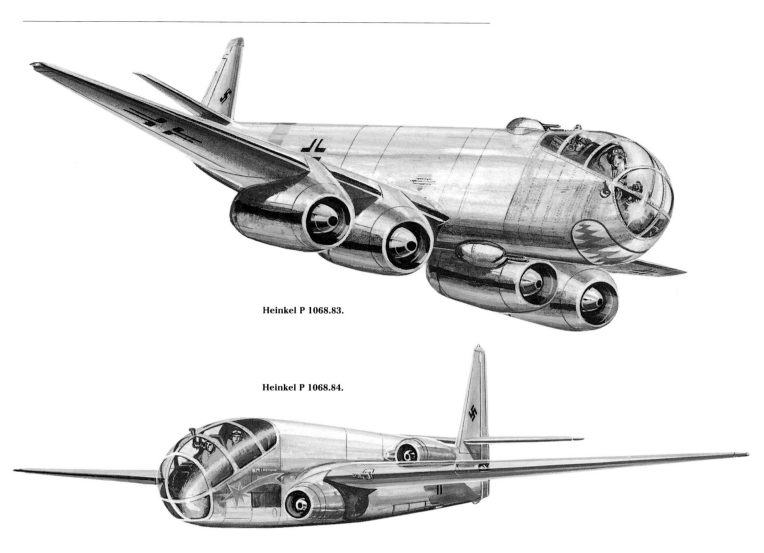

Heinkel P 1068.83.

Heinkel P 1068.84.

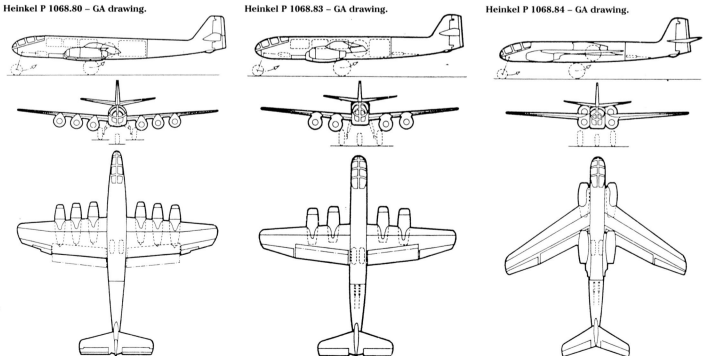

Heinkel P 1068.80 – GA drawing.

Heinkel P 1068.83 – GA drawing.

Heinkel P 1068.84 – GA drawing.

Messerschmitt Me P 1073 –
Project Study for a Long-Distance Bomber with Ultra-Long Range

Messerschmitt P 1073A, a long-distance bomber project designed for an extreme range of almost 18,000 km (11,178 miles). Three on-board fighters were carried to defend it against enemy fighter attack in the target area.

Messerschmitt Me P 1073A – data

Crew	Ten	
Dimensions		
Span	63.00 m	206 ft 8 in
Length	39.30 m	128 ft 11 in
Height	6.10 m	20 ft 0 in
Wing area	330 m²	3,552 ft²
Aspect ratio	12	
Wing loading	388 kg/m²	79 lb/ft²
Weights		
Loaded weight	128,000 kg	282,112 lb
Performance		
Service ceiling	13,000 m	42,640 ft
Max. Speed	600 km/h	373 mph
Range	17,950 km	11,147 miles

The initial aim in 1940 had been for a long-distance aircraft which could not only play a part in the U-boat war by locating and shadowing Allied convoys and attacking shipping, but could also be employed as a long-range bomber against land targets.

In the course of further operational requirement studies, these roles were widened to include deployment as a guided-weapons carrier able to mount nuisance raids on cities and industrial complexes along America's eastern seaboard.

To provide defence against enemy fighters over the target area, it was proposed to carry three parasite fighters within the aircraft's fuselage, these being launched and recovered during flight by an extendable ventral lock and hook arrangement. The three on-board fighters would be lowered individually, via a conveyor, through an opening in the floor of the fuselage and then released to fly under their own power.

Drawings prepared by the Messerschmitt design bureau in September 1940 show that Project P 1073A was to be powered by eight 2,240 hp Junkers Jumo 9-223 twenty-four cylinder diesel engines arranged in tandem in four nacelles, each nacelle having both a tractor and a pusher propeller.

Three remotely-controlled dorsal barbettes, plus one in the tail, and two ventral barbettes provided the necessary means of direct self-defence.

The all-metal construction Project P 1073A had a span of 63.00 m (206 ft 8 in), a length of 39.30 m (128 ft 11 in) and a wing area of 330 m² (3,552 ft²). Calculated speed was 600 km/h (373 mph). Carrying a 6,000 kg (13,224 lb) bomb load and with the three parasite fighters on board, the P 1073A's loaded weight of 128,000 kg (282,112 lb) would have made it the heaviest land-based aircraft of its time.

Messerschmitt P 1073B, the on-board fighter component of the P 1073.

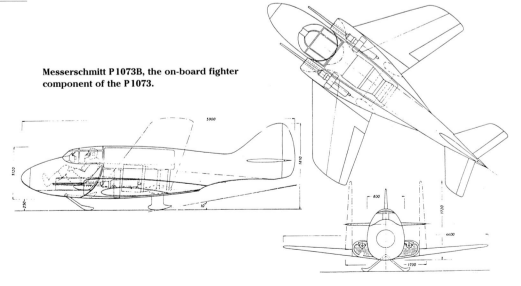

Messerschmitt Me P 1073B – The On-Board Fighter

A low-wing design featuring an oval cross-section fuselage and single fin and rudder. The stubby laminar-profile wings had a sweep of 35°. The air intakes and pair of MG 151/20 cannon were situated on the lower sides of the fuselage ahead of the wing roots. A nose-skid and retractable main landing skid were fitted in place of an orthodox wheeled undercarriage. The BMW 109-003 jet engine was located in the rear half of the fuselage with the exhaust outlet beneath the tail. For loading purposes the wings could be folded upwards immediately outboard of the intake nacelles. In 'transport mode' the Me P 1073B was thus almost exactly square in cross-section; being 1.73 m (5 ft 8 in) wide and 1.72 m (5 ft 7½ in) high.

Messerschmitt Me P 1073B – data

Powerplant	1 x BMW 109-003 turbojet	
Dimensions		
Span	4.40 m	14 ft 4½ in
Length	5.90 m	19 ft 4 in
Height skids extended	1.81 m	5 ft 11 in
Fuselage width	0.80 m	2 ft 7½ in
Wing area	6.50 m²	70 ft²
Weights		
Loaded weight	1,620 kg	3,570 lb

Messerschmitt P 1107 – An Ultra High-Speed Bomber

After many years of searching, the authors were finally able to locate an original copy of the manufacturing specifications of one of Messerschmitt's last jet bomber projects, the P 1107 of 25th January 1945.

The uniqueness of this document warrants the reproduction of the original text in full on this page. It serves as witness not only to the advanced state of German aviation technology, but also to the unshakable optimism of the designers only weeks before the war's end.

The experiences gained during the development of the Me 264 long-range bomber in terms of aerodynamics, weights and assembly methods were incorporated into the P 1107. Series production of the P 1107 was scheduled to commence in the year 1948.

Messerschmitt Me P 1107/I
Bomber Aircraft – calculated data

Dimensions		
Wing area	60 m²	646 ft²
Span	17.30 m	56 ft 9 in
Length	18.40 m	60 ft 4 in
Height	4.96 m	16 ft 3 in
Wing sweep	35°	
Weights		
Take-off weight	29,000 kg	63,916 lb
Fuel capacity	15,000 kg	33,060 lb
Bomb load	4,000 kg	8,816 lb
Performance		
Max speed	990-1,020 km/h	615-633 mph
Range	7,400 km	4,595 miles
Total endurance	8 hrs 27 mins	

Messerschmitt Me P 1107/I
Reconnaissance Aircraft – calculated data

Dimensions		
Wing area	60 m²	646 ft²
Span	17.30 m	56 ft 9 in
Length	18.40 m	60 ft 4 in
Height	4.95 m	16 ft 2½ in
Wing sweep	35°	
Weights		
Take-off weight	29,400 kg	64,798 lb
Fuel capacity	19,400 kg	42,758 lb
Performance		
Max speed	990-1,020 km/h	615-633 mph
Range	9,600 km	5,962 miles
Total endurance	11 hrs 6 mins	

g.Kdos. (Secret Communication)
No. 28/5778 of 25th January 1945.

Short Description of the Messerschmitt P 1107 Long-Range Jet Bomber with the proposed Model Designation Me 8-462.

Oberammergau, dated 16th January 45
signed Messerschmitt

The following is a brief description of the jet bomber:

Role: High-speed bomber for long ranges.

Crew: 4 in pressurised cabin.

Powerplant: 4 x Heinkel-Hirth HeS 109-011 turbojets each rated at 1,300 kg (2,865 lb) st. thrust.

Fuel tankage: Fuel to be carried in mid-fuselage and in the wings.

Armament: Initially weapon load only.

Construction: Four-jet cantilevered mid-wing machine initially with centre-line vertical tail surfaces and retractable tricycle undercarriage.

Materials: Wings and tail unit primarily of wood, fuselage of steel and Duralumin.

Stability: Stability Group H3.

Airframe (Fuselage): Circular cross-section spindle body taken over from Me 264. Fuselage mid-section: Fuel tank(s) and bomb bays, aft fuselage supporting tail unit.

Wing: Preliminary variant wooden wing, detachable at fuselage wall. Wooden wing structure with load-bearing central box-spar of glued pine. Engines attached below aft section of wings. Final variant of metal construction, outer wing sections of wood, normal split flaps, automatic wing leading-edge slots.

Tail unit: Swept V-tail (P 1107/I) proposed as standard arrangement. Horizontal tail surfaces on top of vertical tail (T-tail).

Undercarriage: Retractable tricycle undercarriage, main members with two 1550 x 575 wheels proposed for all take-off weights. Main undercarriage to retract rearwards into fuselage.

Powerplant: Installation of four Heinkel-Hirth HeS 109-011 turbojets, two in each wingroot aft of the main spar.

Equipment: Pressure cabin, cabin heating. Radio equipment: FuG 10, FuG 15, FuG 15a, FuG 25a, FuG 101, FuG 120 and FuG 244 Berlin.

Performance: Calculated constant cruise speed of 900 km/h (558 mph) for long-distance flight. Maximum permissible engine power for normal flight 90% full throttle. Range may be increased by external tanks under wing outer sections, by towed fuel tanks or by aerial refuelling.

Armament: Initially only weapon load. 4,000 kg (8,816 lb) carried internally in fuselage. 4 x 1,000 kg (2,204 lb) SC 1000 bombs, or one 1,500 kg (3,306 lb) SC 1500 and two 500 kg (1,102 lb) SC 500 bombs. 2 torpedos, guided bombs, special air-to-ground missiles etc. Armour-plating not proposed.

Operational deployment: P 1107 suitable for operations against enemy supply lines at sea or on land, as well as for wide-ranging reconnaissance missions.

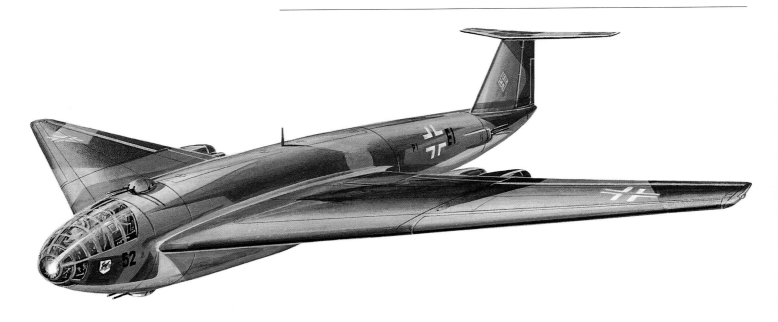

The Messerschmitt P 1107/I, a project for a long-distance bomber, was to have a take-off weight of 29 tons and be able to attain a maximum speed of 1,020 km/h 633 mph.

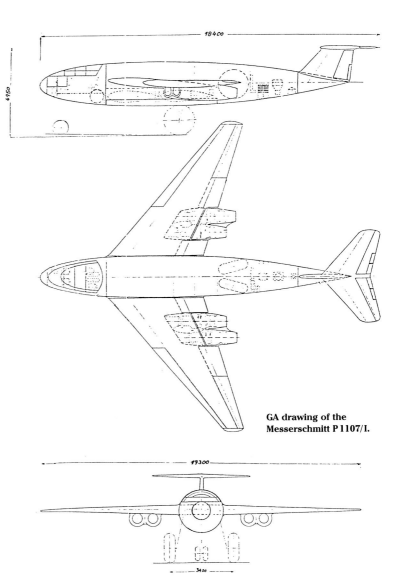

GA drawing of the Messerschmitt P 1107/I.

Professor Dr-Ing Willy Messerschmitt, designer, company director and creator of the legendary Me 109 and Me 262 fighters, as well as the Me 264 strategic heavy bomber, was one of the most enterprising aircraft manufacturers of his generation.

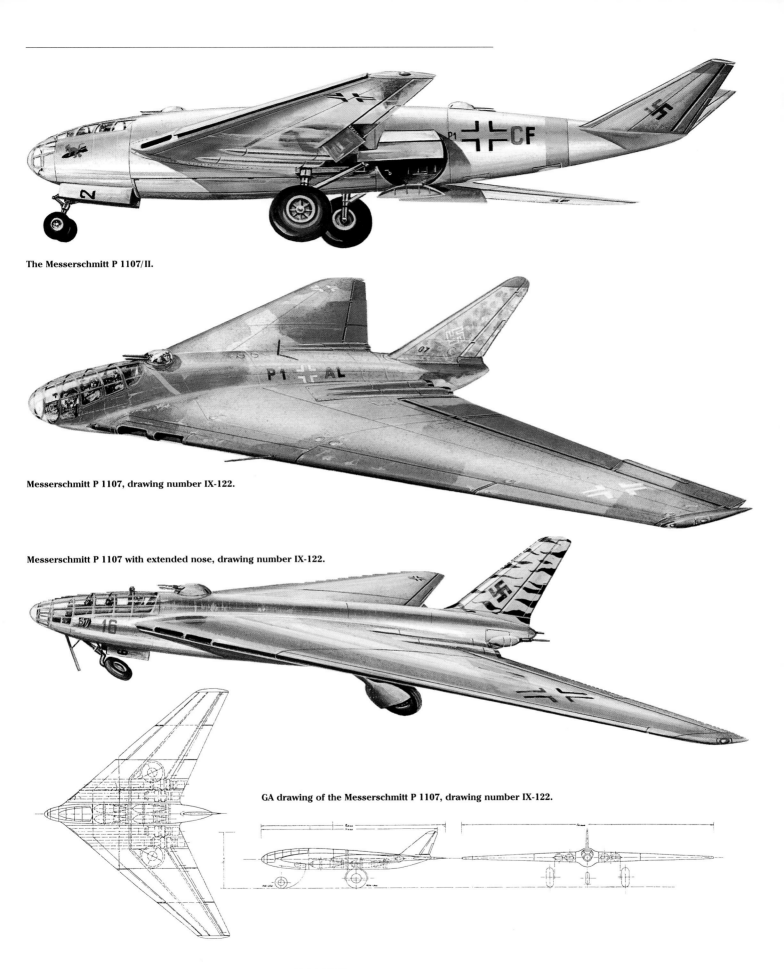

The Messerschmitt P 1107/II.

Messerschmitt P 1107, drawing number IX-122.

Messerschmitt P 1107 with extended nose, drawing number IX-122.

GA drawing of the Messerschmitt P 1107, drawing number IX-122.

The Messerschmitt P 1108 – Long-Range Bomber Project

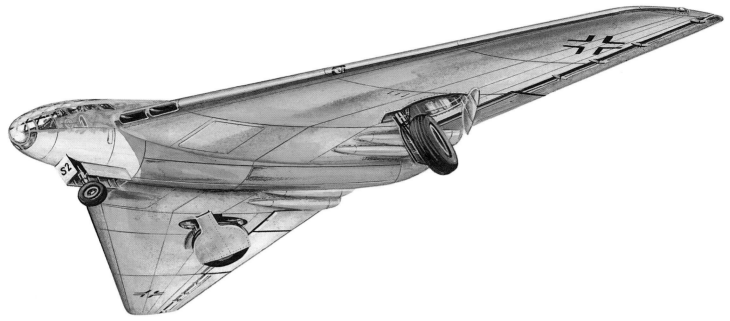

The Messerschmitt projects of this development series – such as the P 1108/I illustrated here – were sensational in both aerodynamic shape and design.

Among the last and most interesting projects submitted to the Main Development Commission (EHK) and the RLM between 1st January 1945 and 23rd March 1945 were the further studies emanating from the P 1107 development series.

The P 1108 series of projects designed by Dipl-Ings. Seifert and Konrad, which included flying-wings – both with and without vertical tail surfaces – as well as more conventionally configured machines, were, in terms of aerodynamics and design, nothing short of sensational. They are published here for the first time.

As practically no original written documentation has survived from either series, the author has attempted to use the few original works drawings which do still exist to reconstruct the missing data and information. These drawings have, at the same time, been used as reference by artist Heinz Rode, whose colour impressions have breathed such extraordinary life into the projects described.

The studies developed and proposed between 12th and 23rd March 1945 for long-range bomber projects P 1108/I and P 1108/II are almost identical in their basic design. There are, however, certain differences in fuselage detail and in their measurements, as well as in powerplant arrangement.

While sharing a common span of 20.00 m (65 ft 7½ in), the P 1108/II has a fuselage length of 16.25 m (53 ft 3½ in) compared to the P 1108/I's 14.30 m (46 ft 11 in). In other words, the former was some 1.95 m (6 ft 4½ in) longer.

The four Heinkel-Hirth HeS 109-011 turbojets of the P 1108/II were faired into the wings; engine air being supplied via trunking from intakes in the leading-edges. The fuselage section was also faired cleanly into the wing surfaces. The abbreviated aft section of the fuselage supported the vertical tail unit.

In profile the P 1108/I, with its shorter nose and cockpit area, and with the wing relocated much further forward, presented an altogether more compact appearance.

A further variant of the P 1108 project series was that identified by Drawing Number IX-123, dated 23rd March 1945. This was a modified and improved P 1108/II. Although closely resembling the basic design, it did vary in wing planform; the centre-section of the three-part wing having straight trailing-edges. In addition, the four Heinkel-Hirth HeS 109-011 jet engines were now attached in pairs to the rear of, and beneath, the wing-centre sections in box-like nacelles. The mainwheels retracted into the wing undersurfaces ahead of these nacelles.

Apart from its increased 21.00 m (68 ft 10½ in) span and a fuselage length of 15.00 m (49 ft 2½ in), no other data are known.

It is clear from the files that this project, the last of the series, was also the last design to be produced by Messerschmitt.

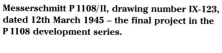

Messerschmitt P 1108/II, drawing number IX-123,
dated 12th March 1945 – the final project in the
P 1108 development series.

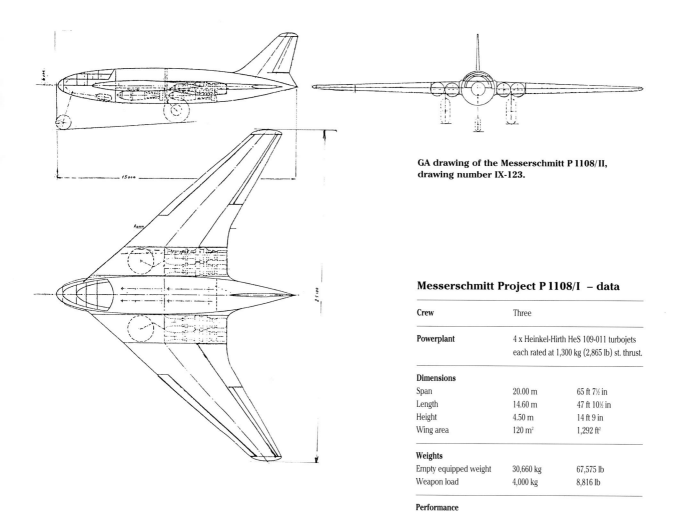

GA drawing of the Messerschmitt P 1108/II,
drawing number IX-123.

Messerschmitt Project P 1108/I – data

Crew	Three	
Powerplant	4 x Heinkel-Hirth HeS 109-011 turbojets each rated at 1,300 kg (2,865 lb) st. thrust.	
Dimensions		
Span	20.00 m	65 ft 7½ in
Length	14.60 m	47 ft 10½ in
Height	4.50 m	14 ft 9 in
Wing area	120 m²	1,292 ft²
Weights		
Empty equipped weight	30,660 kg	67,575 lb
Weapon load	4,000 kg	8,816 lb
Performance		
Range	7,000 km	4,347 miles
Speed	800-980 km/h	497-609 mph

The Messerschmitt Me P 1108 Project
of 12th January 1945

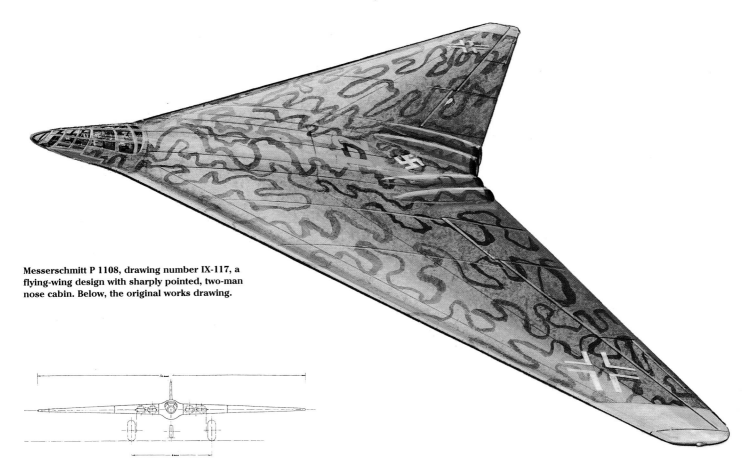

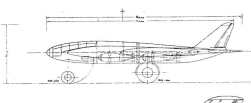

Messerschmitt P 1108, drawing number IX-117, a flying-wing design with sharply pointed, two-man nose cabin. Below, the original works drawing.

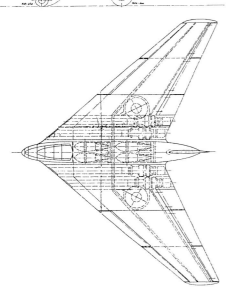

Drawing Number IX-117

This project study of the P 1108 development series was for a long-range bomber of flying-wing design, incorporating a 45° sweep, intended for high speeds. Its four Heinkel-Hirth HeS 109-011 turbojet engines were positioned at a 10° angle from the aircraft's axis to provide effective thrust equalization.

The extremely narrow fuselage, which was an integral part of the wing structure, incorporated a sharply pointed nose which provided accommodation for the crew of two in a pressurised cabin.

A major difference from the other projects in the series was the unusual tandem undercarriage. Span was 20.00 m (65 ft 7½ in), fuselage length 12.40 m (40 ft 8 in), length overall 17.00 m (55 ft 9 in) and the height 2.85 m (9 ft 4 in). The width of the undercarriage track was 4.80 m (15 ft 9 in) for the inner pair of mainwheels and 8.50 m (27 ft 10½ in) for the outer. No other data are known. The Messerschmitt works drawing is published here for the first time.

Drawing Number IX-126

The Me P 1108 'fuselage aircraft', was shown in drawing number IX-126 of 28th February 1945. The four Heinkel Hirth HeS 109-011 turbojets were housed in box-like nacelles beneath the wings and projected beyond the training-edges as 'engine gondolas'. The wing had a span of 19.80 m (64 ft 11½ in) and was swept 35°; the fuselage length being 18.20 m (59 ft 8½ in). Of particular note is the V-tail, used here for the first time in this project series. For deployment as a 'high-speed long-distance bomber' a 4,000 kg (8,816 lb) bomb load would be combined with an estimated speed of some 1,030 km/h (640 mph). Loaded weight was 35,000 kg (77,140 lb). Incorporating the most modern aerodynamic features, this project was intended for civil use after the successful conclusion of the war; flying passenger and freight services on the Frankfurt am Main-New York route in a time of some six to seven hours.

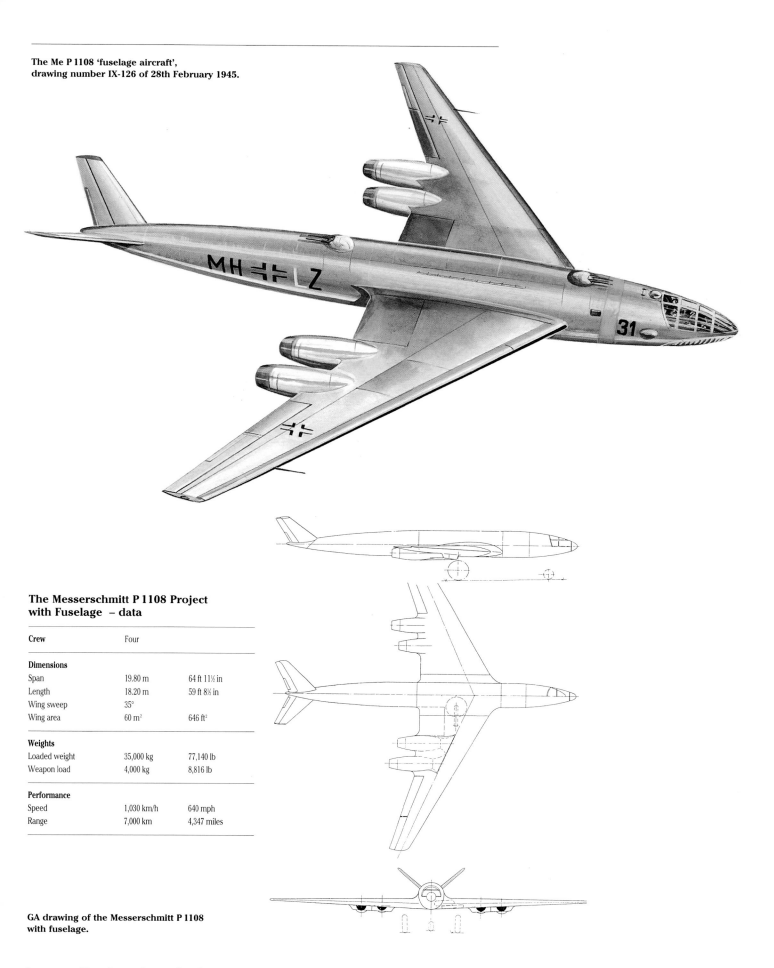

The Me P 1108 'fuselage aircraft',
drawing number IX-126 of 28th February 1945.

The Messerschmitt P 1108 Project with Fuselage – data

Crew	Four	
Dimensions		
Span	19.80 m	64 ft 11½ in
Length	18.20 m	59 ft 8½ in
Wing sweep	35°	
Wing area	60 m²	646 ft²
Weights		
Loaded weight	35,000 kg	77,140 lb
Weapon load	4,000 kg	8,816 lb
Performance		
Speed	1,030 km/h	640 mph
Range	7,000 km	4,347 miles

GA drawing of the Messerschmitt P 1108
with fuselage.

Arado E 555/1 – Long-Range Flying-Wing Bomber Project

In mid-December 1943 the development group (TE) of the Arado works in Landeshut/Silesia, under the leadership of Dr-Ing W Laute, began work on flying-wing projects featuring a completely new wing planform.

The project series, under the collective designation E 555, comprised some 15 individual designs – all with the new wing planform – intended for a variety of roles, from that of long-range bomber to fighter aircraft. These developments were based on the studies of Dipl-Ings. Kosin and Lehmann (Arado), which were entitled 'Flying-Wing Aircraft for Long Ranges and High Speeds'.

On 20th April 1944 a conference, chaired by *Flugbaumeister* Dipl-Ing Scheibe and Ing Haspe (RLM), was convened at the RLM where, together with representatives from Arado, the final specifications for the jet bomber were drawn up.

In mid-1944 the Arado development group received an order from the RLM to produce design studies for a long-range bomber featuring the new wing planform and along the guidelines already established.

The specification called for a flying-wing bomber, powered by up to eight jet engines, which would be capable of flying long distances at high speeds. Precise requirements included the ability to carry a bomb load in excess of 4,000 kg (8,816 lb) over ranges of some 5,000 km (3,105 miles). These demands could best be met by an aircraft of flying-wing design, the wings incorporating both sweep and high-speed laminar profile. The use of swept wings – and a correspondingly large wing area – would obviate the necessity for a normal fuselage and tail unit.

The Arado E 555/1 was to be of light alloy and steel construction, with the rudders using some 5% fabric. The fuselage was of circular cross-section and designed to modern aerodynamic requirements. The three-man crew were housed in a pressurised, fully-glazed cabin located ahead of the centre of gravity. The twin fin and rudder assemblies were situated on the wing upper surfaces 6.20 m (20 ft 4 in) from the aircraft's centre-line. The four-wheel main undercarriage bogies retracted inwards, their width determining the thickness of the wing inner section. The rearward-retracting twin nosewheels were housed in a centre-section bay aft of the pressure cabin.

With a normal 4,000 kg (8,816 lb) bomb load, calculated take-off weight was 24 tons. A jettisonable auxiliary undercarriage, similar to that of the Me 264, would be used to sup-

port the main undercarriage and to permit an overload of a further 2.5 tons.

Calculations of the total thrust delivered by the proposed six turbojets showed that a much higher speed and a greater range could be achieved by the use of four larger and more powerful jet engines. For better thrust equalization, and to reduce occupied surface area, a powerplant arrangement divided between wing upper and lower surfaces would probably have been the more practical solution. To increase the range, as demanded by the RLM, it was proposed to install four of the more powerful BMW 109-018 turbojets, which would also have made possible a more satisfactory aspect ratio.

Defensive armament of the E 555/1 was to comprise two fixed forward-firing MK 103 cannon in the wing roots, plus a pair of rearward-firing MG 151/20s in a remotely-controlled dorsal barbette in the cabin roof. In addition, a tail barbette, similarly armed with two MG 151/20s, would be remotely controlled via a periscope sight from a pressurised weapon station to the rear of the crew cabin.

On 28th December 1944 the Main Development Commission (EHK) ordered the immediate cessation of all work on the Arado E 555/1 project. Like a large number of other highly developed projects from other aircraft manufacturers, the Arado design, which offered so much promise, had fallen victim to yet one more inexplicable decision from the RLM.

Arado E 555/1 – data

Powerplant	6 x BMW 109-003A	
Dimensions		
Wing area	125 m²	1,345 ft²
Aspect ratio	3.6	
Span	21.20 m	69 ft 6½ in
Height	5.00 m	16 ft 5 in
Performance		
Ceiling	13,000-15,000 m	42,640-49,200 ft
Combat radius/normal	3,200 km	1,987 miles
Combat radius/LR tanks	4,800 km	2,980 miles
Cruising speed	715 km/h	440 mph
Max speed	860 km/h	535 mph

An artists impression of this type is used to illustrate the dust jacket of this book

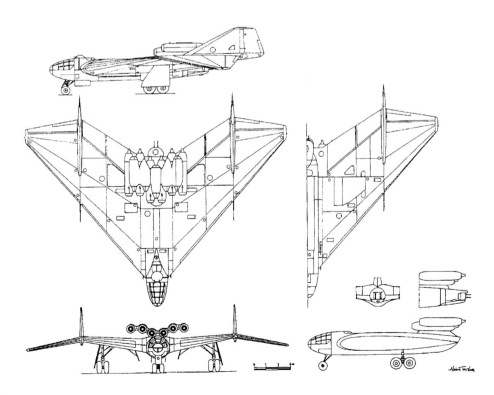

Junkers EF 130 –
A Long-Range Flying-Wing Bomber

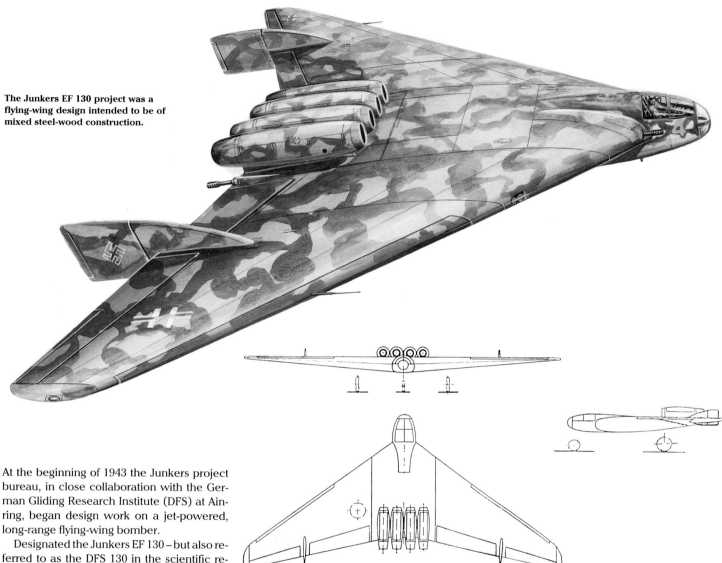

The Junkers EF 130 project was a flying-wing design intended to be of mixed steel-wood construction.

GA drawing of the Junkers EF 130.

At the beginning of 1943 the Junkers project bureau, in close collaboration with the German Gliding Research Institute (DFS) at Ainring, began design work on a jet-powered, long-range flying-wing bomber.

Designated the Junkers EF 130 – but also referred to as the DFS 130 in the scientific reports of the German Aviation Experimental Establishment (DVL) – this project was to have been of mixed construction: a metal fuselage centre-section married to wooden wing outer sections.

The gondola-type fuselage, which faired cleanly into extremely thick wing roots, was to accommodate not only the bomb load but also part of the fuel tankage. The main undercarriage members retracted into the wing centre-section, and the nosewheel into the fuselage behind the glazed and pressurised three-man crew cabin, from where the defensive armament on the wing upper surfaces was remotely-controlled. With a 4,000 kg (8,816 lb) bomb load, range was to have been in the order of 7,000 km (4,347 miles). However the EF 130 did not progress beyond the design and model stage.

Junkers EF 130 – data

Powerplant	4 x BMW 109-003C turbojets each rated at 1,030 kg (2,270 lb) static thrust	
Dimensions		
Span	24.00 m	78 ft 9 in
Wing chord centre-section	9.10 m	29 ft 10 in
Wing area	120 m²	1,292 ft²
Weights		
Loaded weight	38,100 kg	83,972 lb
Performance		
Max speed	950 km/h	590 mph
Ceiling	6,000-11,500 m	19,680-37,720 ft
Range	7,500 km	4,657 miles

Blohm & Voss P 188.01 –
A Heavy Jet Bomber

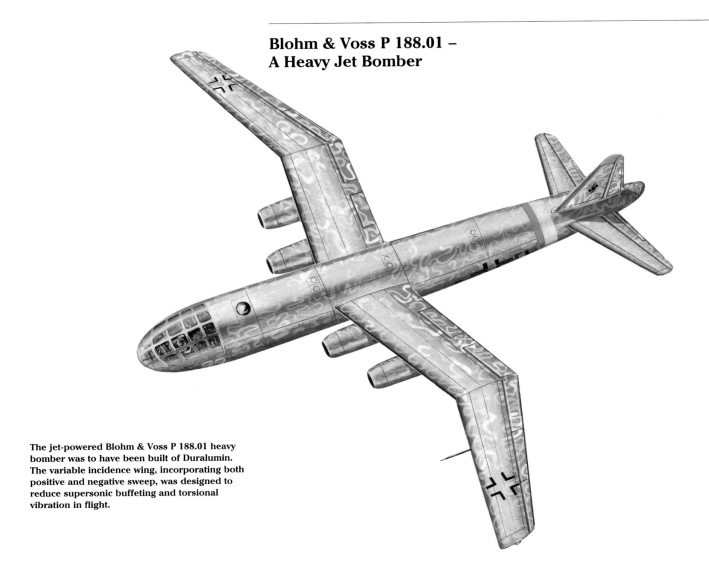

The jet-powered Blohm & Voss P 188.01 heavy bomber was to have been built of Duralumin. The variable incidence wing, incorporating both positive and negative sweep, was designed to reduce supersonic buffeting and torsional vibration in flight.

Blohm & Voss P 188.01 to .04 – data

Crew	Two	
Powerplant	4 x Junkers Jumo 109-004C-1 turbojets	
	each rated at 1,300 kg (2,865 lb) st. thrust	
Dimensions		
Span	27.00 m	88 ft 6½ in
Length	17.60 m	57 ft 8½ in
Height	4.10 m	13 ft 5½ in
Wing area	60 m²	646 ft²
Weights		
Loaded weight	26,800 kg	59,067 lb
Bomb load	3,000 kg	6,612 lb
Performance		
Speed	860-910 km/h	534-565 mph
Range	4,800 km	2,980 miles

In designing the P 188.01 project, consideration was given first and foremost to accommodating the bomb load, a large quantity of fuel and the innovative undercarriage.

These three items were all housed in the mid-section of the fuselage close to the aircraft's centre of gravity. As well as the highly individual configuration common to all P 188 variants, the tandem mainwheels beneath the fuselage were particularly noteworthy. The variable incidence of the entire wing guaranteed that the fuselage would remain constantly in the horizontal during take-offs and landings. The combined positive and negative sweep of the wing was intended to reduce the effects of supersonic buffeting as well as to dampen torsional vibration in flight. The fuselage consisted of three interconnected, but detachable, parts:

1 The pressurised nose cabin for the two-man crew;
2 The mid-section containing the bomb bay, fuel tanks and main undercarriage;
3 The aft fuselage section with tail unit and tail brake.

The load-bearing box spar of the wing centre-section was constructed of steel and also served as an auxiliary fuel tank. The whole wing structure, apart from this spar, was made of Duralumin, only the tail control surfaces and the landing flaps being of wood.

In contrast to the single tail units of the P 188.01 and P 188.03, the P 188.02 and .04 variants were equipped with twin fin and rudder assemblies. The four jet engines were to have been mounted beneath the wings either individually or in pairs. In place of the remotely-controlled tail barbette, the P 188.02 could instead be equipped with a new type of tail-cone lattice airbrake, which could be opened like an umbrella to retard speed in steep nose-down attitudes.

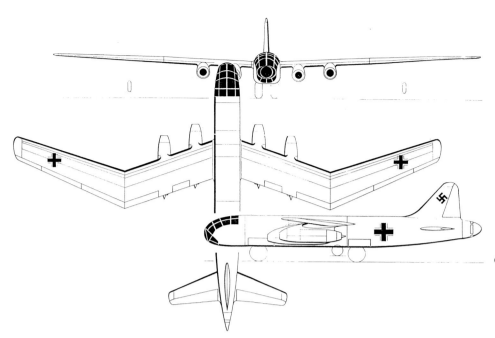

GA drawing of the Blohm & Voss P 188.01.

The Blohm & Voss P 188.02 variant
featured a twin tail unit with endplate fins
and a remotely controlled tail barbette.

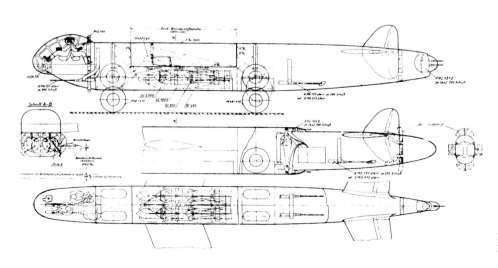

Blohm & Voss P 188.02 –
Fuselage arrangement drawing.

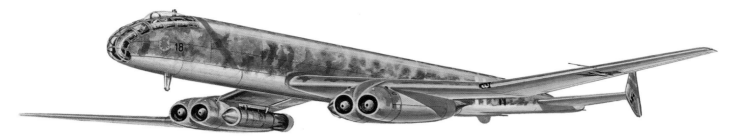

Blohm & Voss P 188.04.

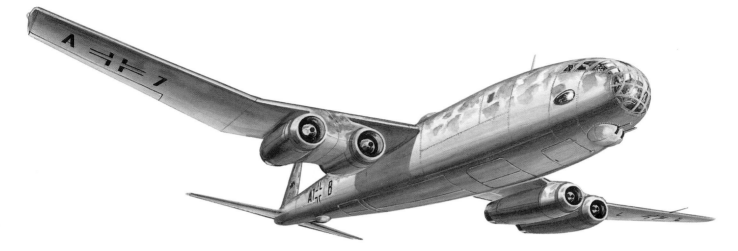

Blohm & Voss P 188.03.

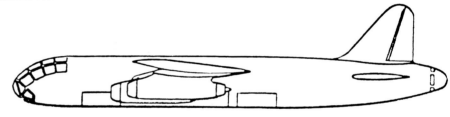

Blohm & Voss P 188.01.

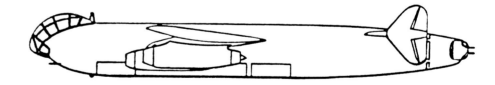

Blohm & Voss P 188.02.

**Comparison profiles of the Blohm & Voss
P 188 series.**

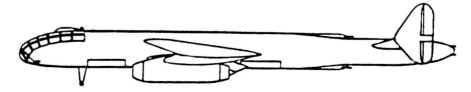

Blohm & Voss P 188.04.

LUFTWAFFE SECRET PROJECTS: STRATEGIC BOMBERS 1935-1945

Blohm & Voss BV 250 –
Land-Based Version of the BV 238 Flying Boat

The BV 250 was intended as a large-capacity transport, long-range bomber and very long-range reconnaissance aircraft. Long before the maiden flight of the BV 238 large flying boat (page 116), the Blohm & Voss design bureau had been engaged in the development of a land-based version of this aircraft.

Of prime importance in the process were the project studies for the BV P 161, from which the BV 250 evolved. Designed and structured for various operational roles, the BV 250 was to be capable of carrying a 45 ton payload over a distance of 2,500 km (1,552 miles). Deployed as a bomber with a range of more than 7,000 km (4,347 miles) it would carry a 20 ton bomb load. As a long-range bomber with a 4,000 kg (8,816 lb) weapon load it would be capable of covering a distance of 10,000 km (6,210 miles), and half as much again, 15,000 km (9,315 miles), as a very long-range reconnaissance aircraft.

All dimensions and structural details were taken over directly from the BV 238 flying boat – with the exception of the underwater hull. In place of the latter the BV 250 was equipped with a twelve-wheel retractable main undercarriage arranged in three twin pairs, one behind the other, under the middle of the fuselage. Stability during take-off and landing would be ensured by two outrigger wheels which were to be fitted in place of the maritime version's outboard floats. In the event, the deteriorating war situation prevented construction of the BV 250.

Blohm & Voss BV 250 – data

Crew	Ten	
Powerplant	6 x 1,950 hp Daimler Benz DB 9-603E	
Dimensions		
Span	57.75 m	189 ft 5 in
Length	46.05 m	151 ft 0½ in
Fuselage height	6.75 m	22 ft 2 in
Fuselage width	3.50 m	11 ft 6 in
Wing area	347 m²	3,735 ft²
Weights		
Loaded weight	108,000 kg	238,032 lb
Performance		
Speed	440 km/h	273 mph
Range according to role	2,500-15,000 km	1,552-9,315 miles

Dr-Ing Richard Vogt

1894 Born in Schwäbisch-Gmünd.

1910 Designed and built an aircraft powered by a three-cylinder Anzani engine.

1914 Volunteered for military service (infantryman on the western front)

1915 Severely wounded, hospitalised in Germany.

1916 Returned to front, trained as pilot.

1918 After end of war employed in the Zeppelin Works at Lindau on Lake Constance.

1919 Began studies at Stuttgart TH.

1922 Certified engineer, Professor of Aviation and Motor Studies at Stuttgart TH.

1923 Qualified as Dipl-Ing Under contract to Dornier, Dr Vogt travels to Japan to work as a designer for Kawasaki.

1932 Designs fighter aircraft and dive-bombers in Japan.

1934 Returns to Germany and establishes aircraft design department at Blohm & Voss (shipbuilders). Designs BV 138, BV 139, BV 142, BV 238 large flying boat, plus a large number of projects.

1945 Goes to America after the war, where he continues his innovative design and development work for various aircraft manufacturers.

1979 Richard Vogt dies in Santa Monica, California on 23rd January 1979.

Dr-Ing Richard Vogt 1894-1979 was head and chief engineer of Blohm & Voss's project bureau. His designs included not only the asymmetrical P 194 ground-attack aircraft and the BV 238 large flying boat, but also a number of strategic bomber projects.

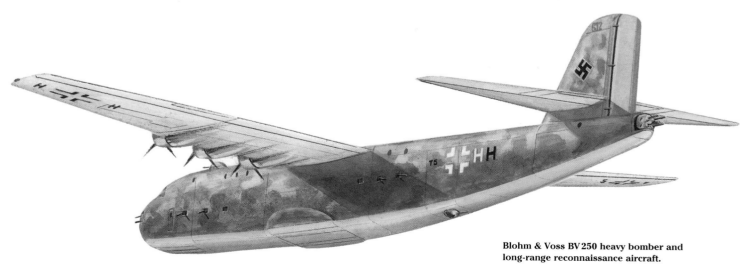

Blohm & Voss BV 250 heavy bomber and long-range reconnaissance aircraft.

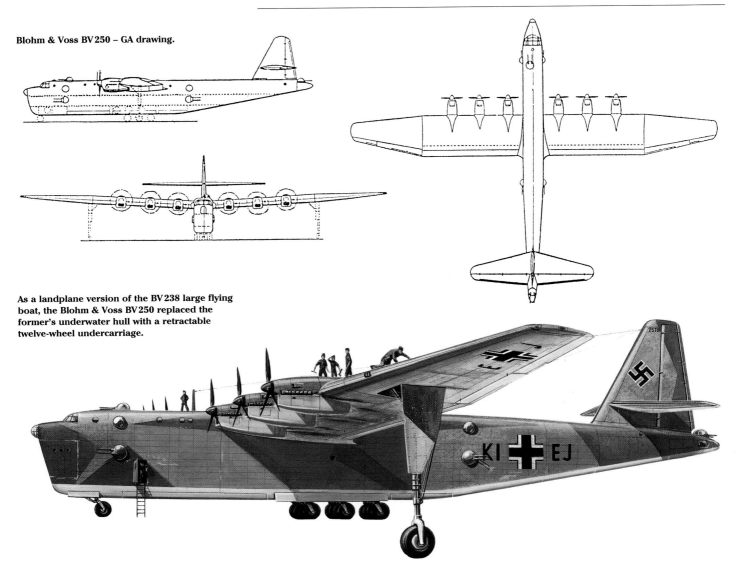

Blohm & Voss BV 250 – GA drawing.

As a landplane version of the BV 238 large flying boat, the Blohm & Voss BV 250 replaced the former's underwater hull with a retractable twelve-wheel undercarriage.

Blohm & Voss P 184.01 – A Long-Range Reconnaissance Aircraft and Bomber

Blohm & Voss P 184.01 – data

Crew	Five	
Dimensions		
Span	35.80 m	117 ft 5 in
Length	17.30 m	56 ft 9 in
Height	6.60 m	21 ft 8 in
Wing area	82 m²	883 ft²
Wing chord	2.20 m	7 ft 2½ in
Weights		
Loaded weight without bomb load	39,225 kg	86,452 lb
Performance		
Range	7,500 km	4,657 miles

The design for a long-range reconnaissance machine and bomber proposed under the project designation P 184.01 was arguably one of the most interesting aircraft to come from the fertile mind of Dr-Ing Richard Vogt, chief designer and head of the project bureau at Blohm & Voss.

It combined the most straightforward of configurations with the extensive use of steel in its construction. The almost untapered wing, with a near constant 2.20 m (7 ft 2½ in) chord, was to be covered by a skin of 2 mm (.079 in) sheet-steel. The wing's main box spar, which doubled as a fuel tank, also served to provide the attachment points for the four 1,950 hp BMW 9-801 twin-row radial engines.

The circular cross-section fuselage was likewise constructed entirely of steel. Dr-Ing Richard Vogt was thus following in the footsteps of Hugo Junkers, who had been responsible for more than a few successful corrugated sheet-steel designs in the past (one only has to think of the Ju 52).

The four individual mainwheels retracted into the rear section of the engine nacelles. The fully-glazed nose offered pressurised accommodation for a crew of five. A periscope sight permitted remote control of all defensive armament, including the tail barbette. In place of the reconnaissance version's camera equipment, the long-range bomber variant could carry a 4,000 kg (8,816 lb) bomb load.

The simple construction and use of steel as a building material ensured that the P 184.01 met all the requirements laid down in the RLM specification.

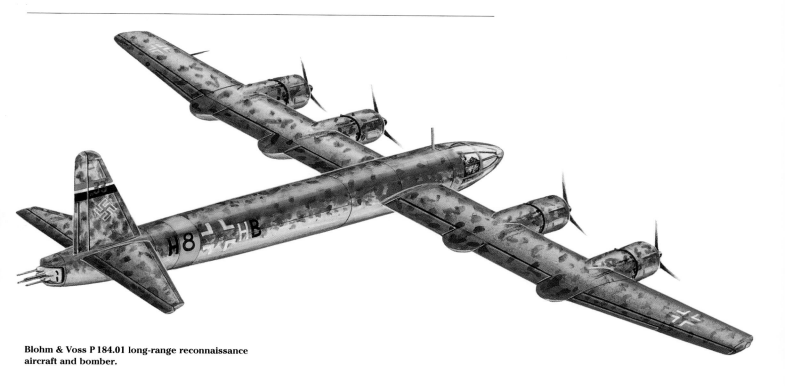

Blohm & Voss P 184.01 long-range reconnaissance
aircraft and bomber.

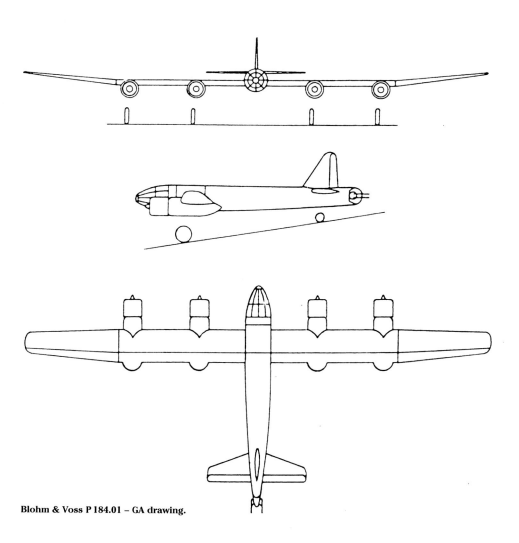

Blohm & Voss P 184.01 – GA drawing.

A Junkers Long-Range Bomber Project of 1945

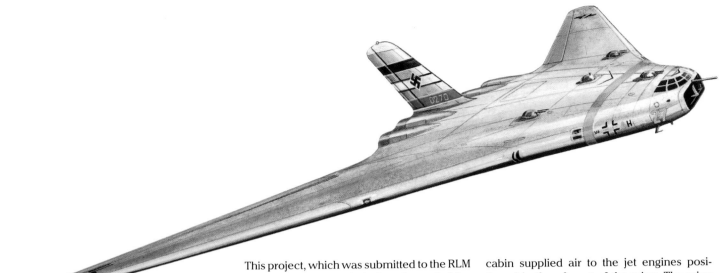

Incorporating a new wing design, Junkers' very-long-range bomber project of 1945 was to have been capable of carrying a 8,500 kg (18,734 lb) bomb load at speeds of up to 1,030 km/h (640 mph). A civil version was projected for post-war transocean passenger and freight services.

This project, which was submitted to the RLM only a matter of weeks before the end of the war, was for a four-jet long-range bomber of flying-wing configuration. It had been developed under the leadership of Prof Dr-Ing Heinrich Hertel, the Technical Director of the Junkers company, by the firm's design bureau in collaboration with the German Gliding Research Institute (DFS).

Incorporating a new wing planform, the 51.30 m (168 ft 3 in)-span project was intended to reach speeds of 1,030 km/h (640 mph) while carrying a bomb load of 8,000 kg (17,632 lb). Range was given as 17,000 km (10,557 miles). Itself made up of two sections, the fuselage was a component part of the wing structure. A wide intake below the crew cabin supplied air to the jet engines positioned in the aft part of the wing. The wing centre-section, which also formed the 3.90 m (12 ft 9½ in)-diameter fuselage section, was above the engine intake trunking. The bomb bays were located to either side of this bifurcated trunking, while the centre-line space between was used to house both the four-wheel main undercarriage bogies and the twin nosewheels. Retractable wingtip outrigger wheels would help to stabilize the 90,000 kg (198,360 lb) aircraft during take-off and landing.

The parlous war situation prevented the RLM from passing any judgement on this project.

Junkers 1945 Long-Range Bomber Project – data

Crew	Eight to Ten	
Powerplant	4 x Heinkel-Hirth HeS 109-011 or	
	4 x Junkers Jumo 109-012 turbojets	
Dimensions		
Span	51.30 m	168 ft 3 in
Length	31.00 m	101 ft 8 in
Wing area	1,100 m²	11,840 ft²
Wing sweep	45°	
Weights		
Loaded weight	90,000 kg	198,360 lb
Performance		
Range	17,000 km	10,557 miles
Speed	1,030 km/h	640 mph

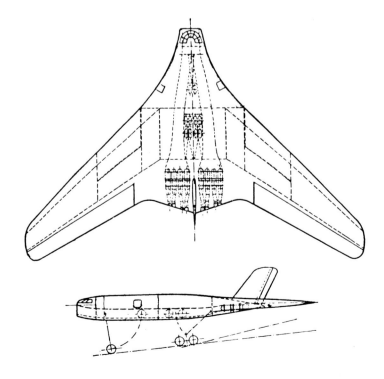

GA drawing of the eight-jet Junkers very-long-range bomber project.

Professor Dr-Ing Heinrich Hertel

1901 Born 13th November in Düsseldorf.

1926 Diploma in aircraft construction studies at Munich TH.

1931 Qualified as Dr-Ing at Berlin TH.

1932 Research scientist at the German Aviation Experimental Establishment (DVL) at Berlin-Adlershof.

1933 Chief technical assistant at the Heinkel works in Rostock.

1934 Heinkel's technical director, headed the teams that produced the He 111, He 100, He 176, He 177 and the He 178.

1939 Appointed to the board of the Junkers company in Dessau.

1940 Junkers' technical director and head of development. Design and construction of the Ju 287, plus other jet bomber projects.

1945 Employed after the war as designer by various French firms and institutes. Development and design of modern large passenger airliners.

1955 Professorship at the Berlin Technical University.

1959 Until retirement in 1970 was head of the Institute for Aircraft Construction at the Berlin Technical University and technical advisor to VFW *(Vereinigte Flugtechnische Werke)* in Bremen. Honorary doctorate at Aachen TH, honorary citizenship of Huntsville/USA (space centre); author of numerous scientific works and papers on modern aircraft construction, with emphasis on biomechanics. His wealth of ideas made Professor Dr-Ing Hertel one of the leading personalities in German aircraft manufacture.

1982 Heinrich Hertel died in Berlin aged 81.

Professor Dr-Ing Walter Blume

1896 Born in Hirschberg/Silesia.

1915 Basic military training, flying school.

1916 Army Aviation Depot A in Strasbourg.

1917 Reconnaissance pilot, promoted Lieutenant.

1918 Awarded Knight's Cross of the Royal House of Hohenzollern and the *Pour le Mérite*.

1919 Flight commander of the Reichswehr's Döberitz airfield.

1920 Courier pilot with 10th Reichswehr Brigade.

1922 Designer at *Rumpler-Flugzeugbau*, graduates as dilpomaed engineer.

1923 Sets up experimental workshop at Berlin-Adlershof, design and construction of light aircraft.

1925 Advisory engineer to the *Heereswaffenamt* (Army Ordnance Directorate) in Berlin.

1926 Chief designer at the *Albatros-Flugzeugwerke*.

1936 After closure of Albatros, Blume goes to Arado in Warnemünde. Under his leadership as manager, director and chief designer, a number of well-known pre-war Arado aircraft are produced.

1939 Continues pioneering design work throughout war; among others the Arado Ar 234, Ar 240 and the E 470 project.

1945 After the end of the war Blume resumed work in the aviation industry; developing the Bl-500/502 passenger aircraft in his Duisburg design office.

1964 Walter Blume died in Duisburg on 27th May 1964.

Professor Dr-Ing Heinrich Hertel 1901-1982, chief designer and technical director of the Junkers Flugzeug- and Motorenwerke, was influential in the design of the He 177 during his time with Heinkel. Among his last wartime works was the Junkers/Hertel flying-wing VLR bomber project. Heinrich Hertel remained a leading light in German aircraft design in the post-war years.

Professor Dr-Ing Walter Blume 1896-1964 was head of the combined project and development department TAE at the Arado works in Brandenburg. Among the designs developed under his leadership were the Arado Ar 234 and those for the E 470 project.

Arado E 470 –
A Long-Distance Bomber

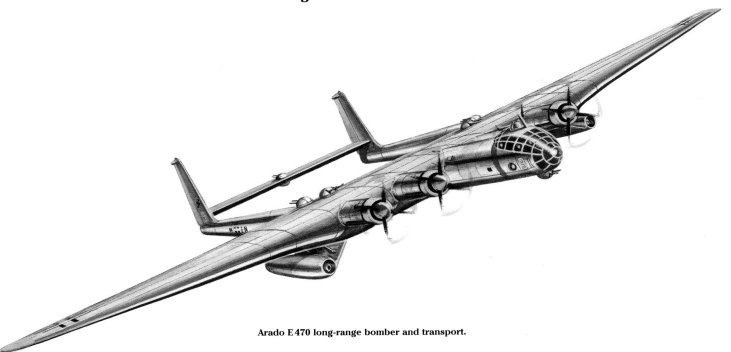

Arado E 470 long-range bomber and transport.

A giant among Arado developments was the E 470 long-distance bomber project. Conceived in 1941, it had a span of 68.50 m (224 ft 8 in) and a loaded weight (including the six 3,500 hp Daimler Benz DB 9-613 coupled engines) of 130,000 kg (286,520 lb). It was intended to carry a 5,000 kg (11,020 lb) bomb load over a distance of 14,900 km (9,253 miles).

In general layout the Arado E 470 was very similar to the long-range bomber proposed by Focke-Wulf with their drawing number P 03.10225-20 (erroneously known as the Fw 261; see page 38). The thickened centre-section, some 2 m (6 ft 7 in) in depth, of the cantilevered wing contained freight holds or bomb bays capable of accommodating the heaviest calibre bombs. The gondola-like central fuselage was attached to the wing and included a pressure cabin for the crew of four. The heavy defensive armament was remotely controlled from this cabin. Unlike the Fw 261, the twin tail booms were connected by a horizontal tail unit and elevator. The twin-wheel main undercarriage members retracted into the wing aft of the outboard engines. The nosewheel was housed in the central fuselage gondola.

Development work was concentrated primarily on the long-range bomber variant, the E 470 E (span 68.50 m (224 ft 8 in); four Daimler Benz DB 9-613s), which had a loaded weight of 130,000 kg (286,520 lb), including a 5,000 kg (11,020 lb) weapon load. There was

also a long-distance transport version, designated the E 470 F. This had the same dimensions as the E 470 E but a lower loaded weight.

A container capable of transporting 39,000 kg (85,956 lb) of freight could be carried beneath the wing centre-section. This cargo container could be detached by quick-release catches and a new one attached in its place in a matter of minutes.

Further variants of the E 470 project series included:

Project A with four Daimler Benz DB 9-613s and 47.30 m (155 ft 2 in) span.
Project B with six Daimler Benz DB 9-613s and 54.00 m (177 ft 1½ in) span.
Project C with four Daimler Benz DB 9-613s and 60.00 m (196 ft 10 in) span.
Project D with six Daimler Benz DB 9-613s and 58.50 m (191 ft 10½ in) span.

The illustration includes a projected addition of auxiliary jet engines to give increased speed, as shown in an original report from 19th December 1941.

This project series, too, was rejected by the RLM without any further reason being given.

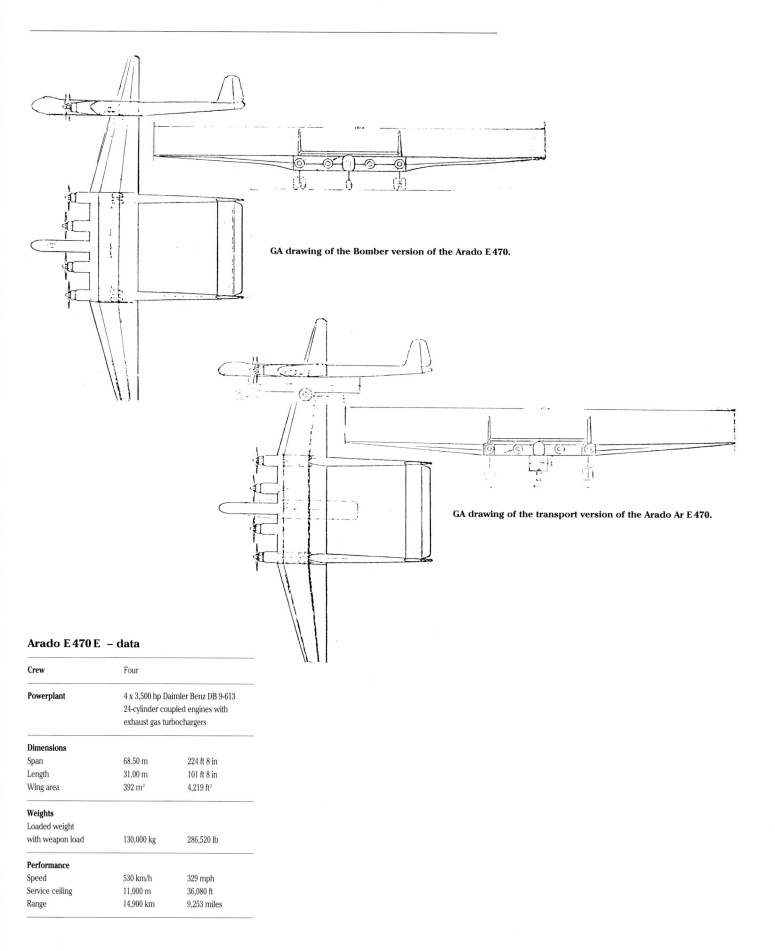

GA drawing of the Bomber version of the Arado E 470.

GA drawing of the transport version of the Arado Ar E 470.

Arado E 470 E – data

Crew	Four	
Powerplant	4 x 3,500 hp Daimler Benz DB 9-613 24-cylinder coupled engines with exhaust gas turbochargers	
Dimensions		
Span	68.50 m	224 ft 8 in
Length	31.00 m	101 ft 8 in
Wing area	392 m²	4,219 ft²
Weights		
Loaded weight with weapon load	130,000 kg	286,520 lb
Performance		
Speed	530 km/h	329 mph
Service ceiling	11,000 m	36,080 ft
Range	14,900 km	9,253 miles

Junkers EF 116 –
A Jet Bomber with a New Type of Wing Planform

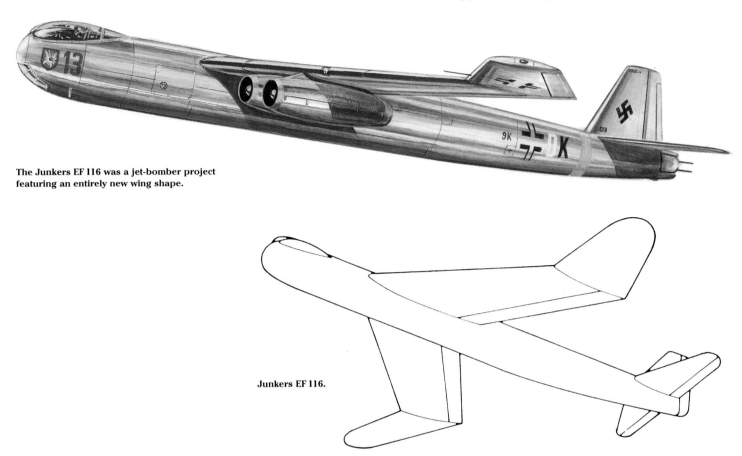

The Junkers EF 116 was a jet-bomber project featuring an entirely new wing shape.

Junkers EF 116.

Junkers EF 116 – data

Crew	Two	
Powerplant	4 x Junkers Jumo 109-004H turbojets each rated at 1,300 kg (2,865 lb) st. thrust	
Dimensions		
Span	26.50 m	86 ft 11 in
Length	22.10 m	72 ft 6 in
Weights		
Weapon load	4,000 kg	8,816 lb
Performance		
Range	5,500 km	3,415 miles
Speed	980 km/h	609 mph
Armament	3 x remotely-controlled barbettes: dorsal, ventral and tail	

The EF 116 was a bomber project which had been developed in 1943 under the design leadership of Prof Dr-Ing Heinrich Hertel and Dipl-Ing Hans Wocke.

The cantilevered shoulder-wing aircraft was to be of all-metal construction. For the first time Junkers were to use an arrow-shaped W-wing incorporating 25° sweep across most of the span, but with 23.5° negative sweep on the final quarter. This innovative wing planform was also proposed for the P 188-01 bomber project designed by Blohm & Voss' Dr-Ing Richard Vogt. Very little was known of the advantages and disadvantages of this wing layout at the time, as the German Aviation Experimental Establishment (DVL) had not begun to conduct wind tunnel tests until 1943.

DVL reports merely stated that part of the wing outer section was angled to give forward (negative) sweep in order to prevent premature wing stall. As well as having high-speed advantages, it also helped to dampen yaw and lessen vibration. At the same time, this positive-negative wing structure resulted in a marked reduction in the mid-wing torque inherent in a normal sharply-swept wing.

Instead of a fully-glazed nose, this cantilevered shoulder-wing design with its circular cross-section fuselage was fitted with individual 'teardrop' canopies for the pilot and bomb-aimer.

A pair of Junkers Jumo 109-004H turbojets, each rated at 1,300 kg (2,865 lb) static thrust, were arranged beneath each positive-sweep wing section. Additional thrust was provided by afterburners.

The main undercarriage retracted sideways into the fuselage and the nosewheel into a bay below the crew cabin.

As all further design work was halted at the end of 1943 on the orders of the RLM, very little data on the EF 116 project are known.

Junkers EF 132 –
A Long-Distance Jet Bomber

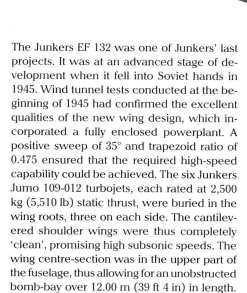

The engines of the Junkers EF 132 were buried in the wingroots in order to avoid disturbing the aerodynamics of the long-distance bomber.

GA drawing of the Junkers EF 132.

The Junkers EF 132 was one of Junkers' last projects. It was at an advanced stage of development when it fell into Soviet hands in 1945. Wind tunnel tests conducted at the beginning of 1945 had confirmed the excellent qualities of the new wing design, which incorporated a fully enclosed powerplant. A positive sweep of 35° and trapezoid ratio of 0.475 ensured that the required high-speed capability could be achieved. The six Junkers Jumo 109-012 turbojets, each rated at 2,500 kg (5,510 lb) static thrust, were buried in the wing roots, three on each side. The cantilevered shoulder wings were thus completely 'clean', promising high subsonic speeds. The wing centre-section was in the upper part of the fuselage, thus allowing for an unobstructed bomb-bay over 12.00 m (39 ft 4 in) in length.

A 1:1 scale mock-up of the EF 132 project was constructed to determine the exact size and shape of the design of the leading-edge engine air intakes as used in the wind tunnel tests. The fully-glazed nose section accommodating the 5-man crew was, in tried and true Junkers fashion, a pressurised cabin from which the defensive armament could also be remotely controlled.

As well as the bomb-bay, the mid-section of the narrow, elongated fuselage – which was more than 30.00 m (98 ft 5 in) long – housed the tandem twin-wheel main undercarriage members and part of the fuel load. The vertical tail surfaces wee modelled on the later developments of the Ju 287 series. At the base of the rudder was a remotely-controlled tail barbette. Other armament comprised two fixed 20 mm cannon fired by the pilot, plus two hydraulically-operated retractable barbettes above and below the fuselage (B- and C-Stand) which were sighted by periscope.

Junkers EF 132 – data

Crew	Five	
Powerplant	6 x Junkers Jumo 109-012 turbojets each rated at 2,500 kg (5,510 lb) st. thrust	
Dimensions		
Span	32.40 m	106 ft 3 in
Length	30.80 m	101 ft 0½ in
Height	8.40 m	27 ft 6½ in
Wing area	161 m²	1,733 ft²
Wing sweep	35°	
Wing loading	404 kg/m²	83 lb/ft²
Weights		
Loaded weight	65,800 kg	145,023 lb
Weapon load	4,000-5,000 kg	8,816-11,020 lb
Performance		
Service ceiling	11,000-14,000 m	36,080-45,920 ft
Speed	930 km/h	578 mph
Range	9,800 km	6,086 miles

Model of the Junkers EF 132 in the wind tunnel.

Chapter Eight

Tactical Bomber Projects 1944-1945

Arado E 560/2 high-speed bomber.

In September 1943 the Luftwaffe High Command issued yet another order banning the development of heavy bombers. Official circles were determined to give precedence to the medium bomber, which now received the new designation of *Arbeitsflugzeug* (lit: work-aircraft). In response, the design bureaux of Heinkel, Arado and Messerschmitt submitted to the RLM in 1944 a number of studies and design proposals for medium bomber types offering high speeds and heavy bomb loads.

Powerplants included not just the very latest high-performance 3,000-4,000 hp piston engines, but also Performance Class II turbojets rated at 2,300 kg (5,069 lb) static thrust and above, as well as 6,500 hp shaft output turboprops.

These project studies were among the last proposals to be submitted to the RLM in the final weeks leading up to the end of the war. Very few documents relating to them have survived. But although far from complete, there is sufficient material to permit artist's impressions and the most important basic data to be presented here. Some of the sensational design features incorporated in these projects caused no little amazement and wonderment in the Allies after the war. In all areas of aerodynamics and powerplant technology the German designs were years ahead of the victors' own aircraft developments.

High-speed wing profiles, variable-geometry wings with sweep of up to 60°, near supersonic speeds combined with long ranges and heavy bomb loads, all this, and more, was under development. While admittedly being intended for the *tactical* rather than the *strategic* role, the authors feel that these projects warrant inclusion in these pages. Published here for the first time, these far-sighted design projects have – after the passage of nearly sixty years – lost little of their immediacy and impact.

Arado E 560/2 High-Speed Bomber Project – data as of 1943/44

Crew	Two	
Powerplant	2 x 4,000 hp BMW 9-803 piston engines	
Dimensions		
Span	18.00 m	59 ft 0½ in
Length	19.10 m	62 ft 8 in
Wing area	49 m²	527 ft²
Weights		
Loaded weight	18,800 kg	41,435 lb
Weapon load	2,500 kg	5,510 lb
Performance		
Speed	890 km/h	553 mph
Range	2,500 km	1,552 miles

106

Arado E 560/4 High-Speed Medium Bomber – data as of 1943/44

Crew	Two	
Powerplant	4 x BMW 109-003E turbojets each rated at 1,200 kg (2,645 lb) static thrust	
Dimensions		
Span	24.00 m	78 ft 9 in
Length	22.30 m	73 ft 2 in
Wing area	57 m²	614 ft²
Weights		
Loaded weight	38,200 kg	84,193 lb
Weapon load	3,000 kg	6,612 lb
Performance		
Speed	950 km/h	590 mph
Range	2,100 km	1,304 miles
Armament	2 x fixed forward-firing MK 103 below cabin, 2 fixed rearward-firing guns in aft fuselage, tail barbette	
Notable feature	Nosewheel undercarriage	

Arado E 560/7 Medium-Range Bomber – data as of 1943/44

Crew	Two	
Powerplant	2 x BMW 109-028 turboprops each of 6,200 hp shaft output plus additional thrust of 650 kg (1,433 lb)	
Dimensions		
Span	19.10 m	62 ft 8 in
Length	16.80 m	55 ft 1½ in
Height	3.95 m	12 ft 11½ in
Wing area	75 m²	807 ft²
Weights		
Weapon load	4,000 kg	8,816 lb
Performance		
Speed	920 km/h	571 mph
Range	3,400 km	2,111 miles
Notable feature	Nosewheel undercarriage	

Arado E 560/8 Medium-Range Bomber – data

Crew	Two	
Powerplant	6 x BMW 109-003 turbojets each rated at 900 kg (1,984 lb) static thrust	
Dimensions		
Span	23.20 m	76 ft 1 in
Length	18.00 m	59 ft 0½ in
Height	3.25 m	10 ft 8 in
Wing area	46.6 m²	502 ft²
Weights		
Weapon load	3,000 kg	6,612 lb
Notable feature	Nosewheel undercarriage	

Arado E 560/11 Medium-Range Bomber – data

Crew	Two	
Powerplant	4 x BMW 109-018 turbojets each rated at 2,300 kg (5,069 lb) static thrust	
Dimensions		
Span	24.00 m	78 ft 9 in
Length	19.10 m	62 ft 8 in
Height	5.10 m	16 ft 9 in
Weights		
Weapon load	4,000 kg	8,816 lb
Loaded weight	28,600 kg	63,034 lb
Notable features	Nosewheel undercarriage Pressure cabin	

Arado E 560/4 high-speed medium bomber.

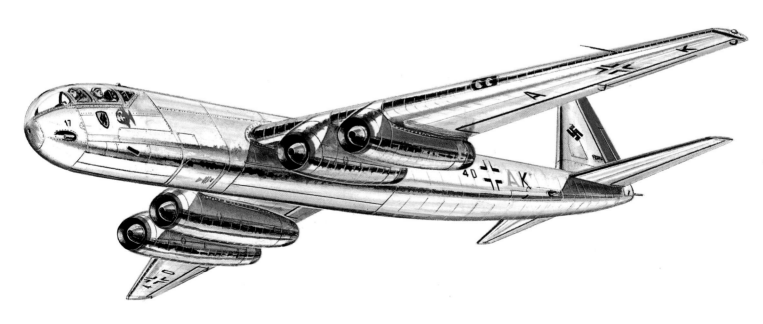

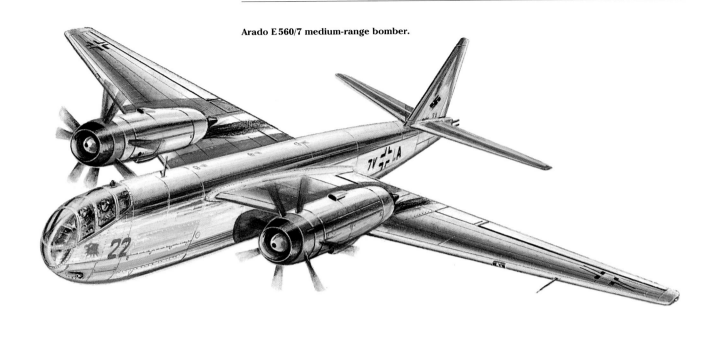

Arado E 560/7 medium-range bomber.

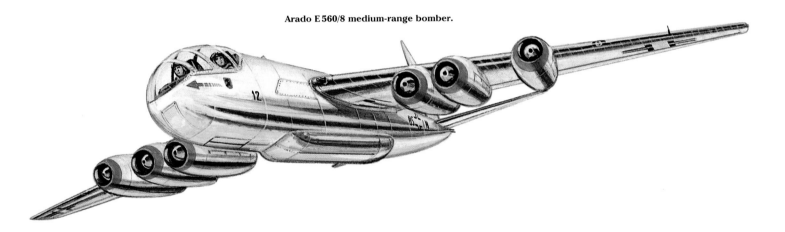

Arado E 560/8 medium-range bomber.

Arado E 560/11 medium-range bomber.

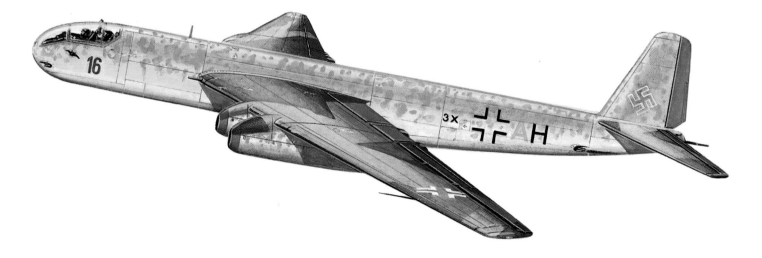

Messerschmitt Me P 1101/101 Variable-Geometry Attack Bomber

With its P 1101/101 project Messerschmitt was proposing an aircraft of a design and configuration which had never before been seen. Featuring a powerplant arrangement at nose and tail, and fitted with a variable-geometry wing which could be swept in flight to an angle of 60°, it was intended to reach a speed of 1,100 km/h (683 mph) at full power, full power being taken to mean the total thrust of all four jet engines.

This fast attack bomber project, part of the P 1101 development series, was to have been capable of carrying a 3,000 kg (6,612 lb) bomb load at high speeds over considerable distances.

Messerschmitt Me P 1101/101 Project – data

Crew	Two	
Powerplant	4 x Heinkel-Hirth HeS 109-011 turbojets each rated at 1,300 kg (2,865 lb) st. thrust	
Dimensions		
Span	18.40 m	60 ft 4 in
Length	17.10 m	56 ft 1 in
Performance		
Max speed	1,100 km/h	683 mph
Armament	4 x fixed forward-firing MK 108 in lower section of nose, 1 x remotely-controlled FDL 108Z dorsal barbette aft of crew cabin, plus 1 x remotely-controlled FDL 108Z ventral barbette	

Messerschmitt Me P 1101-XVIII/102 High-Speed Bomber

Also part of the P 1101 development series, the P 1101/102 project was a design study for a four-jet, fast attack bomber incorporating varying leading-edge wing sweep. The structure and aerodynamics of this project were also intended to achieve high-speed, near-supersonic flight. Of particular note is the differing wing sweep: 60° on the inner sections (with the air intakes for the two turbojets fully buried in each wing root), transitioning to 50° on the outer sections. This arrangement avoided the complicated and, at that time, as-yet unresolved problem of in-flight variable geometry, an otherwise essential prerequisite for high speeds.

In addition to its intended deployment as a fast bomber, this design was also proposed for the role of heavy fighter capable of carrying additional equipment fits and special armament; this latter comprising so-called 'thrust-bombs' – rocket-propelled bomb-shaped projectiles to be used against Allied heavy bomber formations

Messerschmitt Me P 1101-XVIII/102 Project – data

Crew	Two	
Powerplant	4 x Heinkel-Hirth HeS 109-011 turbojets each rated at 1,300 kg (2,865 lb) static thrust	
Dimensions		
Span	19.80 m	64 ft 11½ in
Length	21.50 m	70 ft 6 in

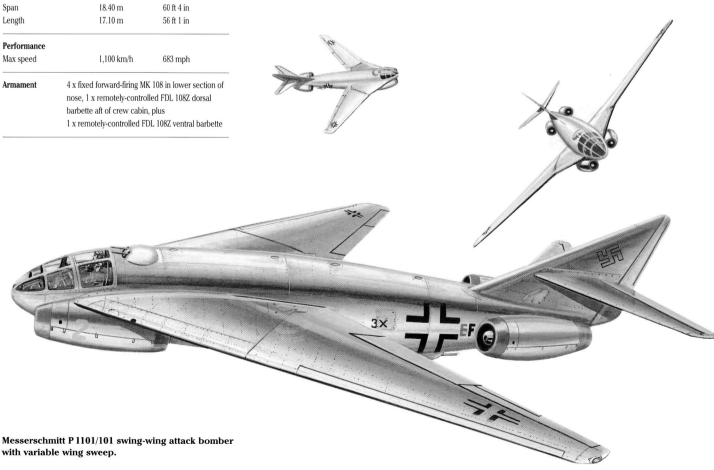

Messerschmitt P 1101/101 swing-wing attack bomber with variable wing sweep.

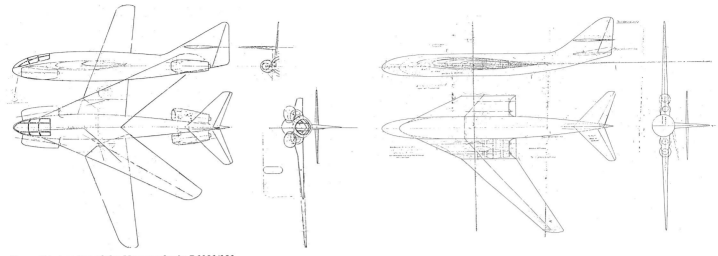

Above: **GA drawing of the Messerschmitt P 1101/101.**

Above right: **Messerschmitt P 1101/102 – GA drawing.**

Messerschmitt Me P 1101/103 Variable-Geometry Bomber

Project 1101, drawing number XVIII/103, was yet another study from Messerschmitt's P 1101 series, which comprised in all some ten different designs. With an unswept span of 19.80 m (64 ft 11½ in), a length of 18.36 m (60 ft 3 in) and an undercarriage track measuring 4.8 m (15 ft 9 in), the project proposed by drawing number XVIII/103 was to have been powered by four Heinkel-Hirth HeS 109-011 jet engines and manned by a crew of two. As a bomber it would have been capable of carrying a bomb load of some 3,000 kg (6,612 lb) over a distance of 2,400 km (1,490 miles). When employed in the heavy fighter or fighter-bomber roles, the P 1101, with its wings swept 50°, had an estimated speed of 1,020 km/h (633 mph). Proposed armament as a fighter was four nose-mounted MK 103 cannon.

As very little documentation exists, the data quoted and the accompanying GA drawing were the only references available for use in the preparation of the artist's impression published here.

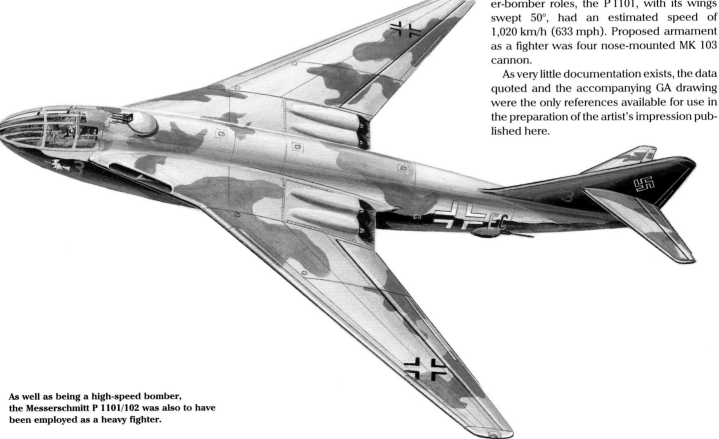

As well as being a high-speed bomber, the Messerschmitt P 1101/102 was also to have been employed as a heavy fighter.

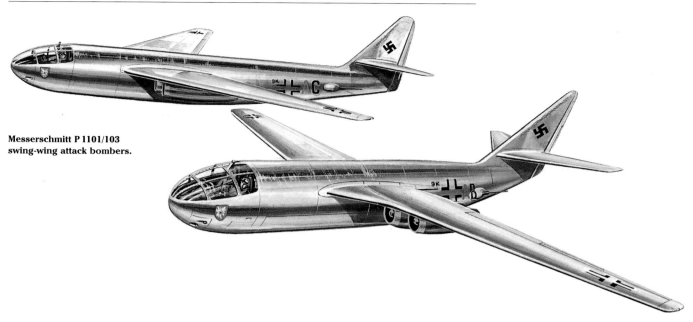

Messerschmitt P 1101/103
swing-wing attack bombers.

Messerschmitt Me P 1101/103 Project – data

Crew	Two	
Dimensions		
Span – extended	19.80 m	64 ft 11½ in
Span – 50° sweep	14.00 m	45 ft 11 in
Length	18.36 m	60 ft 3 in
U/c track	4.80 m	15 ft 9 in
Fuel capacity	11,000 ltrs	2,420 gals
Weights		
Weapon load – Bomber	3,000 kg	6,612 lb
Performance		
Range	2,400 km	1,490 miles
Armament		
Fighter	4 x MK 103 cannon	

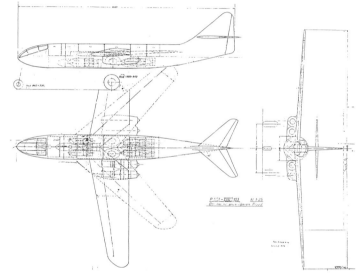

Messerschmitt
P 1101/103 –
GA drawing.

**Among other roles, the Messerschmitt P 1101/105 was
envisaged as a weapons carrier for close target work
and attacking heavy bomber formations.**

Messerschmitt Me P 1101-XVIII/105 – A Fast Bomber and Heavy Fighter

Intended as a counterpart to the Arado Ar 234, Messerschmitt's P 1101/105 project was a four-jet fast bomber featuring a new type of wing design. This so-called 'sickle-wing' incorporated a laminar profile and varying sweep which transitioned from 45° on the inner section to 40° on the outer. In terms of structure and dimensions the P 1101/105 otherwise corresponded with the rest of the designs in the P 1101 project series.

Carrying a 3,000 kg (6,612 lb) weapon load, the bomber variant had an estimated range of fully 2,400 km (1,490 miles), and that at a speed of 1,020 km/h (633 mph).

The P 1101/105 was also intended as a heavy fighter and weapons platform for close-attack and anti-bomber operations. Its armament was to have comprised one 7.5 cm and three MK 108Z cannon in the nose, six obliquely upward-firing MK 108Zs in the mid-fuselage and a remotely controlled FDL-108Z ventral barbette in the aft fuselage level with the leading-edge of the butterfly tail.

Messerschmitt Me P 1101/105 Bomber Project

Crew	Two	
Dimensions		
Span	17.35 m	56 ft 11 in
Length	18.10 m	59 ft 4½ in
Performance		
Range	2,400-3,100 km	1,490-1,925 miles
Speed	1,020 km/h	633 mph

Dimensions and performance of the Heavy Fighter Project are identical to the above

Messerschmitt Me P 1102/105 – A Variable-Geometry Bomber and Fighter

As with the P 1101 development series, the designs comprising the P 1102 project series were also similar to each other in dimensions and performance.

This fast bomber was powered by three turbojets, one on each side of the nose and the third in the aft fuselage. The variable-geometry wing could be swept between the angles of 15° and 50° to meet relevant flight requirements, the former being selected for take-off and landing, the latter enabling the aircraft to reach a speed of 1,010 km/h (627 mph)

As well as operating as a fast bomber, a fighter role was also envisaged for this design.

After the end of the war the documentation relating to this series, too, was seized by the Americans. It was used in the development of a number of new aircraft. The P 1102/105 project's unusual three-engine powerplant arrangement, in particular, was employed on the American Martin XB-51 high-speed attack-interceptor which first flew in mid-1949.

Messerschmitt Me P 1102/105 project – data

Crew	One
Powerplant	3 x Heinkel-Hirth HeS 109-011
Dimensions Wing sweep	As for those of the Me P 1101 series – 15° to 50°
Performance	Range with 3,000 kg (6,612 lb) bomb load 1,900 km 1,180 miles

US Martin XB-51 – comparison data

Powerplant	3 x General Electric 147-GE7-13	
Dimensions		
Span	16.15 m	52 ft 11½ in
Length	24.38 m	79 ft 11½ in
Performance		
Speed	1,030 km/h	640 mph
Range	2,580 km	1,602 miles

Messerschmitt P 1101/105 – GA drawing.

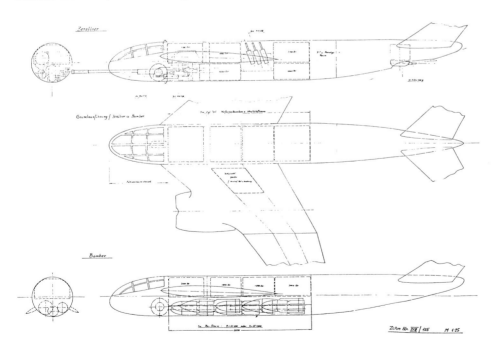

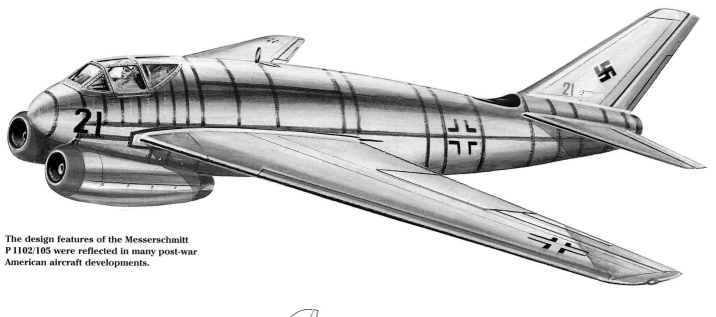

The design features of the Messerschmitt
P 1102/105 were reflected in many post-war
American aircraft developments.

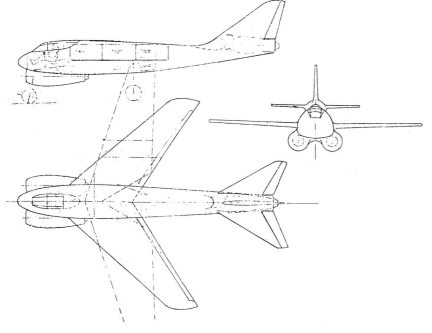

Messerschmitt P 1102/105 – GA drawing.

The US Martin XB-51 bomber
incorporated the same powerplant
arrangement as the Messerschmitt P 1102/105.

Chapter Nine

Strategic Long-Range Flying Boat Projects

The Blohm & Voss BV 222.

Blohm & Voss BV 222 – A Flying Boat for Long-Range Reconnaissance, Transport and Bomber Operations

The Blohm & Voss BV 222 was the largest flying boat to see operational service in the Second World War. It had been designed in 1938 by Blohm & Voss' chief designer, Dr-Ing Richard Vogt, for Deutsche Lufthansa's transatlantic routes. Maiden flight of the BV 222 V1 (civil registration D-ANTE) took place on 7th September 1940.

Some 30 BV 222s had been built by 1945. The original variants, BV 222 V1 to BV 222 V6, received the military designations BV 222A, B and C. These had all been powered by six 1,000 hp BMW-Bramo 323R engines which, from the V7 onwards, were replaced by six 1,000 hp Junkers Jumo 207-C diesels. Under the military designation BV 222C-1, this later series had an increased wing span, a slightly shorter fuselage and heavier armament.

Blohm & Voss BV 222C-1 – data

Crew	Ten	
Powerplant	6 x 1,000 hp Junkers Jumo 207C-2 diesels	
Dimensions		
Span	46.00 m	150 ft 10½ in
Wing area	255 m²	2,745 ft²
Length	37.00 m	121 ft 4½ in
Height	10.90 m	35 ft 9 in
Weights		
Take-off weight	45,900 kg	101,164 lb
	50,000 kg	110,200 lb
	with overload take-off assistance rockets	
Performance		
Speed	390 km/h	242 mph
	at 5,000 m	at 16,400 ft
Range	6,000-9,000 km	3,726-5,589 miles
Endurance	29 hrs	
Service Ceiling	7,300 m	23,944 ft
Armament	3 x MG 151 and 5 x MG 131	

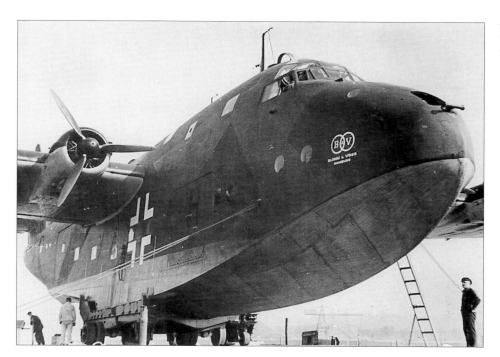

Three-quarter frontal views of the mighty Blohm & Voss BV 222. The flowing lines of the hull are clearly apparent.

The BV 222 is towed to the slipway.

Rear view of the BV 222.
Note the tethering stays as protection against wind gusts.

Blohm & Voss BV 238 –
A Large Bomber and Transport Flying Boat

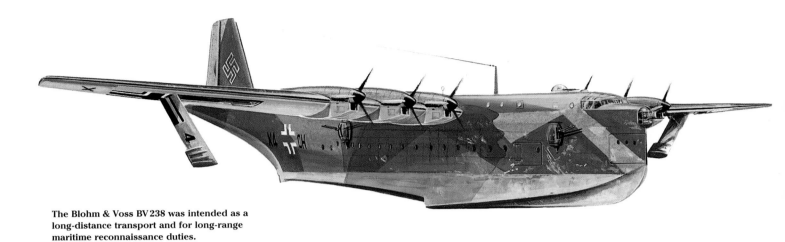

The Blohm & Voss BV 238 was intended as a long-distance transport and for long-range maritime reconnaissance duties.

Blohm & Voss BV 238 V1 – data

Powerplant	6 x 1,750 hp Daimler Benz DB 603C	
Dimensions		
Span	57.60 m	188 ft 11 in
Length	46.02 m	150 ft 11½ in
Weights		
Empty equipped weight	54,660 kg	120,470 lb
Payload	20,000 kg	44,080 lb
Loaded weight	94,345 kg	207,936 lb
Performance		
Speed	410 km/h	255 mph
Range	3,750-6,600 km	2,329-4,099 miles

The BV 238 large flying boat resulted from a contract awarded by the RLM at the beginning of 1941 for a model to replace the BV 222. Structurally very similar to its predecessor, the aerodynamically refined double-decker fuselage permitted the transport of the bulkiest and heaviest of loads. For defensive armament the ten-man crew of this long-range transport and maritime reconnaissance flying boat were provided with no fewer than twelve weapons stations distributed along the length of the fuselage.

The maiden flight of the BV 238 V1 took place in August 1943. During trials it displayed excellent handling and flight characteristics; being able to remain aloft on only three engines, all on the same side.

But imminent series production was halted during the course of 1943 after Generalfeldmarschall Milch announced that: '... *the house is burning, first we've got to put out the fire, fighters are more important!*'

After the introduction of the so-called Emergency Fighter Programme, the BV 238 V1 was flown to Lake Schaal near Hamburg. Here it was maintained at constant readiness for possible long-range missions. However, despite being well camouflaged, it was spotted by American fighter-bombers two weeks before the end of the war. Making pass after pass, they continued to strafe the huge machine until it finally sank. The fuselage of the second prototype was discovered by the Allies in the Blohm & Voss yards; this had slightly smaller dimensions than those of the V1 version.

The BV 238 V1 moored on Lake Schaal near Hamburg.

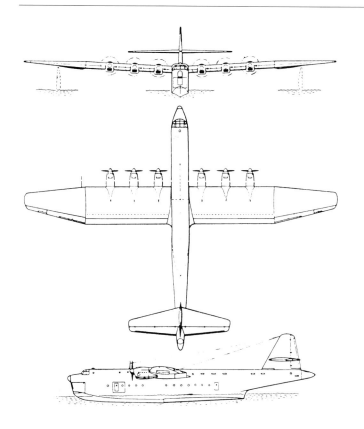
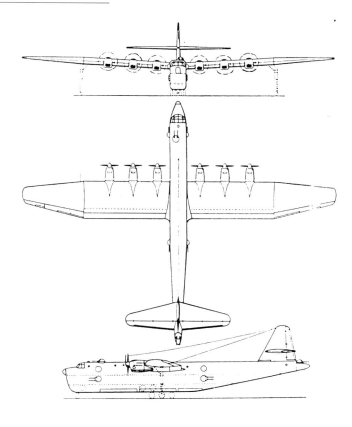

GA drawings of the Blohm & Voss BV 238 in the water (left) and in its land-based form as the BV 250.

A 'jolly jack tar' leans out of the bow doors to secure the BV 238's mooring rope.

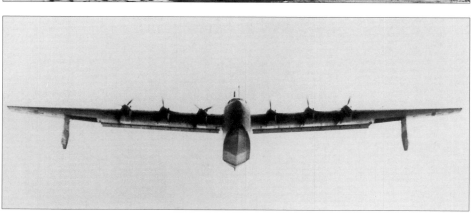

With a wing span of almost 58 m (190 ft) and a length of just over 46 m (150 ft), the Blohm & Voss BV 238 made an imposing spectacle when it took to the air.

Dornier Do 214 –
A Flying Boat for the Strategic Role

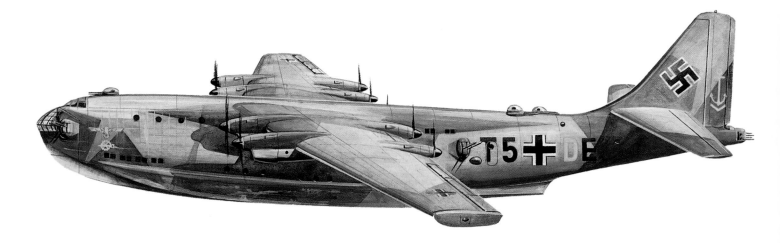

The Dornier Do 214 – alias the P 192-04 – was intended for the role of 'flying milch cow' to supply long-range U-boats in distant waters.

Artist's impression by Gerd Heumann of the Dornier Do 214 in flight.

The large flying boat developed for Deutsche Lufthansa in 1940 under the project designation Dornier Do P 93 was originally intended for civil transatlantic service. With a loaded weight of more than 100 tons it was to have been used on the Lisbon-New York route.

At the beginning of the year the RLM ordered the conversion of the Do 124 for military use as the Project P 192.

Powered by eight Daimler Benz DB 613 engines and with a considerably higher loaded weight of 145,000 kg (319,580 lb), its envisaged role was now that of a strategic flying boat. The eight engines were arranged in tandem pairs in four nacelles either side of the fuselage. Each engine was served by its own individual oil and coolant circuits, which meant that, in the event of engine failure, the propeller of any defective engine could continue to rotate under power from the other engines.

All eight engines were monitored from a central console by the flight engineer. The eight propellers were four-bladed VDM variable pitch; the front four (tractor) being of 3.0 m (16 ft 5 in) diameter, the aft four (pusher) measuring 4.60 m (15 ft 1 in). They were driven via extension shafts; those to the rear being hinged – as on the company's earlier Do 26 flying boat – which allowed the pusher propellers to be raised during take-off to keep them clear of spray.

There were as many as nine proposed variants of the P 192 project:

P 192-01: Transport, to carry a 33,000kg (72,732 lb) payload. Ten remotely controllable weapons stations for heavy machine guns and/or cannon would have made the P 192 a veritable 'Flying Fortress'.

P 192-02: Troop transport for 333 personnel.

P 192-03: Heavy cargo transport with a 82,000 kg (180,728 lb) payload.

P 192-04: U-boat supply aircraft.

P 192-05: Aerial minelayer.

P 192-06: Fuel transporter and flying tanker.

P 192-07: Military transport for fully-armed and equipped troops.

P 192-08: Air ambulance.

P 192-09: Long-range bomber and guided weapons carrier.

However in 1943, without giving any further reasons, the RLM ordered all work on the Do P 192 to cease.

Dornier Do P 192 – data

Dimensions

Span	60.00 m	196 ft 10 in
Length	51.60 m	169 ft 3 in
Height	14.30 m	46 ft 11 in
Wing area	500 m²	5,382 ft²

Weights

Loaded weight	145,000 kg	319,580 lb

Performance

Speed	490 km/h	304 mph
Service ceiling	7,000 m	22,960 ft
Range	6,600-8,100 km	4,099-5,030 miles

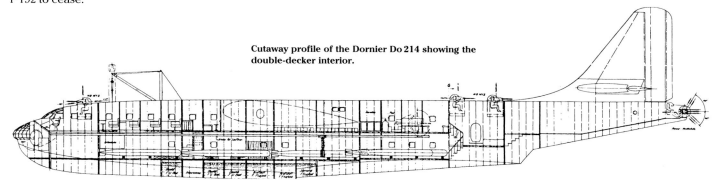

Cutaway profile of the Dornier Do 214 showing the double-decker interior.

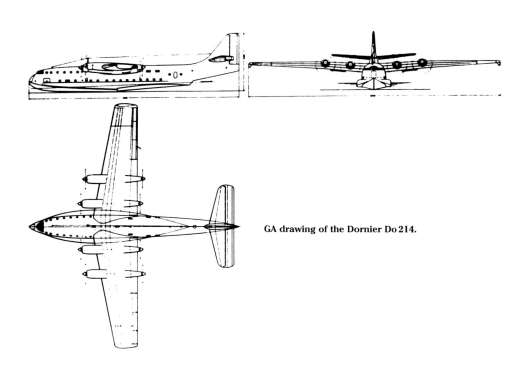

GA drawing of the Dornier Do 214.

Dornier Do 216 –
A Long-Range Flying Boat for Anti-Shipping Operations

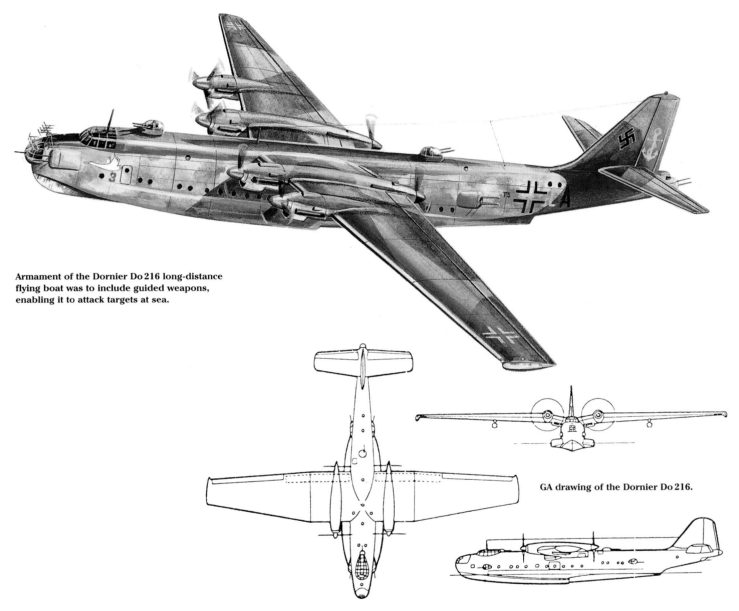

Armament of the Dornier Do 216 long-distance flying boat was to include guided weapons, enabling it to attack targets at sea.

GA drawing of the Dornier Do 216.

Dornier Do 216 (P 174/I) – data

Crew	Six	
Dimensions		
Span	48.00 m	157 ft 5 in
Length	42.30 m	138 ft 9 in
Height	7.90 m	25 ft 11 in
Wing area	310 m²	3,337 ft²
Weights		
Loaded weight	85,000 kg	187,340 lb
Performance		
Speed	490 km/h	304 mph
Range	4,500-6,700 km	2,794-4,160 miles

After the RLM cancelled work on the Do 214 in mid-1943, Dornier developed a smaller, more refined flying boat – initially under the project designation P 174/I, but later given the RLM designation Do 216 – which was intended as a replacement for the Do 214. The proposed powerplant for the Do 216/1 was to be four 2,500 hp Junkers Jumo 223 24-cylinder diesel engines.

The fuselage was generally similar to that of the Do 214, albeit only a single-, rather then a double-decker. In addition to the glazed nose and two cheek stations, there were to be six further remotely controlled weapons stations. This flying boat was to be capable of carrying a 5,000 kg (11,020 lb) weapon load, including guided missiles underwing. But the RLM rejected this very promising project too, as ostensibly there was no requirement for a flying boat of this class.

The same was said of a modified version of the Dornier P 174/II, the P 174/III, which had the same dimensions as the former but was to have been powered by six Daimler Benz DB 603C engines.

Blohm & Voss P 144 – A Flying Boat as Long-Range Reconnaissance Aircraft, Tanker and Weapons Carrier

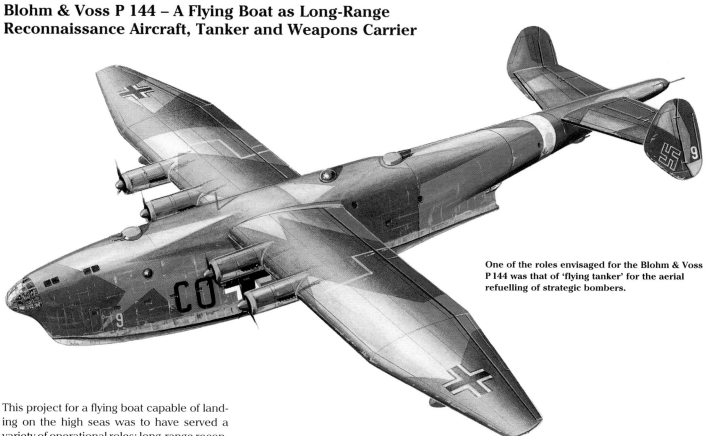

One of the roles envisaged for the Blohm & Voss P 144 was that of 'flying tanker' for the aerial refuelling of strategic bombers.

This project for a flying boat capable of landing on the high seas was to have served a variety of operational roles: long-range reconnaissance aircraft, U-boat support aircraft, bomber and weapons carrier, surface minelayer and aerial tanker for the refuelling of strategic bombers.

In contrast to the Blohm & Voss BV 238 flying boat, the P 144 project featured a twin fin and rudder; this arrangement being chosen to provide the remotely controlled dorsal weapons stations with an improved field of fire. The outboard underwing floats were fixed and non-retractable.

The stepped hull was of standard aero- and hydrodynamic configuration, but rose perpendicularly at its after end. In the angle

where this vertical stern-post met the underside of the aft fuselage there was a glazed weapons station which also doubled as a control and aiming station for air-launched guided weapons. The weapons themselves were carried on ETC racks beneath the wings. As well as underwing guided missiles, aerial torpedoes and mines, bombs could be carried in, and dropped from, a watertight bomb bay. Over a range of 8,650 km (5,371 miles) the total permissible payload was 6,000 kg (13,224 lb).

The P 144 project was intended for operations along America's eastern seaboard. But in 1944 this project was also cancelled by the RLM; the reason given being a lack of operational potential.

Blohm & Voss P 144 – data

Crew	Ten	
Powerplant	4 x 2,500 hp Junkers Jumo 223	
Dimensions		
Span	53.00 m	173 ft 10 in
Length	40.00 m	131 ft 2½ in
Height	6.20 m	20 ft 4 in
Wing area	280 m²	3,014 ft²
Weights		
Loaded weight	56,000 kg	123,424 lb
Range	7,500 km	4,657 miles

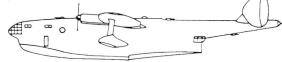

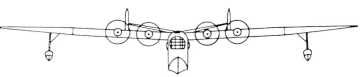

GA drawing of the Blohm & Voss P 144.

Heinkel He 220 –
A Large Flying Boat for Transocean Operations

The Heinkel He 220 large flying boat was originally developed at the behest of Deutsche Lufthansa for service on its transatlantic routes.

Heinkel He 220 – data

Powerplant	4 x 3,500 hp Daimler Benz 613	
Dimensions		
Span	57.30 m	187 ft 11½ in
Length	42.50 m	139 ft 5 in
Height	11.60 m	38 ft 0½ in
Weights		
Loaded weight	85,000 kg	187,340 lb
Performance		
Range	8,550 km	5,310 miles
Max speed	510 km/h	317 mph

One of the most interesting flying boat projects laid before the RLM was the Heinkel He 220 large capacity flying boat for transocean operations.

Developed at the beginning of 1940 under a contract from Deutsche Lufthansa, it may be regarded as a competitor to the Blohm & Voss Bv 222 and the Dornier Do 214, both of which also emanated from requirements drawn up by the national airline.

After a decree from the Luftwaffe High Command of 28th September 1940, which restricted civilian aircraft manufacture to all but a few examples, Lufthansa withdrew their specification. The project studies were then submitted to the RLM, who examined them for their military adaptability and ordered the

necessary modifications. After much to-ing and fro-ing the RLM finally gave the go-ahead for a military version of the BV 222. Despite further project proposals from both Dornier and Heinkel, the RLM remained firm in their decision for the BV 222. Heinkel persevered into 1943. At the beginning of that year, with the presentation of the He 220 design, they offered the RLM a flying boat which bore a certain structural resemblance to the BV 222, but which was superior to the latter in terms of performance and operational capabilities.

Powered by four 3,500 hp Daimler Benz DB 613 coupled engines the He 220 had a loaded weight of 135 tons and combined a calculated range of 8,550 km (5,310 miles) with an 8,000 kg (17,632 lb) weapon load.

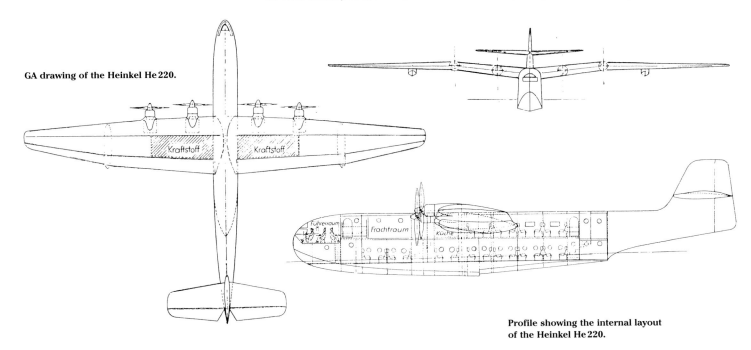

GA drawing of the Heinkel He 220.

Profile showing the internal layout of the Heinkel He 220.

Heinkel He 120 –
A Further Flying Boat for Transocean Operations

The He 120 was another flying boat project from Heinkel. Its basic design had been initiated by Dipl-Ing Walter Günter as early as 1937. After Günter's death in 1938 the work was carried on by Dipl-Ing Karl Schwärzler. Development was at the behest of Deutsche Lufthansa, but after the outbreak of war the project contract was annulled in favour of the Blohm & Voss Bv 222.

Heinkel He 120 – data

Powerplant	4 x 900 hp Junkers Jumo 9-207	
Dimensions		
Span	35.70 m	117 ft 1 in
Length	26.40 m	86 ft 7 in
Weights		
Loaded weight	29,600 kg	65,238 lb
Performance		
Range	6,900 km	4,285 miles

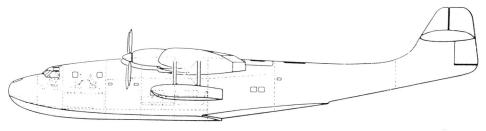

Side-view of the Heinkel He 120.

WFG P 2136 and P 2138 –
A Long-Range Reconnaissance Aircraft and Minelayer

The design bureau of the *Weser Flugzeugbau AG* (Weser Aircraft Manufacturing Co), under the leadership of Dr-Ing Helmut, had been working on the development of flying boat projects for Deutsche Lufthansa's transocean routes since 1938.

Upon the outbreak of war in 1939 these civil projects were halted on the orders of the RLM; their further development being dependent upon a military role being found for them.

As is evident from project documentation still in existence, modification work involving the fitting of more powerful engines, defensive armament and mine-laying equipment was begun. Despite this, the two 'boats, which differed in design and dimensions, were rejected by the RLM. Work on both projects ceased in the middle of 1940.

WFG P 2136 – data

Crew	Eight	
Powerplant	6 x 830 hp Junkers Jumo 109-207C diesel engines	
Dimensions		
Span	53.40 m	175 ft 2 in
Length	39.80 m	130 ft 6½ in
Height	8.40 m	27 ft 6½ in
Fuselage width	3.50 m	11 ft 6 in
Weights		
Loaded weight	72,000 kg	158,688 lb
Range	8,000 km	4,968 miles

WFG P 2138 – data

Crew	Eleven	
Powerplant	4 x 2,500 hp Junkers Jumo 9-223 coupled engines driving contra-rotating propellers	
Dimensions		
Span	70.00 m	229 ft 7 in
Length	41.80 m	137 ft 1½ in
Weights		
Loaded weight	125,000 kg	275,500 lb
Performance		
Range	10,900 km	6,769 miles

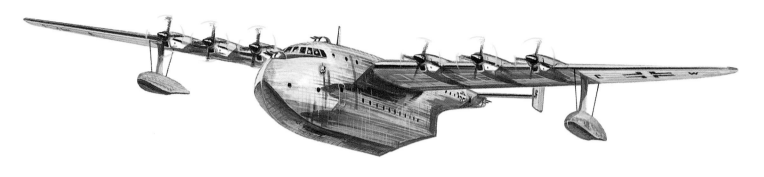

The WFG P 2136 of the Weser Flugzeugbau AG;
a minelayer and long-range reconnaissance flying boat.

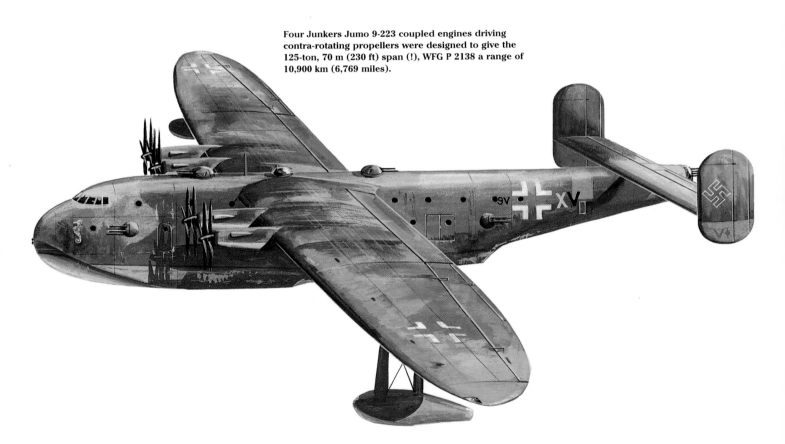

Four Junkers Jumo 9-223 coupled engines driving
contra-rotating propellers were designed to give the
125-ton, 70 m (230 ft) span (!), WFG P 2138 a range of
10,900 km (6,769 miles).

STRATEGIC LONG-RANGE FLYING BOAT PROJECTS

Chapter Ten

Allied War Booty

The Allied armies had hardly crossed the Rhine before British, American, French and Soviet teams of specialists began the search for all surviving records from German research institutes and design bureaux.

These documents were gathered in by the ton and transported to Allied collection and evaluation centres. Among them were aviation projects in advanced stages of development which some Allied scientists, at first glance, dismissed as products of over-ripe imaginations – but which within a few months, or even years later, were being built in the USA, the Soviet Union, in France and Great Britain – or which at least had a huge influence on the design of new projects in these countries. This 'transfer of scientific knowledge' could fill volumes. Just a few examples are quoted here to give the reader some idea of the actual events of the time. Anyone who today reads the commentaries and reports on the German aviation industry written by some acknowledged experts in the immediate post-war Allied aviation journals can only shake their head in disbelief.

The Americans, for example, initially ridiculed the German practice of arranging jet engines in the open airstream; in other words, suspending them in nacelles below the wings or placing them atop the fuselage (as on the Heinkel He 162). But, after inspecting captured German powerplants, high-ranking RAF officers and engineers from Rolls-Royce had to admit that their own industry had not succeeded in producing a fully serviceable jet engine before the war's end. They went further, stating that the BMW 003 axial-flow turbine developed by Dr-Ing H Oestrich was at least two years ahead of British axial-flow development. After studying German documents, British engineers Morgan and Davis of the Farnborough aviation research establishment remarked: *'We realised within a matter of minutes that our entire aircraft development programme was already out of date ...'*

Morgan further confirmed that Germany's aviation experts led the field in swept-wing research. Until that time British and American designers had been unaware of the advantages offered by wing sweep.

The complex calculations relating to high-speed airflow behaviour over wings and fuse-lages were foreign to them. Sydney Camm, the chief designer of the Hawker Hurricane, even laughed at the swept-wings of the German aircraft. Other experts shrugged off these developments with such comments as: 'After all, we were the ones who won the war...'

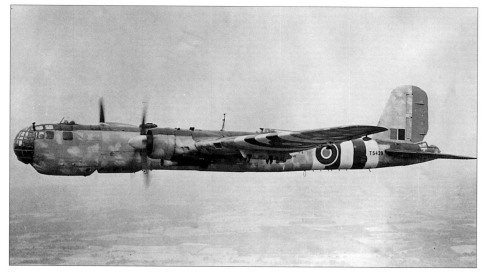

In post-war years the Heinkel He 177 was thoroughly tested by the Allies. In 1945 the British aviation journal *The Aeroplane* wrote: 'We were very lucky that the Heinkel He 177 was not ready to enter service earlier'. This particular machine fell into French hands shortly after the invasion (hence the D-day striping) and was flown to Farnborough in September 1944 for testing by the RAF.

In contrast to this, W S Farren, the Director of Farnborough, wrote to the British Aviation Minister on 9th July 1945 stating that, when visiting German research plants, he had been confronted by facilities, buildings and equipment on a scale and of a lavishness which had exceeded all his imaginings. The plant at the 'Hermann Göring' aviation research institute at Volkenrode was dismantled and re-built at Farnborough, were it helped to provide the British aviation industry with one of the most modern research facilities of the post-war years.

The then British Minister of Trade, Sir Stafford Cripps, could not resist adding his own comment regarding these scientific windfalls: 'One can only tolerate the Germans by squeezing their knowledge out of them as quickly as possible and then having nothing more to do with them ...'

For along with the countless tons of paper – construction drawings, project studies, blueprints, etc. – the victors' war booty also included a whole host of the scientists themselves.

Dipl-Ing Dietrich Küchemann, for example, who during the war had been in charge of the DVL's supersonic wind tunnel at Brunswick, was brought to England where he became one of the United Kingdom's most successful aircraft designers. Perhaps more than any other, Küchemann was in a position to translate his theoretical and experimental knowledge into practice. Together with colleagues Dr-Ing Johannes Weber and Dipl-Ing Karl Doetsch, he exerted a major influence on research at Farnborough. Thus, for example, the German scientists played a leading role in the design of the Anglo-French Concorde supersonic airliner. Showered with honours and decorations, they eventually became British citizens.

In a manner of speaking, the Soviet Union had the Americans to thank for its first rocket-powered supersonic aircraft. This was the experimental DFS 236 aircraft developed by the German Gliding Research Institute, which, at the war's end, and surrounded by a veil of secrecy, was in the final stages of assembly at the Siebel Aircraft Works in Halle. It would become the Soviet counterpart to America's

Bell XS-1 experimental rocket aircraft.

The town of Halle had originally been occupied by the Americans. Several weeks later, however, Soviet troops moved into that part of central Germany under the terms of the post-war partition agreement between the Allies. The American commandant of Halle did not give a second thought to handing over the Siebel aircraft works, including the experimental department, to the Soviets lock, stock and barrel. Even the workforce had, without exception, to be in their proper places – from chief designer Dipl-Ing Heinson, through works test-pilot Flugkapitän Zise, down to the humblest cleaning lady. After the Soviet take-over, work at the Siebel factory got under way again immediately.

Russian engineering officers had very quickly realised just what an undreamed-of prize had fallen into their laps.

One of the greatest items of scientific booty for the Allies – and not just in terms of physical size alone – was the Munich Aviation Research Institute's high-speed wind tunnel located in the Ötz Valley in the Tyrol. Codenamed 'Building Project 101', this plant, which had been almost completed by the war's end, was at that time the largest wind tunnel facility in the world. Hydroelectric Pelton turbines with an output of 76 megawatts (the equivalent of 100,000 hp), could produce winds and airflow speeds of up to supersonic levels in the 18 m (59 ft) diameter, 140 (460 ft) long measuring chamber.

The Americans wanted to ship the wind tunnel to the United States, but these plans faced violent opposition from their French allies. After some vehement controversy and tough bargaining as to where the wind tunnel was to be rebuilt, the French finally won the day. Dismantling of the Ötz Valley complex began in October 1945, and the first of no fewer than 13 complete goods trains carrying components of the tunnel was soon heading towards France. The wind tunnel was reassembled at Modane in the Savoy Alps with the help of German specialists. The French aviation research establishment had thereby acquired one of the most modern and advanced test and measuring facilities in the world. It is still in use today.

As war booty, this Heinkel He 111 was also exhaustively flown by the British.

May 1945: Professor Dr Albert Betz left of the Göttingen Aerodynamic Experimental Institute AVA hands over German research material on the swept wing to US scientist Dr Theodore von Karmann.

US scientists inspect the powerplant of a V2 rocket in the underground plant at Nordhausen in Thuringia.

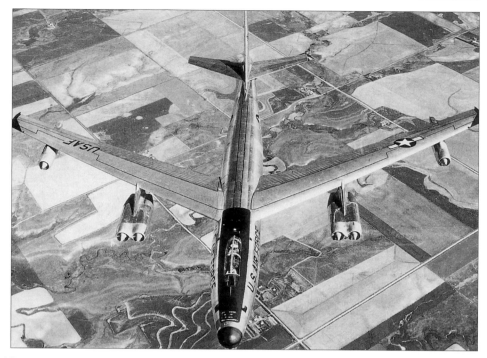

America's Boeing B-47 Stratojet, which made its first flight in December 1947, also embodied the results of German research into wing sweep. Boeing's chief designer, George S Schairer, was already busy collecting important material from the German Aviation Research Centre at Volkenrode on 10th May 1945 – just forty-eight hours after the end of the war. It would prove of inestimable value to his company.

Dr Adolf Busemann, Germany's foremost aero-dynamicist in swept-wing research, was another of the aviation scientists head-hunted by the Americans after the end of the war and taken to the United States.

Dipl-Ing Hans Multhopp, one-time chief aero-dynamicist with Focke-Wulf in Bremen, played a major part in the design of the Ta 183 jet fighter. At the end of the war the British took him to Farnborough. He subsequently held several key positions with the Martin company in America.

Dr-Ing Anselm Franz was head of jet turbine development at Junkers. Under his leadership t he company produced, among others, the Jumo 109-004 turbojet engine. In 1945 Dr Franz was taken to the USA, where he developed modern jet engines for the Lycoming company. His gas turbines, for example, were used to power the well-known Bell Huey series of helicopters.

The Anglo-French Concorde supersonic airliner, in whose development the German engineers Weber, Doetsch and Küchemann played leading roles.

The high-speed wind tunnel complex in the Ötz Valley in the Tyrol was one of the most valuable war prizes to fall into Allied hands.
With an output of 100,000 hp, it was the largest wind tunnel facility in the world.

One of the wind tunnel's turbine wheels. The two men perched by the blades give some idea of its enormous size.

View of the wind tunnel complex nearing completion.

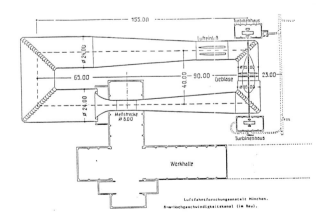

GA schematic of the Ötz Valley wind tunnel.

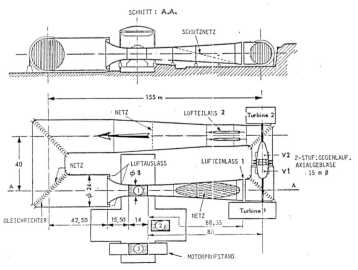

BILD 1: GESAMTANSICHT DES GROSSEN HOCHGESCHWINDIGKEITS - WINDKANALS VON ÖTZTAL

Powerplants, Weapons and Equipment

This section is intended to give a brief overview of some of the engines, special powerplants, guided weapons, guided free-fall and powered bombs, defensive armament and weapons stations, which were either in part already being used – or were scheduled for use – as powerplants, weapons and equipment on the bomber projects described in the preceding pages.

Engines and Special Powerplants

Daimler Benz DB 603 ASM. 2,250 hp 12-cylinder injection engine, with additional MW-50 boost, which required C3 special fuel.

Daimler Benz DB 604C. 3,500 hp 24-cylinder injection X-engine. After production had begun, the entire DB-604 programme was cancelled on 4th September 1942 upon the orders of the RLM.

Daimler Benz DB 605 ASB. 1,850 hp 12-cylinder injection engine with single-stage special supercharger; a high-altitude engine which was to power various bomber projects.

Daimler Benz DB 606B. 2,700 hp 24-cylinder coupled, or 'double', engine comprising 2 x DB 601Es, which was used to power the Heinkel He 177.

Daimler Benz DB 610 A-B. 3,000 hp 24-cylinder coupled engine comprising 2 x DB-605s.

Daimler Benz DB 613 C-1. 4,000 hp 24-cylinder coupled engine. Construction as DB 606 and DB 610; comprising 2 x DB 603 E/Gs.

Daimler Benz DB 621. 1,620 hp 12-cylinder high-altitude engine, developed from the DB 605 with two exhaust gas turbochargers.

Daimler Benz DB 623. 2,300 hp 12-cylinder high-altitude engine with turbocharger and charge cooling.

Daimler Benz DB 624A. 1,900 hp 12-cylinder high altitude engine with exhaust gas turbocharger.

Daimler Benz DB 625C. 1,755 hp further development of the DB 605D with exhaust gas turbocharger.

Daimler Benz DB 627B. 2,000 hp 12-cylinder in-line engine with two-stage supercharger and charge cooling. A further development of the DB 603G.

Daimler Benz DB 628. 1,600 hp 12-cylinder high-altitude engine with two-stage large supercharger.

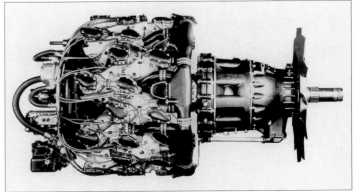

BMW 802. 2,800 hp 18-cylinder twin-row radial engine with exhaust gas turbocharger, intended to power various bomber projects.

Top and above: **BMW 801 TJ**. 2,000 hp 14-cylinder twin-row high-altitude radial engine with exhaust gas turbocharger and charge cooling.

Deutz DZ 710. 3,100 hp 16-cylinder two-stroke engine developed by Klöckner-Humbold Deutz AG. With fuel injection and exhaust gas turbocharging, this was one of the most powerful piston engines intended for use in various long-distance bomber projects. A further development as a 6,000 hp 32-cylinder coupled engine, designated the DZ 720, was to have powered large flying boats.

BMW 803. 4,500 hp 28-cylinder liquid-cooled four-row radial engine with boost injection.

Junkers Jumo 213E. 2,100 hp 12-cylinder high-altitude engine with two-stage supercharger. The Jumo 213 was a masterpiece of German aerodynamic development. A special version, comprising two Jumo 213s coupled in tandem, produced 5,000 hp. This large powerplant was intended for use in long-distance bombers and large flying boats.

Junkers Jumo 222. 2,500 hp 24-cylinder liquid-cooled multi-row radial engine designed to power the projects developed under the Bomber-B Programme.

Junkers Jumo 224. 4,000 hp opposed-piston diesel engine with single-stage exhaust gas turbocharger. Driving contra-rotating propellers, this engine was to be fitted in large flying boats operating in strategic roles.

Argus As 109-044. 500-750 kg (1,102-1,653 lb) static thrust pulse-jet. The As 109-044 propulsive duct was a further development of the Argus As 109-014 pulse-jet which powered Fieseler's Fi 103 flying-bomb, better known as the V1. It was intended for use, among other projects, on the Messerschmitt Me 328 parasite fighter.

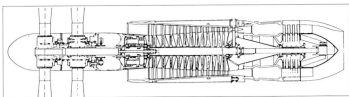

BMW 109-028. 6,700 hp shaft output turboprop version of the BMW 109-018 jet engine. Driving four-blade contra-rotating propellers and delivering 1,200 kg (2,645 lb) additional thrust, the BMW 109-028 turboprop was to have powered the BMW High-Speed Bomber Projects I and II.

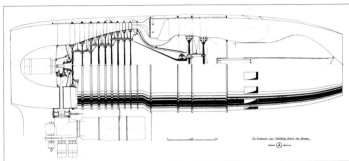

Daimler Benz DB 109-016. 13,000 kg (28,652 lb) static thrust large turbojet. The DB 109-016, developed by Daimler Benz AG in March 1945 and designed for the DB very-high-speed bomber project (Project number 3.10 256-05), was at that time the most powerful turbojet engine in the world. With a length of 6.70 m (21 ft 9 in) and a diameter of some 2 m (6 ft 7 in), it could have been fitted to only the largest of bomber projects.

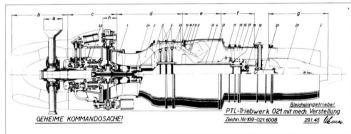

Daimler Benz DB 109-021. 3,300 hp shaft output turboprop version of the Heinkel-Hirth HeS 109-011 jet engine, delivered 1,100 kg (2,424 lb) additional thrust.

BMW 109-003R. A combination powerplant consisting of a BMW 109-003 turbojet plus a BMW 109-718 liquid fuel rocket engine, delivering 1,250 kg (2,755 lb) static thrust, mounted on a bearer above the jet engine's exhaust pipe. This combination was to have been used on tactical bomber projects.

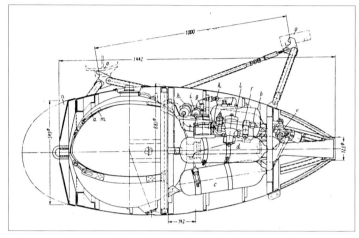

Walter 109-500A Take-Off Assistance Rocket. Delivering 500 kg (1,100 lb) static thrust during its 30-second burn-time, the 109-500A worked on the so-called cold principle – developing no heat, but relying on a chemically produced thrust reaction. These rockets were used to assist the take-off of heavily-laden bombers and transports, such as e.g. the BV 238 large flying boat (see page 116).

A Heinkel He 111H-16 begins its take-off run with the assistance of two 109-501 rockets.

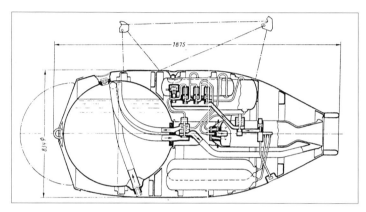

Walter 109-501 Take-off Assistance Rocket. Compared to the 109-500A, this rocket was considerably more powerful; its 30 seconds of 'combustion' producing 1,500 kg (3,306 lb) of static thrust. The 109-501 weighed 502 kg (1,106 lb), which included 220 kg (485 lb) of H_2O_2, 20 kg (45 lb) of kerosine and 12 kg (26 lb) of catalyst solution. It was mounted underwing and, after burning out, was jettisoned to return to earth by parachute.

Guided Weapons

Launch of a L 10 torpedo glider from a Heinkel He 177A-5.

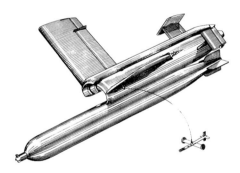

L 11 glider at moment of release from the aerial torpedo.

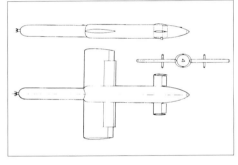

Schematic of the L 11 'Schneewittchen'.

Blohm & Voss L 10 *'Friedensengel'* ('Angel of Peace') Torpedo Glider

The L 10 torpedo glider, unpowered but with a tri-axial guidance system, was developed by Blohm & Voss to carry a standard LT 950 aerial torpedo over a distance of some 8,000-9,000 m (8,750-9,840 yards) towards its intended target. This approach flight was made in a 14° dive at a speed of 310 km/h (192 mph). After having released the L 10, the launch aircraft triggered a time fuse, thereby deploying a small kite which was towed behind the glider on a 25 m (82 ft)-long cable. When the weapon hit the surface of the water, sensors in the kite would detach the glider body, allowing the torpedo to continue its run submerged.

Technical Data

Length of glider		
without torpedo	3.89 m	12 ft 9 in
Span	2.73 m	8 ft 11½ in
Control	via Lotfe 7D bombsight and FuG 200 radio	

Blohm & Voss L 11 *'Schneewittchen'* ('Snow-White') Torpedo Glider

The L 11 was a further development of the L 10 torpedo glider capable of being launched from carrier aircraft flying at much higher speeds. The glider was 'aimed' by the carrier aircraft's being pointed towards the intended target at the moment of launch. The launch speed of more than 500 km/h (310 mph) was retarded by a braking parachute which slowed the torpedo before it entered the water. Upon striking the surface, the glider part of the combination – two clamshell fuselage sections each fitted with wing and tail units – would be released by the same towed kite arrangement as used by the L 10. The torpedo would then continue its submerged run, independent of the carrier aircraft, controlled by its own biaxial guidance system.

Technical Data

Span	3.43 m	11 ft 3 in
Length overall	6.34 m	20 ft 9½ in
Total weight	1,050 kg	2,314 lb
Angle of glide	12°	

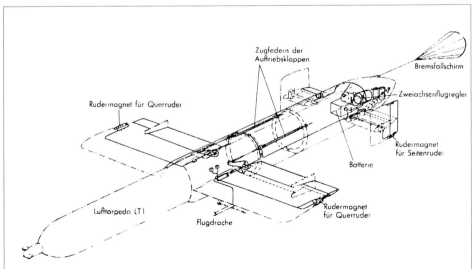

Zugfedern der Auftriebsklappen

Bremsfallschirm

Rudermagnet für Querruder

Zweiachsenflugregler

Rudermagnet für Seitenruder

Batterie

Luftorpedo LT 1

Flugdrache

Rudermagnet für Querruder

GA drawing of the L 11 'Schneewittchen'.

Blohm & Voss BV143A-1 Torpedo-Bomb

The BV143A-1 was a torpedo-bomb which could be either air-launched, or fired from a ground ramp as a flying-bomb against land or sea targets.

Similar in layout to the BV143A-2 (see below), this weapon was powered by a bi-fuel rocket motor. Gyro-controlled, it approached its intended target at a velocity of 730 km/h (453 mph).

Technical Data

Span	3.17 m	10 ft 5 in
Length	6.35 m	20 ft 10 in
Range	8,000 m	8,750 yards
Warhead	210 kg	463 lb
Powerplant	1 x Walter 109-502 rocket motor rated at 1,500 kg 3,306 lb static thrust.	

Above: **Views of the BV143A-1 torpedo bomb**

Below: **Views of the BV143A-2 on its transporter trolley.**

Blohm & Voss BV143A-2 Torpedo-Bomb

The BV143A-2 was a steerable torpedo, which was launched at a height of 1,500 m (4,920 ft); its bi-fuel rocket motor then enabling it to approach a target over a 6,000 m (6,560 yard) range in level flight.

After release from the launch aircraft, a feeler was extended from the underside of the torpedo. When this made contact with the surface of the water it activated a compressed-air cylinder which controlled the inertial guidance system. The BV143A-2 made its run-in to the target at a height of just 12 m (39 ft) above the waves, power being provided by a Walter 109-502 liquid fuel rocket motor which delivered 1,500 kg (3,306 lb) static thrust for 40 seconds.

Technical Data

Length	5.98 m	19 ft 7 in
Span	3.38 m	11 ft 1 in
Weight	1,130 kg	2,490 lb
Warhead	180 kg	397 lb

Blohm & Voss BV 143B-1 Glide-Bomb

The BV 143B-1 was a rocket-powered glide-bomb designed for launch from a carrier aircraft at an altitude of 3,500 m (11,480 ft). The tandem arrangement of the lifting surfaces gave it a glide angle of 1:20. Developed under contract to Blohm & Voss by the German Gliding Research Institute (DFS), it was intended for use against both land and sea targets. The warhead was a 1,000 kg (2,204 lb) armour-piercing PC 1000 bomb. This was encased in an aerodynamic body together with a rocket motor, the latter giving the weapon a speed of 350 km/h (217 mph) upon burn-out. No information is available regarding the method of guidance or overall dimensions.

LMA III Aerial Mine

The LMA and LMB were originally designed as sea mines to be dropped by parachute. The LMB IV was a further development intended for use against land and/or surface targets. Rate of fall was 55 m (180 ft) per second. Weight depended upon the type and amount of explosive filling; the LMB IV's 910 kg (2,006 lb) of Amatol 39 gave it a total weight of 1,080 kg (2,380 lb). The thin-walled mine had a length of 3.22 m (10 ft 7 in) and a diameter of 82.9 cm (33 in.)

These aerial mines were to have been dropped by the Messerschmitt Me 264 long-distance bomber in attacks on cities along the east coast of the USA.

Fieseler Fi 103
Radio-Controlled Flying Bomb

Initially developed as a ground-to-ground missile, and known as the *Vergeltungswaffe* (Revenge weapon) V1, the Fi 103 could also be employed as an air-to-ground weapon launched from carrier aircraft. With a loaded weight of 2,200 kg (4,849 lb) – 800 kg (1,763 lb) of which was made up of the explosive charge – the Fi 103 was released some 8,000-10,000 m (8,747-10,933 yds) from its intended target, towards which it would be aimed under the power of its own Argus As 109-014 pulse-jet. It was intended to equip the Fi 103 with the more powerful As 109-044 in order to increase both its range and speed.

The illustration shows an air-launched Fi 103 flying-bomb in its normal carrying position beneath the starboard wingroot of a Heinkel He 111H-22 bomber.

Blohm & Voss BV 8-246 *'Hagelkorn'* ('Hailstone') Glide-Bomb

The BV 8-246 was an unpowered glide-bomb designed for attacking surface targets over long distances. Carrying an explosive charge of 435 kg (959 lb) of Amatol 39, the BV 8-246's angle of glide after release was 1:30, a figure not attained by any other such missile. Its approach to the target was gyro-controlled in horizontal flight.

Technical Data

Span	6.40 m	20 ft 11½ in
Length	3.52 m	11 ft 6½ in
Weight	730 kg	1,609 lb

Henschel Hs 293 Glide-Bomb

The Hs 293 was a radio-controlled glide-bomb carrying a 510 kg (1,124 lb) explosive charge of Triolen 106. The Walter 109-507 rocket motor attached to the underside of the bomb delivered 590 kg (1,300 lb) static thrust and had a burn-time of 10 seconds. Control was by means of a FuG 203 'Kehl' transmitter and FuG 230 'Straßburg' receiver housed in the aft section of the Hs 293. At a launch range of 12 km (7.5 miles) the bomb's target diagram was just 5 x 5 m (16 x 16 ft).

Technical Data

Length	3.40 m	11 ft 2 in
Span	2.90 m	9 ft 6 in
Weight	722 kg	1,591 lb

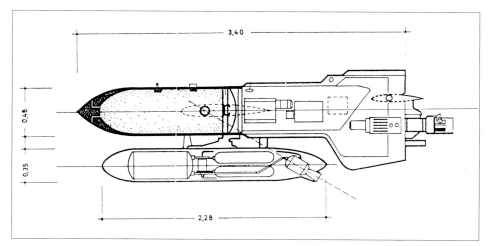

Cutaway profile of the Hs 293

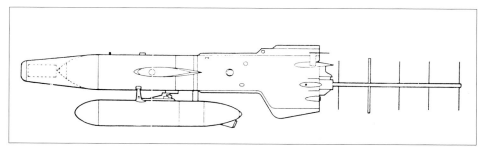

The Hs 293D – a further development of the Hs 293 equipped with 'Tonne-Seedorf' TV guidance. The 45 cm 18 in extension, containing a TV camera, fitted to the nose of the bomb improved its accuracy to an even greater degree.

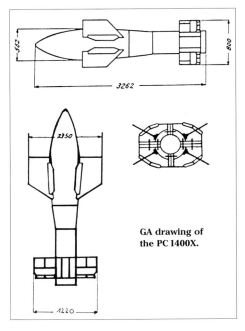

GA drawing of
the PC 1400X.

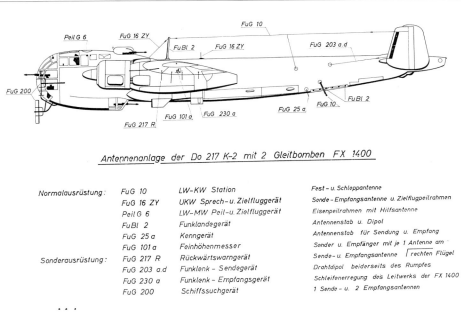

Antennenanlage der Do 217 K-2 mit 2 Gleitbomben FX 1400

Normalausrüstung:	FuG 10	LW-KW Station	Fest- u. Schleppantenne
	FuG 16 ZY	UKW Sprech-u. Zielfluggerät	Sende-Empfangsantenne u. Zielflugpeilrahmen
	Peil G 6	LW-MW Peil-u. Zielfluggerät	Eisenpeilrahmen mit Hilfsantenne
	FuBl 2	Funklandegerät	Antennenstab u. Dipol
	FuG 25 a	Kenngerät	Antennenstab für Sendung u. Empfang
	FuG 101 a	Feinhöhenmesser	Sender u. Empfänger mit je 1 Antenne am
Sonderausrüstung:	FuG 217 R	Rückwärtswarngerät	Sende- u. Empfangsantenne ⌐ rechten Flügel
	FuG 203 a.d	Funklenk – Sendegerät	Drahtdipol beiderseits des Rumpfes
	FuG 230 a	Funklenk – Empfangsgerät	Schleifenerregung des Leitwerks der FX 1400
	FuG 200	Schiffssuchgerät	1 Sende- u. 2 Empfangsantennen

. . .

Line illustration of the Dornier Do 217K-2 carrying the PC 1400X free-fall bomb underwing and identifying, among others, the radio antennae associated with its use.

PC 1400X Controlled-Trajectory Bomb

Developed by the German Aviation Experimental Establishment (DVL), this controlled free-fall bomb could be steered towards the land or sea target by means of tail-mounted spoilers. An enlarged version of the PC 1400X, incorporating a nose scanner, permitted corrections to the trajectory to be made independently. The PC 1400X was produced by Rheinmetall-Borsig in Berlin-Marienfelde.

Technical Data

Length	3.26 m	10 ft 8½ in
Span	1.35 m	4ft 5 in
Weight	1,570 kg	3,460 lb
Warhead	300 kg	661 lb
Rate of fall	290 m/sec	951 ft/sec
Release height	4,000-8,000 m	13,120-26,240 ft
Penetration	13-28 cm	5-11 in armoured steel

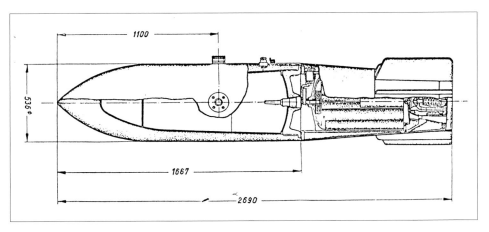

PC 1800 RS Armour-Piercing Powered Bomb

Similar in design and construction (apart from weight and measurements) to the PC 1000 RS, this bomb weighed 2,057 kg (4,534 lb), was 2.69 m (8 ft 10 in) long and had a diameter of 53.6 cm (21 in). It could penetrate 25-35 cm (10-14 in) of armoured steel or reinforced concrete. Its one-piece, thick-walled casing was of tempered steel with an extra-hardened tip. It was carried externally underwing on a PVC 1006 bomb rack and was released electrically.

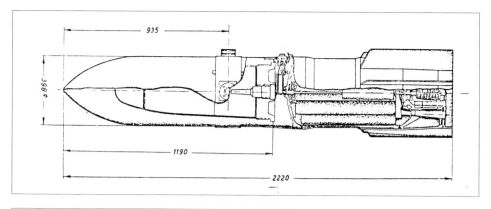

PC 1000 RS Armour-Piercing Powered Bomb

This rocket-propelled armour-piercing (thrust) bomb was a fin-stabilized explosives delivery system powered by a solid fuel rocket motor of 3 seconds burn-time. Weighing just 978 kg (2,155 lb), the PC 1000 RS was 2.20 m (7 ft 2½ in) long and had a diameter of 39.8 cm (15½ in).

At a release trajectory of 60° it could penetrate 18-22 cm (8-9 in) of armoured steel. The PC 1000 RS was carried externally underwing on an ETC 2000 bomb rack.

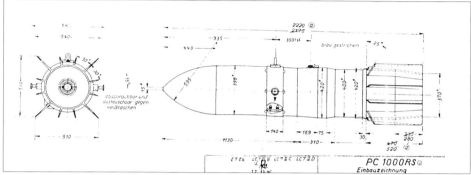

Front and side views of the PC 1000 RS.

Arado E 377 Radio-Controlled Glide-Bomb

One of the last glide-bomb developments to be laid before the RLM at the end of 1944 was Arado's aircraft-like E 377 project, in both powered and unpowered versions. Working in collaboration with Rheinmetall-Borsig, Arado had designed a glide-bomb which could be carried beneath an Arado Ar 234C or a Heinkel He 162 fighter and which, after launch, could be directed – either by remote control or by a target guidance system – against ships or other surface objectives. The project documentation submitted to Department E 2/II of the RLM met every requirement contained in the original RLM specification. Structurally, the E 377, which was to be made of wood, resembled an aircraft. The turned, circular cross-section fuselage housed a 2-ton explosive warhead (and, in its unpowered version, also served as an additional fuel tank for the carrier aircraft). The wings of the E 377 were also designed as fuel tanks which, like the fuselage tank, were coated with a preservative sealing compound.

The dorsal and ventral vertical tail surfaces were symmetrical, the former mounting a rectangular tailplane. Control and rudder movements to guide the E 377 to its target were carried out by means of a so-called 'Fighter Control' device, which was operated by the carrier aircraft after launch, or by a system of 'straight-ahead' tracking. Transfer of fuel from the tanks of the unpowered version of the E 377 'Verlustgerät' (literally 'Expendable device') was by jet pressure driven by a compressor in the powerplant of the carrier aircraft. This system, which in effect transformed the glide-bomb into a temporary auxiliary fuel tank, afforded a considerable increase in range.

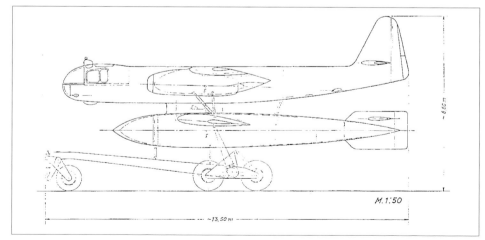

For take-off both components – carrier and bomb – were brace-mounted in trays on a special trolley. Release from the trolley could be effected by disengaging a single strut. The trolley, designed by Rheinmetall-Borsig, was a further development of the three-wheeled

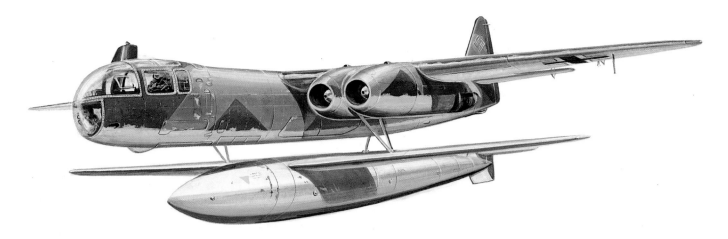

Arado Ar 234C-2 with E 377 glide-bomb.

Arado E 377 Glide-Bomb – data

Span	14.40 m	47 ft 3 in
Length	10.90 m	35 ft 9 in
Wing area	27 m²	291 ft²
Aspect ratio	7.65	
Wing loading	442 kg/m²	90 lb/ft²
Take-off weight with trolley	10,000 kg	22,040 lb
Warhead	1,800-2,000 kg	3,967-4,408 lb
E 377A Powerplant	2 x BMW 109-003 or	
	2 x Porsche 109-005 turbojets	
Weight of take-off trolley inc. 4 x Walter retro-rockets and drag chute		
	4,000 kg	8,816 lb
Fuel capacity	4,500 kg	9,918 lb

take-off trolley used for the Arado Ar 234A-2; its overall weight being increased to 4,000 kg (8,816 lb) by extension of the lateral end bearers and addition of an extra pair of wheels.

After the composite (Ar E 377/Ar 234C-2 combination) had lifted off from the trolley, the latter was braked by means of both retro-rockets and a drag chute. Concerns regarding the yaw forces generated during take-off led to Heinkel's He 162s being considered for the role of carrier aircraft. The Arado technicians planned to use explosive bolts to separate the E 377 bomb component from the carrier aircraft.

Assembling the composite prior to operations was carried out with the aid of a special frame and twin-trestle, enabling the carrier aircraft to be fitted on top of the Arado E 377.

The projected version of the bomb to be employed in combination with the Heinkel He 162 was designated the Arado E 377'A' (to distinguish it from the version using the Arado carrier, which was identified by a small 'a').

Two BMW 109-003 turbojets would enable the powered variant of the E 377 to approach its target at a speed of 750 km/h (466 mph).

The warhead of the Arado E 377 comprised a hollow charge containing 2,000 kg (4,408 lb) of Trialen 105, a highly-explosive material which was particularly suited to anti-shipping operations. For area bombing it was intended to use a thin-walled bomb casing to achieve the blast effect of an aerial mine. In addition, 500 kg (1,202 lb) of incendiary liquid was carried in the bomb's aft fuselage section; this serving also as a counterbalance. In place of the 2-ton explosive warhead, a standard SC 1800 bomb (minus tail fin) could be accommodated in the E 377's fuselage.

A piloted version of the Arado E 377 – a so-called SO-*Gerät* (suicide device), along the lines of the Japanese 'Baka' suicide bomb – was also planned.

The end of the war prevented assembly and operational use of the E 377.

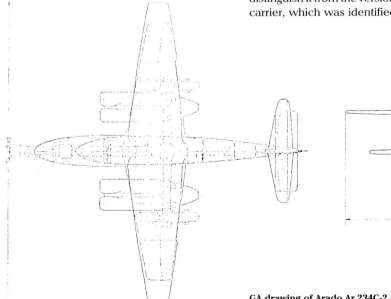

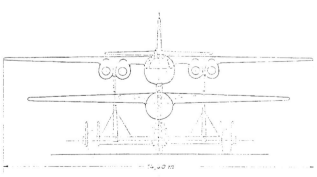

GA drawing of Arado Ar 234C-2 carrier aircraft and Arado E 377 glide-bomb on take-off trolley.

Arado Ar 234A at moment of take-off and release of trolley. The trolley is falling back to earth and the drag chute is starting to open.

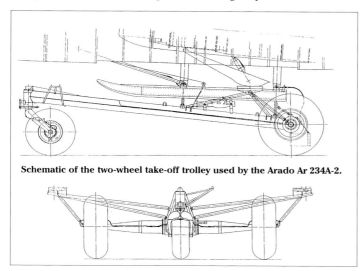

Schematic of the two-wheel take-off trolley used by the Arado Ar 234A-2.

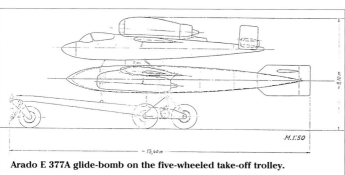

Arado E 377A glide-bomb on the five-wheeled take-off trolley.

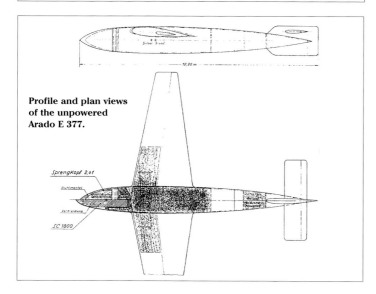

Profile and plan views of the unpowered Arado E 377.

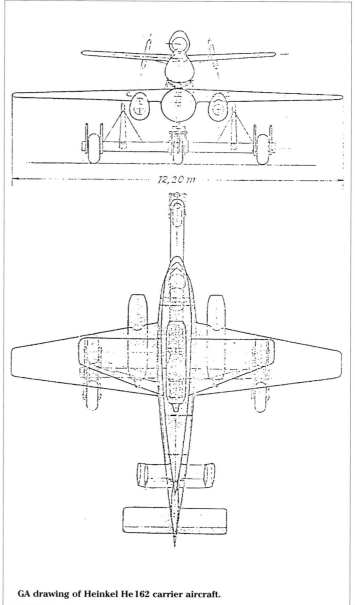

GA drawing of Heinkel He 162 carrier aircraft.

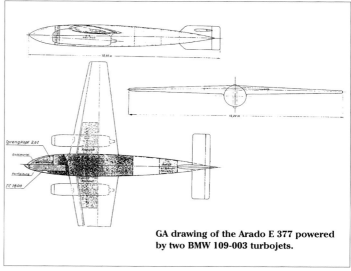

GA drawing of the Arado E 377 powered by two BMW 109-003 turbojets.

Weapons and Weapons Stations

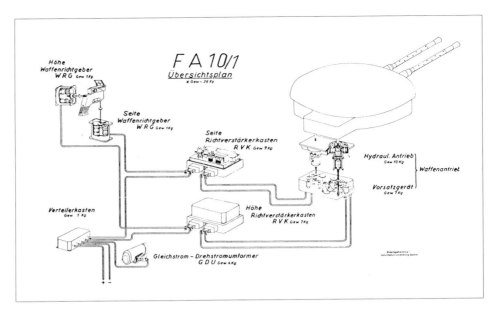

Schematic of the remotely controlled FDL-131/Z barbette.
The FA 10/1 remote control system was developed by AEG specifically for use in heavy and long-range bombers. The guns were aimed and fired via a gun-sight entirely separated from the weapons station. Driven by servo-motors, the FDL-131/Z was armed with two MG 131s and could be located either above or below the fuselage. Because of its flat, compact construction it was also considered for use on wing surfaces. Note: FDL = *Ferngerichtete Dreh-Lafette* – remotely-controlled revolving barbette.

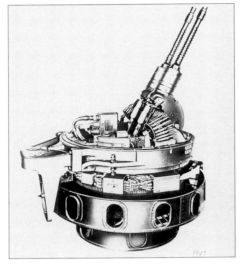

Right: **The FDL-131/Z barbette minus casing.**

Far right: **HDL-131/V Manned Tail Turret**
Designed by Rheinmetall-Borsig, the HDL-131/V was a quadruple gun turret, mounting four MG 131/20s, intended as tail armament for the Heinkel He 177B. An improved version with hydraulic controls and a target acquisition system was to have been installed in the Tank Ta 400, He 277, Ju 290B-1 and Ju 290Z bomber projects.

Below: **MK 108 Machine Cannon**
Developed in 1944 by Rheinmetall-Borsig, the 30 mm MK 108 machine cannon was the main armament of a number of fighter aircraft. Its reliability and compact design – overall length 1.57 m (5 ft 2 in), weight 58 kg (128 lb) – made it an ideal defensive weapon for long-range bombers. The MK 108Z twin-gun installation, with a rate of fire of 600 rounds (per barrel) per minute, was a particularly fearsome weapon.

Right: **Rheinmetall-Borsig HL-151/20 Tail Gun Mounting.**
Still undergoing trials at the war's end, this tail mounting was armed with two MG 151/20s. The long-range 20 mm MG 151/20, which would today be classed as an automatic cannon, fired high-explosive shells at a rate of 720 rounds per minute. The HL-151/20 was also envisaged for use on long-range bombers.

GA drawing of the MK 108.

MK 108 cannon in the nose of a Me 110G night-fighter.

We hope that you enjoyed this book . . .

Midland Publishing titles are edited
and designed by an experienced and enthusiastic
trans-Atlantic team of specialists.

Further titles are in preparation but we welcome
ideas from authors or readers for books they would
like to see published.

In addition, our associate company, Midland
Counties Publications, offers an exceptionally wide
range of aviation, spaceflight, astronomy, military,
naval and transport books and videos for sale by
mail-order around the world.

For a copy of the appropriate catalogue, or to order
further copies of this book, please write, telephone,
fax or e-mail:

Midland Counties Publications
Unit 3 Maizefield,
Hinckley, Leics, LE10 1YF, England

Tel: (+44) 01455 233 747
Fax: (+44) 01455 233 737
E-mail: midlandbooks@compuserve.com

*The first volume of Luftwaffe Secret Projects, dealing with Fighters 1939-1945
is still available at £29.95 / $44.95. ISBN 1 85780 052 4.*

INDEX